# CLOSET QUEENS

*Also by Michael Bloch*

The Duke of Windsor's War (1982)

Operation Willi: The Plot to Kidnap
the Duke of Windsor (1984)

Wallis & Edward: The Intimate Correspondence
of the Duke and Duchess of Windsor (1986)

The Secret File of the Duke of Windsor (1988)

The Reign and Abdication of Edward VIII (1990)

Ribbentrop (1992)

The Duchess of Windsor (1996)

FM: The Life of Frederick Matthias Alexander,
Founder of the Alexander Technique (2004)

(ed.) The Diaries of James Lees-Milne (3 vols, 2006–8)

James Lees-Milne: The Life (2009)

Jeremy Thorpe (2014)

# CLOSET QUEENS

## SOME 20TH CENTURY BRITISH POLITICIANS

## MICHAEL BLOCH

Little, Brown

LITTLE, BROWN

First published in Great Britain in 2015 by Little, Brown

1 3 5 7 9 10 8 6 4 2

A CIP catalogue record for this book
is available from the British Library.

ISBN 978-1-4087-0412-7

Typeset in Minion by M Rules
Printed and bound in Great Britain by
Clays Ltd, St Ives plc

Papers used by Little, Brown are from well-managed forests
and other responsible sources.

MIX
Paper from
responsible sources
FSC® C104740

Little, Brown
An imprint of
Little, Brown Book Group
Carmelite House
50 Victoria Embankment
London EC4Y 0DZ

An Hachette UK Company
www.hachette.co.uk

www.littlebrown.co.uk

*To Richard Davenport-Hines*

# CONTENTS

# LIST OF ILLUSTRATIONS

## PLATE SECTION ONE

1. The 5th Earl of Rosebery, Liberal Prime Minister 1894–5, and the 7th Earl Beauchamp, Liberal cabinet minister 1910–15 (and model for Lord Marchmain in *Brideshead Revisited*), were cousins through their mothers, and partly owed their success to handsome looks. Both were hounded by vindictive fellow noblemen who claimed to have proof of their homosexual activities.

2. Reginald 'Regy' Brett, 2nd Viscount Esher, and Lewis 'Loulou' Harcourt, 1st Viscount Harcourt – intriguers in the realms of both politics and forbidden love.

3. George Wyndham worshipped his political mentor Arthur Balfour, but lacked his icy ruthlessness, and died a broken man.

4. Winston Churchill with fellow Sandhurst cadets in the 1890s: he later won a libel action after allegations that he had engaged with them in 'acts of gross immorality of the Oscar Wilde type'.

   Churchill as Undersecretary for the Colonies with his private secretary 'Eddie' Marsh, whom he described as 'a friend I shall cherish and hold on to all my life'.

5. Churchill, aged forty-two, as a battalion commander of the Royal Scots Fusiliers in 1916 with his second-in-command and beloved protégé, 'Archie' Sinclair, aged twenty-five.

   Churchill with his son Randolph, his adoration of whom almost led to a rift with his wife.

6. Three homosexual imperialists: Lord Kitchener, who surrounded himself with handsome young officers and was described as possessing 'a taste for buggery'; Cecil Rhodes, who was devastated by the death of the intimate friend with whom he lived; and George Lloyd, seen here enrobed as Governor of Bombay in the 1920s, whose struggle with his proclivities inspired a novel.

7. Sir Samuel Hoare ('Slippery Sam') skates on thin ice, while his wife Lady Maud looks on.

   Sir Philip Sassoon – MP, millionaire aesthete, and admirer of airmen.

8. Two rakes and risk-takers – a fresh-faced Bob Boothby soon after his election to parliament in 1924 as 'the Baby of the House', and a raddled-looking Tom Driberg in 1953: their long survival in politics was a tribute to their sharp wits.

## PLATE SECTION TWO

1. Henry 'Chips' Channon and Alan Lennox-Boyd enjoyed long and successful political careers while leading racy homosexual lives behind the scenes; intimate friends, they married sisters, Guinness heiresses.

2. Harold Nicolson, diplomatist, politician and man of letters, and Viscount Hinchingbrooke, pictured after marrying his second wife Anne Holland-Martin in 1962, were friends in the wartime House of Commons. They were also both homosexuals married to lesbians: Nicolson had two sons by his marriage to Vita Sackville-West, 'Hinch' no fewer than seven children by his first wife Rosemary.

# FOREWORD

## *by Matthew Parris*

The intending author of a book like this faces three big difficulties. All three should be acknowledged. All three should be seen as reasons for reserve. But none can be accepted as an argument against going ahead.

The intending reader should respond likewise.

The first difficulty is that especially when it comes to politicians, stories about sexual scandal are inherently interesting, but often for salacious reasons rather than the pursuit of truth.

Sex sells. It may help us understand history better – I believe it does – but much else that helps us understand history, though capable of careful research and earnest presentation, will not attract readers. Sex does. Gossip about secret homosexuality has always invited prurient curiosity. To devote several years – and a book – to the pursuit of sexual rumour opens an author to the charge of exploiting history rather than furthering its study.

To this I reply that it lays upon the author the duty to take great care not to overstate, not to blur the distinction between fact and rumour, and to bear always in mind that the more thoughtful reader will be looking to understand the whole person better, rather than gasp or snigger.

The second difficulty is that although homosexuality is not these days considered by most as a disgrace or a reason for shame, some whiff of embarrassment does still (for many) hang around the subject. It shouldn't. Might a book called *Closet Queens* be accused of encouraging an aura of taboo?

To this I reply that it might. It depends how the book is written. A reputable author should not trade on, and a reputable reader should not seek, any kind of a tut-tut or finger-wag. The secret lives of deceased politicians should be treated respectfully and in the most factual and unjudgemental way.

The third difficulty is, if you like, historiographical: if a study's focus is on an aspect of people's lives that the world (and perhaps they themselves) considered shameful and potentially ruinous, we can assume that reports would have been unlikely to see the light of day, while the individual concerned, and his intimates and successors, will have taken every possible precaution to bury or destroy the evidence. To put it bluntly (as Michael Bloch does) if these rumours were based on fact, it's likely we have been left only with the rumour. A study like this will therefore, and inevitably, be dominated by speculation and supposition, and open to the charge that much has been alleged but nothing proved.

To this I reply that that is certainly true, and always a reason for caution, but cannot be allowed to call off the very idea of pursuing the story.

Three objections, then: are we behaving like peeping Toms? Are we encouraging the view that homosexuality is shameful? And is all this just unsubstantiated tittle-tattle anyway?

Mr Bloch's study, and the way he has conducted and presented it, answers these challenges convincingly.

First: his treatment of his subjects is careful and respectful. If readers are looking for mere titillation they will not find it in these pages. Bloch's approach is forensic and never over-heated. It is left to the reader to decide whether the inclinations or behaviour of his subjects matter. His chapter on the late Sir Edward Heath is a model in this respect.

Secondly: this is not an unkind study. You will not find here a censorious word, and the author remains studiously morally neutral, though the implications of (for instance) 'Loulou' Harcourt's behaviour are shocking. For the most part – pae-dophilia excepted – Bloch's study does invite sympathy for men in public life who were forced by popular prejudice to hide from the world something quite important about them-selves; and the reader will certainly not end up on the side of the curtain-twitchers or moralisers. But the author himself stands back from judgement, allowing the reader to judge.

Thirdly: this is history that knows and acknowledges its lim-itations. Michael Bloch is very, very careful to distinguish between rumour, report and incontrovertible fact. Nobody whom these accounts touch could complain that smoke has been turned into fire.

But the smoke fascinates me. I am only one reader, but as such I confess I do find gossip interesting and I'm not free from mere curiosity. The book can be read just for fun.

But you will not read it without being drawn deeper into a sense of the tangle of history and the mess people can make of their lives privately, while presenting a front of rationality and control. You will not read it without thinking harder and more carefully about the extent to which private turmoil, even shame, does – and the extent to which it may not – exert a hidden influence on the public man. The links between the unseen and the seen are never far from the author's mind, and will not be far from yours.

Finally, you will often enough chuckle. There is considerable half-concealed humour in some of these stories, and one senses that Michael Bloch relishes it. I shall not forget his report of Sir Winston Churchill's remark one November on hearing that a minister had been caught cavorting with a guardsman in the bushes of St James's Park: 'On the coldest night of the year? It makes you proud to be British.'

# INTRODUCTION

During the 1990s I wrote a biography of Jeremy Thorpe, the charismatic politician, born in 1929, who led Britain's historic Liberal Party (which subsequently merged with the Social Democrats to form the Liberal Democrats) from 1967 to 1976. (Never intended to appear in his lifetime, it was only published on his death in December 2014, Thorpe, who had suffered for more than thirty-five years from Parkinson's disease, having astonished the world by his longevity.) Thorpe possessed outstanding political gifts, and transformed his party's fortunes: having received 2.3 million votes at the general election of 1966, the Liberals won 6 million in 1974 and could, had they wished (which for various reasons they did not), have entered into a governing coalition with the Conservatives. He was a dazzling performer, who claimed that he would have gone on the stage had he not launched himself into politics; his inspirational personality was largely responsible for the Liberal upsurge. At the same time he was a master of the 'dark arts' of politics – intrigue, presentation and manipulation – and an accomplished political risk-taker. (It should be added that, while Thorpe tended to be extremely popular with the public, with his party's rank-and-file and with those he met socially, he was not always liked by those who had dealings with him, many of whom regarded him as devious, flashy, egotistical and superficial.)

Though he enjoyed the company of women, many of whom found him very attractive, Thorpe was fundamentally gay by nature: during his life he enjoyed several close relationships with other men, and numerous sexual escapades. As all homosexual activity was illegal in England until 1967, and continued to attract intense social disapproval for a quarter of a century after that (the annual *Social Attitudes* survey suggested that half of the population still considered it to be 'always wrong' as late as 1993), this was something that Thorpe, like so many others, had to keep secret from the world at large. Any public exposure of his sexual activities, apart from putting him at risk of criminal prosecution, promised to spell the ruin of his political career amid circumstances of the utmost disgrace. He therefore led a double life: while pursuing a homosexual 'rake's progress' behind the scenes, he was always gallant with 'the ladies', married twice (his first wife, by whom he had a son, died as the result of a car crash), and acted the part of a respectable family man. To use a crude but trenchant expression which came into fashion in the 1960s, he was (like almost all other politicians of the time of a similar persuasion) a 'closet queen'. Thorpe was, indeed, somewhat unusual in that he continued to lead an active homosexual life after he had become a well-known public figure; many politicians, fearful of the risks and ambitious for their careers, repressed their homosexuality as they 'climbed the greasy pole', and in some cases led entirely celibate lives, while continuing to have feelings which they were anxious to keep secret. The fate of Thorpe himself suggested they had good reason to do so: in 1976 he was obliged to resign as Liberal leader when details emerged of an affair with a younger man fifteen years earlier (when it was still illegal); and in 1979 he found himself tried at the Old Bailey for having allegedly conspired to have the man in question murdered: though he was acquitted, the evidence which the trial revealed of his homosexual past and his efforts to cover it up left him a discredited figure.

While this was not a point to which I drew undue attention in my biography, it often occurred to me while I was writing it that the skills which Thorpe developed as a clandestine homosexual were not dissimilar to those which made him such an effective politician. These skills may be said to fall into four categories: (1) quick wits and sharp antennae; (2) acting ability – enabling one to put on a good show, play on the emotions of one's audience, and cover up and dissemble where necessary; (3) a talent for intrigue and subterfuge (surely a necessary part of the equipment of even the most 'virtuous' politician); (4) a capacity for taking calculated risks, allied to an aptitude for dealing with threatening situations. Another factor in Thorpe's story was that there seemed to be a psychological link between the thrill of 'feasting with panthers' (as Oscar Wilde described the dangerous allure of casual homosexual encounters) and the general excitement of politics. Intrigued by these coincidences, I conceived the idea of producing a literary survey of homosexual or bisexual male politicians* in twentieth-century Britain, with a view to investigating how they coped with the double lives they were usually obliged to lead, and whether the duplication of 'closet queen' and political qualities, so evident in Thorpe's case, generally held true. It occurred to me that the proportion of men who fell into this category was likely to be greater in politics

---

* I have not included lesbians, partly because there were few female politicians of note in Britain until the final third of the century, partly because lesbianism has never been illegal in Britain, and has thus given rise to rather different social pressures.

than in other walks of life, for two reasons. First, the very fact that they were actors, risk-takers, intriguers, etc. would tend to draw them towards the profession. Secondly, many of the century's parliamentary politicians were educated at all-male boarding schools,* which (while officially proscribing homosexuality on pain of expulsion) fostered intense and often sexual friendships among their pupils, and also provided training in 'playing the game' (which from the closet-queen point of view meant presenting a conventional front to the world and ensuring that one did not get caught – or alternatively, breaking the rules and getting away with it).

However, I soon realised that there was a serious obstacle in the way of this project. For closet queens are by nature intensely secretive. They do not, as a rule, keep diaries or write letters casting light on their sexuality, nor, if they can help it, do they allow gossip to circulate regarding their tastes. They often destroy their papers or arrange for them to be destroyed after their deaths. If their biographies are written, their families usually ensure that this aspect of their lives is barely mentioned.† How, therefore, is one to find out about their *modus operandi*? (It is true that 'Chips' Channon kept a diary which is rumoured to contain information about the sex lives of both himself and other 'queer' politicians; but all such references were carefully expurgated from the edition which was published in 1967, since when no historian, so far as I am

---

* But one must not exaggerate: of the twenty persons (one of them female) who served as prime minister during the twentieth century, only ten went to such schools – five to Eton, two to Harrow, one to Haileybury, one to Rugby and one to Fettes – and they held sway for rather less than half the time.

† Regarding this branch of literature, the prize certainly goes to Sir Robert Rhodes James, who, as well as editing the diaries of 'Chips' Channon so as to remove all overt reference to his homosexuality, managed to write biographies of Lord Rosebery and Victor Cazalet without referring to the widespread contemporary rumours that they were homosexual, and in his biography of Lord Boothby mentioned such rumours merely to dismiss them.

aware, has been granted access to the originals. It is also true that two men who feature in these pages, Tom Driberg and Ian Harvey, wrote memoirs dealing more or less frankly with their homosexuality, while Nigel Nicolson, the son of another, wrote a book mentioning his father's proclivities; but these publications – all of which took place during that interesting decade, the 1970s, and caused some sensation at the time – were exceptional.) In Thorpe's case it was possible to discover quite a lot, because his period of activity was relatively recent, because he had led a promiscuous life and taken extraordinary risks, leaving a trail of evidence, and because he encountered serious trouble resulting in a sensational trial, as a result of which he was the subject of extensive investigations, both public and private. But most of my potential subjects were long dead, they had (even if they succeeded in leading fulfilling romantic lives) behaved discreetly, and they had managed to avoid serious trouble. Indeed, it may be that some (even fairly prominent) politicians of the past were entirely successful in concealing their homosexuality from all but their closest intimates, their secret going with them to their graves. And this is merely to speak of those who led active sex lives. How is one to get a picture of the emotions of those who chose to remain largely or entirely celibate?

Here, nevertheless, for what it is worth, is my survey of homosexual, bisexual and sexually ambiguous British politicians of the last century. I have cast the net wide, including some who managed to be fairly open about their tastes while avoiding trouble, others who led complex double lives, often married with children, and some who to a greater or lesser degree repressed their sexuality,* along with some who seem to

---

* While this is not a subject I have consciously explored in this book, sexual repression is itself a condition with potentially positive aspects, in so far as it enables some men to excel in other directions.

have been genuinely bisexual, and some who would normally be considered heterosexual but who had homosexual pasts, or who exhibited a strong vein of platonic homosexuality in their relationships with young men. (I have also included a few who had no discernible sexual feelings – though who knows what lurked in the hidden depths?) Inevitably, the result is more a bird's-eye glimpse of the subject than a thoroughgoing analysis: much remains shrouded in mystery; bricks have had to be made with limited straw; cautious use has sometimes been made of oral testimony whose value can be difficult to assess. My choice of subjects and the manner in which I have approached them are unashamedly idiosyncratic: to some I have devoted a chapter, to others a few lines; where appropriate, I have dealt with them in pairs, comparing and contrasting. (My list is not intended to be exhaustive, and I should be interested to hear from anyone who knows of other candidates.) While I hope the study will prove instructive, I have tried not to draw too many conclusions, leaving it to the reader to decide what patterns (if any) emerge.

In the not so distant past, to describe anyone (let alone a public figure) as a homosexual was a slur, and a book dedicated to so describing a whole group of people would have been regarded as potentially libellous in the case of the living, a cruel attack on those who cannot answer back in the case of the dead, and altogether in poor taste. But now that, in most Western societies, homosexuality is generally accepted as a normal preference, and psychologists usually consider that an element of it, acknowledged or otherwise, resides in us all, it is surely time to try to understand the strain of 'closet-queenery' which runs through recent political history and has made a significant (and by no means entirely negative) contribution to it. And it implies no disrespect to these often brave and gifted men, and to the tribulations and disappointments they

endured, to suggest that the phenomenon, viewed retrospec-
tively, of professing one set of mores for public consumption
and adhering (if only mentally) to another for private satisfaction possesses comedic possibilities: I make no apology for
the fact that this book aims to entertain as well as enlighten. It
might be said that such lives were hypocritical. But hypocrisy
is not one of the seven deadly sins; it can spare feelings, avert
trouble, and act as a useful social lubricant. It is said to be a very
British quality.

Something must be said about the sexual climate in which
these men operated. From the dawn of English history until
recent times, sexual acts between males were severely
penalised by various laws: in particular, under the Buggery
Act of 1533 (repealed in 1861) sodomy was a capital offence.
Nevertheless, provided reasonable discretion was exercised,
it was generally possible to indulge one's tastes and form relationships while avoiding trouble, especially for those of rank
or wealth. London seems to have had a vibrant homosexual
subculture for centuries (though one hesitates to use the
word 'homosexual', with all its modern connotations, in connection with the era before the coining of the word in the
1890s); and homosexual behaviour traditionally flourished in
all-male societies such as schools and colleges, the army and
navy, and religious houses, as well as at the royal court and in
the theatrical and musical worlds. However, a new factor
during the Victorian period was the rise of Evangelical
Christianity and the associated 'purity movement' which
sought to cleanse the land of 'vice' and contain the 'scourge'
of prostitution (including male prostitution) which had
become endemic in the capital. This tendency triumphed
with the passage of the Criminal Law Amendment Act of
1885, which raised the age of (heterosexual) consent from

thirteen to sixteen, and incidentally – through the notorious amendment proposed by the Liberal MP Henry Labouchere, owner and editor of the journal *Truth* which dedicated itself to 'exposing corruption and moral degeneration' – introduced the crime of 'gross indecency' between males: this was undefined, but was later taken to apply to almost any homosexual behaviour down to a mere act of touching.

During the closing years of the nineteenth century, the 'homophobic' public mood was intensified by two widely publicised scandals. In the Cleveland Street affair of 1889, police discovered a male brothel operating in the thoroughfare of that name, staffed by 'telegraph boys' working at London's main post office nearby and including well-known aristocrats among its clients. The authorities were anxious to cover up the affair, especially as the Queen's senior grandson, Prince Albert Victor, was rumoured to have visited the establishment; the brothel-keeper was allowed to escape abroad, as were some prominent clients (notably the Prince of Wales's equerry Lord Arthur Somerset), and though some of the boys and their 'minders' were prosecuted, they received light sentences. After a muted beginning the affair raised an outcry in the press, as well as in parliament (where the government was lambasted by Labouchere for its exculpatory role); it left an impression on the public of homosexuality as an aristocratic vice which led to the corruption of working-class youths. This impression was spectacularly reinforced a few years later by the case of Oscar Wilde (1895), the most famous dramatist of the day, who, following the collapse of his foolish libel action against the 9th Marquess of Queensberry, was convicted under the Labouchere Amendment and given the maximum sentence of two years' hard labour after a series of criminal proceedings which had featured the evidence of a procession of rent boys, luridly reported by the popular press. (Another result of the exposure of Wilde, who as a leading light of the 'aesthetic' movement had affected outrageously camp mannerisms, was that homosexuality became closely associated in the public imagination with effeminacy – in earlier times, the stereotype of the 'bugger' had rather been that of a butch predator.)

As the twentieth century began, therefore, homosexuals operated in an unprecedented climate of fear (described in E. M. Forster's novel *Maurice*, written in 1913 but only published in 1971 after his death). Another discouraging factor was that the public schools, and all-male youth associations such as the Boy Scouts (founded in 1908 by the repressed homosexual Robert Baden-Powell), while providing fertile ground for homosexual behaviour, preached a fierce cult of abstinence based on the idea that all sexual activity outside marriage was both sinful and unhealthy. Yet it is easy to exaggerate the tribulations undergone by middle-class British homosexuals, at least during the first half of the century. Certainly, one needed to be secretive about one's inclinations and discreet in one's associations; but the need to operate clandestinely lent an extra spice to life, and one was generally safe so long as one drew one's partners and confidants from a trusted circle of friends. Thus homosexuality flourished within the confines of fraternities such as the Bloomsbury Group. (During the 1930s a clandestine fraternity of this kind may be said to have existed in the House of Commons: homosexual MPs such as Bernays, Boothby, Bracken, Bullock, Cartland, Cazalet, Channon, Latham, Lennox-Boyd, Macnamara, Nicolson and Sassoon knew each other well, were aware of each other's tastes and often met socially.) The police investigated complaints, and sometimes harassed those who 'importuned' in streets, bars and clubs, or who engaged in sexual activity in public parks and lavatories, but until the 1950s they did not usually concern themselves with what went on behind closed doors, and investigations unprompted by complaints were rare. Thus of those relatively few twentieth-century politicians whose careers were effectively terminated by their exposure as homosexuals, just one (Freeth) came to grief as the result of an official investigation, and two others (Harcourt and Latham) on account of inquiries caused by a complaint. Of the remainder, two (Beauchamp and Thorpe) fell because they were hounded by individuals determined to expose and ruin them; two (Fletcher-Cooke and, possibly, Crookshank) because they engaged in risky associations which came to the notice of the authorities; four (Field, Harvey, Hampson and Davies) because of alleged misbehaviour in public places; and several in the 1980s and 90s because they were 'outed' by the press (something which would have been unimaginable in previous decades). So far as one can tell, the political careers of the other fifty-odd men mentioned in this book do not seem to have been seriously endangered by their homosexuality (which in several cases, indeed, was repressed, 'platonic', or confined to episodes in the past). It is, of course, possible that some of them received the attentions of blackmailers (this being the main terror faced by gay men until recent times), or had to talk or bribe their way out of trouble; but if so they seem to have handled these situations effectively, as few traces now remain.*

The climate altered from decade to decade. In his fascinating book *Queer London, 1918–57* (University of Chicago Press, 2005), Matt Houlbrook shows that, in the metropolis, there were times when the police were particularly active in

---

* Exceptions include the case of George Thomas, as Leo Abse, who helped him out of blackmail situations, later wrote about the fact; and those great risk-takers Boothby, Driberg and Thorpe – there is fairly clear evidence that Boothby and Thorpe coped with blackmailers, while Driberg boasted to friends that he was 'an expert at bribing the police'.

their harassment of homosexuals, and others when they were relatively inactive and it was possible to operate without great risk. The two world wars – during which millions of sex-starved youths were drafted into the armed services, men lived for the moment and the blackout provided anonymity – witnessed an explosion of more or less unregulated homosexual behaviour; in the immediate aftermath of those conflicts, thanks to an austere public mood induced by the loss and suffering, and the protests of the 'purity brigade' about the collapse of public morals, there was something of a 'crackdown'. Owing partly to the male camaraderie which had been instilled by wartime service, partly to a sharp reaction against pre-war morality, homosexuality became rather fashionable in the 1920s, and not merely among such socially privileged groups as the 'Brideshead generation' at Oxford: this was a period when women bobbed their hair, dressed so as to look flat-chested and generally tried to appear 'boyish' in order to attract men. It was still necessary to exercise considerable discretion (indeed, the sense of belonging to a 'secret society' was part of the thrill); but homosexual circles of one kind or another proliferated.

By far the most hazardous decade for homosexuals was the 1950s – a case of the darkest hour occurring before the dawn. On the one hand, a fiercely homophobic Home Secretary, Sir David Maxwell Fyfe,* aided by an equally puritanical Director of Public Prosecutions, Sir Theobald Matthew, was determined to 'rid England of this plague'; on the other hand, the defection to Moscow in 1951, at one of the 'hottest' moments of the Cold War, of two raffish Soviet agents working at the

* Except on the issue of homosexuality, Maxwell Fyfe was regarded as a fairly liberal Home Secretary: he helped draft the European Convention on Human Rights, opposed corporal punishment, and introduced a bill restricting the operation of the death penalty.

Foreign Office, Guy Burgess and Donald Maclean, of whom the first was homosexual and the second bisexual, reinforced the official view that all homosexuals were 'security risks' who had to be 'rooted out' in the national interest, a view encouraged by the Americans who were then convulsed with McCarthyite paranoia about such matters. The result was that the police started treating homosexuals as a dangerous fraternity who had to be systematically identified and rounded up: those arrested were promised leniency if they revealed their contacts, who were in turn arrested; search warrants were obtained to raid private premises with a view to obtaining 'incriminating' private correspondence. This was a terrible period, during which many men who had done no more than engage in occasional private consensual encounters, such as the cryptographer Alan Turing and the writer Rupert Croft-Cooke, suffered prosecution and disgrace. The most notable victims of the witch-hunt were three distinguished men – the glamorous Lord Montagu of Beaulieu, the Dorset landowner and war hero Michael Pitt-Rivers, and the journalist Peter Wildeblood – who at a highly publicised trial in Winchester in March 1954 were convicted and sentenced to a year's imprisonment for having allegedly committed illegal acts with two RAF servicemen at a beach hut on Lord Montagu's Hampshire estate. Two aspects of the case cast light on the prevailing hysteria. The previous year Montagu had been charged with similar offences involving boy scouts, but the case had collapsed when the boys withdrew their evidence; it would seem that the authorities, wishing to 'make an example' of a high-profile victim, were determined one way or another to 'get' the young peer (he was then twenty-six) whose homosexuality was well known in society circles. And the trail of evidence which led to the conviction began when RAF personnel throughout the world had their kit examined specifically with a view to finding letters indicating 'suspicious' male friendships.

However, even before the Montagu trial ended, Maxwell Fyfe was recommending to the cabinet that they establish a royal commission to reconsider the law regarding homosexuality, seeing that there was 'a considerable body of opinion which regards the existing law as antiquated and out of harmony with modern knowledge and ideas'; the cabinet was not keen, as the matter was so controversial and the government with its small parliamentary majority would soon have to face the electorate, but Maxwell Fyfe was insistent, and finally it was agreed to appoint a less 'public' departmental committee to examine the subject: this was announced in April 1954 and set up in July under the chairmanship of the Vice-Chancellor of Reading University, John Wolfenden. Why the homophobic Maxwell Fyfe, who was then orchestrating the unprecedented national persecution of homosexuals, should have gone out of his way to persuade a reluctant cabinet to institute this body is something of a mystery. When, in September 1957, the Wolfenden Committee, after deliberating for three years, reported with a majority recommendation that homosexual acts committed in private between consenting males over the age of twenty should cease to be criminal, Maxwell Fyfe, now Viscount Kilmuir and Lord Chancellor, declared that he was 'not going down in history as the man who made sodomy legal'. The idea of an official investigative body had originally been suggested to Maxwell Fyfe in 1953 by a fellow Conservative MP, Sir Robert Boothby (who was himself bisexual, though few of his colleagues were aware of this as he had for years been conducting a highly visible affair with the wife of another prominent Conservative, Harold Macmillan). Boothby and Maxwell Fyfe had been fellow Oxford undergraduates after the First World War, and it may be that Boothby knew of some

secret in Maxwell Fyfe's past (possibly even a youthful homosexual escapade) which enabled him to put pressure on the
minister to take the (for him) bizarre step of recommending
the Committee's establishment.* In any case, the cabinet of
1957 agreed with Kilmuir that no steps should be taken to
implement the Wolfenden recommendations, and they
remained unimplemented for another ten years. It is one of the
many ironies of this saga (as described in Chapter 11) that the
Macmillan government of 1957–63 which blocked Wolfenden
seems to have contained more closet queens than any other of
the century – during the years 1959 and 1960, for example, the
cabinet included a homosexual or bisexual Foreign Secretary,
Chancellor of the Exchequer, Colonial Secretary, Health
Secretary and Minister of Labour, and was presided over by a
Prime Minister who was rumoured to have been expelled from
Eton for homosexuality.

Although public opinion (in so far as it is possible to gauge
it) remained opposed to changing the law, a growing consen-
sus in the media, the arts, the churches and the professions
(including the legal and medical professions) supported
Wolfenden, and by the mid-1960s this included a majority in
both houses of parliament (the Lords expressing their support
before the Commons). The Labour government which came
to power in 1964 showed itself just as reluctant as its
Conservative predecessor to introduce the necessary legislation; but thanks to two of its more enlightened members, the
Home Secretary Roy Jenkins and the Leader of the House of
Commons Richard Crossman, both of whom had enjoyed

* In his book *The Other Love* (Heinemann, 1970), my late friend H. Montgomery
Hyde argues that it was the public furore resulting from the Montagu trial which
led to Wolfenden. Although Hyde was an MP at the time, and an ardent supporter
of homosexual law reform, he was evidently unaware that Maxwell Fyfe had first
raised the matter in cabinet in February 1954, one month prior to the proceedings against Montagu and his co-defendants at Winchester.

homosexual adventures in their youth, time was allowed for a Sexual Offences Bill which was privately introduced in the House of Lords by the 8th Earl of Arran and piloted through the House of Commons by Leo Abse MP, and which passed into law in July 1967. That marked just the start of a long campaign to secure legal equality for homosexuals, and the excitements and tribulations faced by gay or bisexual politicians were far from over – as will be described in the Epilogue.

During the dozen years I spent thinking about this book, and the couple of years I devoted to researching and writing it, many people helped me in various ways, and I should like to thank Andrew Best, Jackie Best, John Black, Simon Blow, David Bonner, Piers Brendon, Peter Brooke, Eva Chadwick, Claudia Connal, Richard Davenport-Hines, Juliana Deliyannis, Patric Dickinson, Antony Fletcher, Sue Fox, Jonathan Fryer, Zoe Gullen, Lady Selina Hastings, Jerry Hayes, Sir Michael Howard, Keith Jeffreys, Jonathan King, James Lees-Milne, Sir Mark Lennox-Boyd, Lord Lexden, Andrew Lownie, Ursula Mackenzie, Philip Mansel, Maddie Mogford, Hugh Montgomery-Massingberd, Alastair Morrison, Charles Orwin, Matthew Parris, John Ranelagh, John Rogister, Tony Scotland, Linda Silverman, Denis Staunton, Richard Thorpe, Moray Watson, Tim Whiting and Ed Wilson. Several helpers asked not to be mentioned, and I'm sorry if I've left anyone out.

Michael Bloch
August 2014

# 1

# ARCHIE, REGY, LOULOU AND BILL

We begin with four distinguished statesmen who, between them, were prominent in British public life from the 1880s to the 1930s – the 5th Earl of Rosebery ('Archie'), the 2nd Viscount Esher ('Regy'), the 1st Viscount Harcourt ('Loulou'), and the 7th Earl Beauchamp ('Bill'). All were educated at Eton, and profoundly affected by that school's ethos. In politics, they were all Liberals. (Esher, who began his career as private secretary to the leader of the Liberal Party, later became a politically neutral figure close to the leaders of both main parties, but remained a radical at heart.) Rosebery was Liberal Prime Minister in 1894–5; Harcourt and Beauchamp were members of the Liberal government of 1905–15; Esher, though never holding government office, exercised great influence behind the scenes of politics for three decades. Rosebery, Harcourt and Beauchamp all served at different times as First Commissioner of Works, ministerial head of the department which looked after the nation's properties (including the royal residences and parks), while Esher, as Secretary to the Office of Works, was for some years the department's presiding civil servant. All were married to rich women, to whom they appear to have been devoted: the marriages of Rosebery, Esher and Harcourt each produced four children, that of Beauchamp no fewer than seven. Yet they were all ruled by homosexual feelings, as a result of which one committed suicide, one was obliged to live most of the last decade of his life in exile, and one was arguably driven to the verge of madness by his repressed emotions. Only Esher managed to combine a successful marriage with a lifetime of fulfilling (though mostly platonic) relationships with young men – though in order to do so he renounced a promising career in conventional politics, contenting himself with the role of *éminence grise*.

On Gladstone's retirement in 1894, Archibald Primrose, 5th Earl of Rosebery (1847–1929), became Queen Victoria's tenth Prime Minister at the age of forty-six. Few premiers in British history have enjoyed so much public popularity on taking office. Rich, handsome, and a celebrated racehorse owner (whose horse twice won the Derby during his premiership), he was a glamorous figure, adored by the popular press. As Chairman of the London County Council, he had won a reputation as a social reformer; during two brief but successful terms as Foreign Secretary, he had shown himself a staunch imperialist at a time when the British Empire had become tremendously popular. He was an outstanding platform speaker, and a brilliant talker; he was also an accomplished writer, whose biography of Pitt the Younger (from whose sister he was descended) had been widely praised. He was the darling of the London crowds, and worshipped in his native Scotland. As his party and its allies appeared to command a comfortable parliamentary majority, and an election was not due for another five years, his premiership looked set to be long and distinguished.* Yet it proved to be the most shambolic of the Victorian era, coming to an ignominious end after only fifteen months in a resounding election defeat which kept the Liberals out of power for a decade.

For all his gifts and charms, Rosebery was a peculiar personality. A hypochondriac given to bouts of depression, he enjoyed little social life during his premiership, which he mostly spent alone at his house in Surrey, brooding melancholically and suffering from a series of mysterious illnesses. His obsessive secrecy led to problems in the business of government; his paranoid suspicion that his colleagues were conspiring against him (though not without foundation) tended to be self-fulfilling; his petulant and egocentric behaviour invited comparison with a spoilt child; his habitual reluctance to accept public office, despite an obvious streak of ambition, struck many as coquettish. Moreover, there were persistent rumours that Rosebery, a widower who surrounded himself with handsome male secretaries,† was homosexual. Oscar Wilde's disastrous libel case against the 9th Marquess of Queensberry, followed by his prosecution for homosexual offences, took place during Rosebery's last weeks in office. Rosebery was implicated in that Queensberry's eldest son, the

---

* These appearances were somewhat deceptive: the Liberals depended for their majority on the votes of the Irish Parliamentary Party, some of whose members, with the passing months, became reluctant to continue supporting the government.

† In 1898 Asquith's nineteen-year-old son Raymond, then staying with Rosebery, wrote of his secretary Waterfield: 'He must have been very handsome ... [and] inclines one to believe the worst of his illustrious master.' (John Joliffe [ed.], *Raymond Asquith: Life and Letters* [Collins, 1980], p. 50.) Rosebery had a close relationship with Ronald Munro Ferguson (1860–1934), a handsome young army officer whom he helped to get elected to the House of Commons and who served for a time as his private secretary: unusually affectionate letters from Rosebery to Munro Ferguson (who later, as Viscount Novar, became Governor-General of Australia) have survived. (Information from Lord Lexden.)

personable Francis, Viscount Drumlanrig, had been his private secretary, and Queensberry had been alleging that
Rosebery had 'consorted' with Drumlanrig just as Wilde was
consorting with his youngest son Lord Alfred Douglas, an
allegation which gained some credence with the dramatic
news that Drumlanrig had shot himself. Indeed, during
Wilde's trial Queensberry hinted that he possessed damning
evidence of Rosebery's proclivities as well as of Wilde's, which
he might make public unless Wilde was convicted. While it
seems fairly clear that Rosebery possessed homosexual leanings, opinion is divided as to whether he enjoyed physical
relationships with other men.

Rosebery was the pretty and precocious son of a Scottish
family with long traditions of public service, ennobled in the
seventeenth century. His father, who as MP for Stirling held
junior office in several Whig administrations, died when he
was three, and he had a difficult relationship with his mother,
who made a second marriage to the 4th Duke of Cleveland.*
Lord Dalmeny (as he was known as heir to the earldom) blossomed at Eton, where his wit, good looks and keen intellect
made him popular with both masters and boys. His great
mentor was William Johnson, an outstanding tutor who also
influenced two other men featured in this book, Balfour and
Esher. Johnson not only gave his pupils a superb education,
accompanied by philosophical advice which prepared them
for life; he also treated them as equals rather than underlings,
thus inspiring their affection and sometimes their love. He was
an unashamed favouritist, concentrating his attention on boys
who were clever and good-looking; he developed intense

---

* Seeing that many of the men mentioned in this book had unusually close
relationships with their mothers, it is worth noting that this was not the case
with the four subjects of this chapter: Harcourt and Beauchamp never knew
their mothers, while Rosebery and Esher did not get on with theirs.

romantic feelings for these protégés, and derived vicarious satisfaction by encouraging them to form intimate friendships among themselves. (He was probably chaste – though the homoerotic atmosphere he engendered led to his dismissal in 1872, some years after Dalmeny had left the school.) Dalmeny saw him as a father-figure and became one of his top favourites – though Johnson warned him that smugness and laziness might prove his undoing, that he was one of those 'who seek the palm without the dust'. It is unclear how far Dalmeny reciprocated Johnson's romantic interest; but he fell madly in love with at least one boy at the school – Frederick Vyner, by whose murder at the hands of Greek brigands in 1870 he was devastated, keeping the anniversary sacred for the rest of his life. He was also close to Edward Hamilton, who remained a lifelong friend (Hamilton, who never married, joined the civil service, and received both promotion and a knighthood during Rosebery's premiership).

As an undergraduate at Christ Church, Oxford, Dalmeny showed promise as a scholar, but (as Johnson had feared) abandoned himself to dissolute pleasures. While he was there his grandfather died and Rosebery (as he became) inherited the earldom, along with a substantial fortune. He used his inheritance to buy a string of racehorses; when told by the Christ Church authorities that this was not allowed for junior members of the college, he showed aristocratic disdain by abandoning his studies and leaving the university. During his twenties (which he largely devoted to racing and foreign travel), Rosebery met and impressed both Gladstone and Disraeli, who tried to recruit him to their respective causes: though he admired Disraeli more, he remained faithful to his family's Whig and reformist traditions, and gave his support to Gladstone. He declined a junior post in Gladstone's first government (which would have made him its youngest member, at twenty-four). However, after the Liberals lost office in 1874, he accepted the role of the party's chief campaigner in Scotland: he toured the country as a platform speaker, arousing great enthusiasm with his romantic looks and brilliant oratory.

In 1878, the thirty-year-old Rosebery, who had never shown much interest in women,* caused surprise by marrying Hannah, only child of the late Baron Meyer de Rothschild, to whom he had been introduced some years earlier by Disraeli. She was probably the richest woman in England, having inherited her father's immense fortune along with Mentmore, his neo-Gothic palace in Buckinghamshire with its fabulous art collection. As she was gauche, unworldly, far from beautiful and already getting fat, it was generally assumed that Rosebery was marrying her for her money, but she possessed other attractions for him – she had an intellect equal to his own, and offered him the uncritical adoration which satisfied his vanity. By his marriage to a Jewess, which scandalised both English society and the Jewish establishment, Rosebery also expressed his patrician contempt for convention. (The two continued to adhere to their respective religions.) He became extremely fond of her – though on the rare occasions when they appeared together in public (for she was happy to stay at home while he went about in society) he was apt to tease her with mildly anti-semitic remarks. She bore him two sons and two daughters: Rosebery was never very close to his elder son Harry, who was rather Jewish-looking, but adored his younger son, the classically beautiful Neil.

Soon after Rosebery's marriage, Gladstone, who had retired

---

* Rosebery's latest biographer Leo McKinstry mentions a few dalliances with actresses; but this was so *de rigueur* for a young nobleman in Rosebery's position that not much can be read into it. He was famously misogynistic and preferred to attend all-male social gatherings.

from politics following his 1874 defeat, decided to make a comeback. Rosebery persuaded him to stand for the Scottish seat of Midlothian (which included Rosebery's estate at Dalmeny), and managed his two famous campaigns there before the 1880 general election: the result was a resounding victory both for Gladstone personally and for the Liberals throughout the country. Rosebery felt that his services entitled him to a place in Gladstone's new cabinet; but Gladstone, though grateful, insisted that Rosebery, who was still in his early thirties and had never held public office, serve first in a junior post. Rosebery sulked for a year before accepting a subordinate position at the Home Office, from which he later resigned in a huff. Gladstone then accepted Rosebery's suggestion that a new ministry be created to deal with the affairs of Scotland; but when he offered to make Rosebery the first Scottish Secretary, Rosebery refused as the office was not yet in the cabinet. Only in January 1885 did Rosebery reluctantly accept the most lowly of cabinet posts as First Commissioner of Works. However, when Gladstone formed his third administration a year later, Rosebery's tactic of 'playing hard to get' finally paid off when he was appointed Foreign Secretary at the age of thirty-eight. Although the administration only lasted five months, Rosebery won golden opinions for his skilful conduct of diplomacy. He defused a dangerous crisis in the Balkans, consolidated the British position in Egypt, and stood up to both Russia and Germany when they threatened British interests, while doing nothing which might risk war.

Rosebery was a lifelong campaigner for reform of the House of Lords: he thought it absurd that the chamber should consist entirely of hereditary legislators, with the Conservatives in a permanent majority. When a reform proposal he put forward in 1888 came to nothing, he wanted to renounce his peerage and stand for the House of Commons, but was advised that this was legally impossible. He therefore stood in the first elections to the new London County Council in 1889, and duly won his seat; at the Council's first session, he made a speech of such brilliance that he was immediately elected Chairman by 104 votes to 17. He served as Chairman for eighteen months, winning widespread admiration for his moulding of the Council into a progressive and non-partisan body which built schools, cleared slums, improved public health and generally got things done. Following this episode, many Liberals began to see Rosebery as a potential successor to Gladstone and future Prime Minister. However, he was shattered by the sudden death of his wife from Bright's disease in November 1890, following which he announced his retirement from politics. Nevertheless, when the octogenarian Gladstone formed his fourth and last administration in August 1892, Rosebery (after the usual hesitations) agreed to resume the foreign secretaryship. His second period in charge of British diplomacy was largely taken up with colonial affairs: he accomplished the British annexation of Uganda, while preventing the French annexation of Siam. He also pressed for an expansion of the Royal Navy, to which the cabinet agreed with reluctance, it being unclear where the extra money would be found.

When the Liberals took office in 1892, their parliamentary majority depended on the support of the Irish Nationalist MPs, whose aspirations Gladstone aimed to satisfy by granting Home Rule. However, in September 1893 the Home Rule Bill was rejected by the House of Lords. Having failed to realise his main objective, Gladstone, who at eighty-three was showing signs of senility, was expected to retire soon. The obvious candidate to succeed him as Liberal leader and Prime Minister was the Chancellor of the Exchequer, Sir William Harcourt, an experienced political heavyweight who had effectively been recognised as Gladstone's deputy since 1886. However, Harcourt had so antagonised his colleagues by his overbearing behaviour that few of them wished to serve under him. The best alternative seemed to be Rosebery: although far younger and less experienced than Harcourt, and a peer at a time when his fellow peers had just thrown out the main item of the government's programme, he was the minister most popular with the public, had been a notable success as Foreign Secretary, and was the candidate favoured by the Queen. Though eager for the premiership, Harcourt was prepared to serve under Rosebery provided he was recognised as the second man in the government, leading it in the House of Commons. But an obstacle to the smooth transfer of power was Harcourt's son Lewis, known as 'Loulou' (to be considered later in this chapter). Loulou had served as his father's private secretary for the previous thirteen years, during which he had schemed to ensure Sir William's eventual succession to Gladstone: he could not bear to think that his efforts had been in vain and that the prize would fall to Rosebery, who did not seem to want it. Loulou succeeded in poisoning the minds of several ministers (notably the Irish Secretary John Morley) against Rosebery; and while his father ignored his advice to refuse to serve under Rosebery, the son's continuing influence ensured that Harcourt would be an obstructive deputy.

These were the inauspicious circumstances in which Rosebery, in March 1894, exchanged the Foreign Office, where he was his own master, for the 'dunghill' (as he called it) of the premiership. Two events during his first weeks in office boded ill for his tenure. Harcourt (who remained Chancellor) introduced his annual budget, in which he raised revenue for the naval expansion desired by Rosebery by introducing a system of graduated death duties: Rosebery, who foresaw that this would lead to the eventual destruction of the landed class to which he belonged, was appalled, but as one of the richest men in Britain was ill-placed to resist. And a colonial scheme on which Rosebery had set his heart, involving an exchange of territory with the Belgian Congo which would have given Britain control of an uninterrupted corridor 'from the Cape to Cairo', foundered on the objections of Harcourt and other ministers (encouraged by Loulou). Having hitherto led a charmed political life, Rosebery took these failures to heart. His only consolation was the widespread jubilation over the victory of his horse Ladas II* at the Derby in June, which (while rather shocking strait-laced nonconformist Liberals) confirmed his continuing public popularity.

Meanwhile a continuing nightmare for Rosebery was Queensberry's vicious campaign against him. On becoming Foreign Secretary in 1892 he had appointed Queensberry's heir Drumlanrig, a handsome charmer, his private secretary; and only a few months later he arranged for Drumlanrig, who was twenty-six and had yet to demonstrate any outstanding talents, to be made a junior member of the government, with a seat in the House of Lords. This enraged Queensberry, who was not himself entitled to sit in the upper chamber.† He suspected Rosebery of having sexual relations with his son, and expressed these suspicions in intemperate letters to various personages including the Queen. In August 1893 Queensberry followed Rosebery to Bad Homburg, where he was taking a cure, with the declared intention of giving him a horse-whipping, and had to be dissuaded by the Prince of

---

* Named after an athlete in the service of Alexander the Great. Ladas I had been Rosebery's first horse, which had come last in the Derby of 1869.

† The Scottish peers, of whom Queensberry was one, elected sixteen of their number to represent them in the House of Lords; Queensberry had in fact been elected as a representative peer, but had been disqualified in 1880 when, as an atheist, he refused to take the oath of allegiance to the sovereign.

Wales who was also staying there. This behaviour could be dismissed as the ravings of a madman; but in October 1894, the eighth month of Rosebery's premiership, Drumlanrig, who was staying with a family to whose daughter he had recently become engaged, detached himself from a shooting party and proceeded to kill himself by firing his gun through the roof of his mouth. The inquest returned a verdict of accidental death, but this seemed improbable, and gossip began to circulate that Queensberry's accusations were true, and that Drumlanrig, with a view to protecting his former lover and current leader, had first made a gesture towards matrimony, and then committed suicide.

Much controversy has raged over Rosebery's rumoured homosexuality. Of his two principal biographers, Robert Rhodes James (1963) does not mention it at all. (It is true that homosexuality was still illegal and almost unmentionable in 1963; but Rhodes James, who was Conservative MP for Cambridge from 1976 to 1992, made a career out of writing biographies of homosexual or bisexual politicians while barely mentioning this aspect of their natures: other subjects treated in this way, to be considered later, include Bob Boothby, Victor Cazalet and Chips Channon.) More recently, Leo McKinstry (2005) examines the evidence and concludes that it is all circumstantial and that, apart from adolescent infatuations at Eton, there is no proof that Rosebery ever had homosexual relations with anyone. But what proof would one expect to find? Rosebery was not just discreet but obsessively secretive. He insisted on opening all his own letters (which did not surprise Loulou Harcourt, 'from my knowledge of what some of them must contain'); and during his later years he not only destroyed many of his own papers, but secured the return of intimate letters he had written to various correspondents (including William Johnson and Frederick Vyner), which he duly burnt. He also took unusual precautions to shield himself from prying eyes: at one of his Scottish residences, Barnbougle Castle, he lived in solitary splendour with a few trusted servants, and not even members of his family were allowed to visit him. Given such cautious behaviour, and his wealth, he would probably have been able to indulge a secret, illicit sex life had he wished to do so, without significant risk of exposure, even to future generations. But whether or not Rosebery engaged in physical homosexual relationships is beside the point. The circumstantial evidence – that he disliked the company of women, and delighted in that of handsome youths; that he married a rich and physically unattractive woman whom he loved as a kind of mother figure; that he was petulant, coquettish, and intensely narcissistic;* that he behaved like a man who possessed a guilty secret; that his favourite holiday destination throughout his life was Naples, the homosexual Mecca of the time; that his closest friends included several men who were clearly homosexual, such as 'Regy' Esher (to be considered presently) and Horatio Brown (historian of Venice and lover of its gondoliers); and that there was much knowing gossip about him in homosexual circles – leaves little doubt that he possessed homosexual tendencies; so that Queensberry's allegations, whether true or not, would have touched a raw nerve.

What is beyond dispute is that, in the months following Drumlanrig's death, Rosebery collapsed both physically and psychologically. He began to suffer from chronic insomnia, and increasingly withdrew to The Durdans, his house near Epsom, discouraging visitors. He took to his bed with a series

---

* A cartoon by Max Beerbohm shows him admiring himself in shop windows (which may have been a homosexual allusion, as gazing protractedly into shop windows was the recognised method at the time of indicating that one was looking to 'pick up' another man in the street).

of ailments, most of them probably psychosomatic, and befud-
dled his mind with drugs. It has been suggested that this
breakdown was mainly provoked by exasperation at the
obstructiveness of cabinet colleagues, but his later recollections suggest a more personal explanation: 'I cannot forget
1895. To lie awake night after night, wide awake, hopeless of
sleep, tormented of nerves, and to realise all that was going on,
at which I was present, so to speak, like a disembodied spirit,
to watch one's own corpse, as it were, day after day, is an experience which no sane man would repeat.' Rosebery was in the
midst of his ailing seclusion when Wilde issued his libel writ
against Queensberry in February 1895. (Despite much provo-
cation over the previous two years, Rosebery had refrained
from taking similar action, which was wise whether or not
there was any truth in Queensberry's insinuations.) Given that
Rosebery and Wilde had been tarred with the same brush by
'the mad marquess', there was speculation that Rosebery's neurotic behaviour arose from a fear that his name would be
mentioned during Wilde's case. Although Rosebery's breakdown had begun well before Wilde launched his disastrous
action, Rosebery would have been right to be concerned – at
a preliminary hearing in the case, a letter from Queensberry
was produced referring to Wilde as 'a damned cur and coward
of the Rosebery type' (i.e., a homosexual). Wilde's case soon
collapsed, Queensberry having produced a host of witnesses
to his proclivities, whereupon he was prosecuted under the
Labouchere Amendment for 'gross indecency'. After his first
trial had ended with the jury's failure to agree, several people,
including Edward Carson who had represented Queensberry
in the libel case, urged the authorities to drop the case against
Wilde, who had already suffered both financial and reputa-
tional ruin; but the government accepted the view of the
Solicitor-General, Sir Frank Lockwood, that Wilde had to be

retried, or else the public might imagine that Queensberry's allegations against Rosebery were true, and that Wilde had 'got off' owing to influence exerted by or on behalf of the premier. Possibly a suspicion that the allegations were backed by some evidence, which Queensberry might reveal (as he was threatening to do) if deprived of Wilde's scalp, also played a role.

Wilde was convicted and sent to prison on 25 May; Rosebery tendered the resignation of his government on 22 June. He did not need to do so, for the Liberals and their allies still possessed a parliamentary majority (though the Irish MPs were becoming restive). But the government had suffered a chance defeat on a minor issue of army supply; Rosebery chose to make this a resigning issue, and his colleagues did not try to dissuade him. He had clearly lost all enthusiasm for the premiership, and no longer seemed capable of exercising it. The programme of his administration lay in tatters, its domestic legislation obstructed by the House of Lords, its foreign policy (guided by Rosebery himself) by Harcourt and his cabinet allies. Its sole practical achievement had been Harcourt's death duties, to which Rosebery had been so opposed. The Conservatives under Salisbury returned to power and held an immediate general election in which the Liberals, rather to Rosebery's satisfaction, fared disastrously. Rosebery soon surrendered the leadership to Harcourt, who no longer wanted it. The Liberals were now split between their imperialist and radical factions: the former, led by Asquith and Grey, still looked up to Rosebery, but he alienated them by his failure to consult them, and by his inaccessibility – he spent most of his time in Scotland or Naples. He was still only in his fifties, and widely expected to make a comeback. He made vague moves towards setting up a new political movement, but most of his potential supporters deserted him after he had shown solidarity with the Conservative government over both Ireland and the Boer

War. When the Liberals returned to power in 1905, Rosebery, who had always displayed such reluctance over accepting office, waited for the call to join the new administration, and was dismayed when it never came. He sniped at the government from the wings, and in 1911 was critical of its legislation to emasculate the upper chamber (preferring a change in its composition to a decrease in its powers), though he begrudgingly voted in favour of the measure, following which he never set foot in the House of Lords again.

As a former Prime Minister, Rosebery published three books which won him a reputation as a historian. His choice of subjects was interesting. Two of them dealt with the bitter last years of two great statesmen, Pitt the Elder and Napoleon. The third was a biography of his late friend, the maverick Conservative politician Lord Randolph Churchill, whose career had fizzled out after a brilliant early start. When Rosebery described Churchill as 'the chief mourner at his own protracted funeral', he was generally thought to be referring to himself.

In 1916, when Lloyd George came to power at a time of national crisis, he invited Rosebery, as an elder statesman, to join his administration in an unspecified capacity. Rosebery refused – though his adored younger son Neil Primrose, a Liberal MP since 1910, accepted junior office in the new government. However, the following year, Neil, who had chosen to interrupt his political career with a spell of military service, was killed fighting the Turks in Palestine, aged thirty-four.* This was a devastating blow from which Rosebery did not

---

* Two years before his death, Neil had married Lady Victoria Stanley, daughter of the Conservative statesman the 17th Earl of Derby. Her second husband, whom she married in 1919, was Neil's close friend and regimental comrade Malcolm Bullock (1890–1966), who served as a Conservative MP from the 1920s to the 1950s, and had a homosexual reputation. (One daughter resulted from each of the marriages.)

recover. Shortly afterwards he suffered a stroke, becoming a pitiable figure during the last years of his life (which was surprisingly long, seeing that he had supposedly been at death's door during his premiership in 1895, thirty-four years before his actual demise in 1929). On his deathbed, he asked for a gramophone record to be played of the Eton Boating Song, the words of which had been written by his beloved William Johnson.

Unlike the other subjects of this chapter, Reginald Baliol Brett, 2nd Viscount Esher (1852–1930), was not an aristocrat of ancient lineage, but the son of a successful barrister who briefly served as Solicitor-General under Disraeli and was ennobled after becoming Master of the Rolls; his mother was French, and probably illegitimate, which lent an exotic touch to his background. 'Regy' Brett (as he was known until his father's death in 1899) was an appealing, clever, rather languid youth of twenty-five when, through various connections, he was appointed private secretary to the Marquess of Hartington in 1878. Hartington was then leader of the Liberal Party, though after the Liberal election victory of 1880 he stood aside to let Gladstone resume the premiership, serving under him as Secretary of State for India and for War. Brett, who from 1880 to 1885 combined his secretarial duties with being MP for Falmouth, seemed on the threshold of a promising career in Liberal politics, but he had other ideas. During his years with Hartington he had discovered an unusual ability to charm the great and win their confidence, along with a talent for intrigue and manipulation. (While still in his twenties, he engineered the appointment of his friend Lord Ripon as Viceroy of India.) For thirty years, from the mid-1880s to the First World War, he was on close terms with the leading figures of both political parties, who confided in him and consulted him: during those years there were few serious issues on which he was not in the know and did not have a say. In particular, he enjoyed the intimate friendship of two men who, like himself, had been protégés of William Johnson at Eton: the Liberal Rosebery and the Conservative Balfour, each destined to become leader of his party and Prime Minister (though while valuing Esher, they never liked each other). Rosebery generally refused to receive cabinet colleagues at home, but was always happy to see Brett; while Brett often called on Balfour before breakfast and sat on his bed, discussing the events of the day. In addition, Brett became a favourite of all three sovereigns under whom he lived, Queen Victoria, Edward VII and George V, who often sought his advice and usually took it: he was especially close to King Edward, who during his reign consulted him almost daily on every subject. He also cultivated leading newspaper editors, such as Buckle of *The Times* and Stead of the *Pall Mall Gazette*, which effectively enabled him to create whatever publicity he wished on any subject that interested him.

Though scarcely known to the public, Esher became one of the most powerful men of the land, and his influence was often resented by the politicians, civil servants, diplomats and courtiers who felt sidelined by him. But it was impossible to hold him to account as he never accepted any major position of responsibility. He only ever held two minor public posts – in the civil service, as Secretary to the Office of Works from 1895 to 1902 (to which he was appointed by his friend Rosebery), and at court, as Deputy Constable and Lieutenant-Governor of Windsor Castle (a sinecure accepted in 1901 from a grateful King Edward). The exalted posts which he was offered and refused included Governor of Cape Colony, Secretary of State for War (twice by the Conservatives and once by the Liberals), and Viceroy of India. (He also declined an earldom, the editorship of two national newspapers, and the job of writing Disraeli's official biography.) In his private diaries, and confidential letters to his younger son, he explained some of the reasons behind his reluctance to accept office. On refusing the South African governorship, he wrote (December 1900) that it would distance him from a private life that was precious to him. On first refusing the War Office, he wrote (September 1903) that 'I really do not think I can sacrifice all independence, all liberty of action, all my *intime* life, for a position which adds nothing to that which I now occupy'. On refusing the viceroyalty, he wrote (October 1908): 'I am confident that in going to India, I should be throwing away the substance of power for the shadow. Besides, every day questions arise of vital importance to our country, when [by remaining in England] I can have my say and sway a decision.' And during the First World War, in which he carried out various important roles without any official status at all, he wrote (March 1915) that 'I am not going to "regularise" my position, which means that someone else can give me orders – I never have'.

What impelled Esher in his quest for power without glory? Clearly he enjoyed exercising influence from behind the scenes; but he was also a patriot, who successfully advanced three long-term causes in which he believed. First, having served under Hartington at the War Office, Esher felt that the antiquated British Army required drastic reform if it was to be ready to fight a European war. Britain's undistinguished military performance in the Boer War gave him his opportunity, and in 1903–4, in the teeth of much opposition but with the support of both Balfour and Edward VII, he chaired a committee which abolished the post of Commander-in-Chief, established a general staff, reorganised the War Office and entrusted future policy to a Committee of Imperial

Defence of which Esher himself became a permanent member. As the military historian Correlli Barnett has written, 'without Esher ... it is inconceivable that the British military efforts of two world wars could have been possible, let alone generally successful'. Secondly, being half-French, a fluent French speaker and a lover of French literature, he was an ardent francophile, who encouraged the Entente Cordiale of 1904 and Britain's subsequent moves towards becoming France's ally. For much of the First World War he effectively managed Anglo-French relations, over the head of the furious British Ambassador to Paris, Lord Bertie. Thirdly, Esher, a romantic royalist, was concerned to enhance the prestige of the British monarchy. At the Office of Works he stage-managed three great royal events – Queen Victoria's Diamond Jubilee in 1897, her funeral in 1901, and King Edward's Coronation in 1902 – establishing a tradition of spectacular royal ceremonial which helped maintain the monarchy's popularity. He persuaded Edward VII to entrust him with the care of the Royal Archives, which he used to produce royalist propaganda, notably by supervising a carefully expurgated edition of Queen Victoria's letters which portrayed the late sovereign (who was in fact stupid, interfering and prejudiced) as a wise, impartial and steadying influence in British public life. Esher himself wrote several historical works which stressed the benign role of the monarchy – it was mostly as an author that he was known to the public.

Esher's shadowy career was mirrored by an equally shadowy private life, dominated by a series of infatuations with adolescent boys and young men. Most of these were probably platonic, but his first serious love clearly contained a physical element. At Eton, Regy Brett (as he then was) fell strongly under the influence of William Johnson, whom he came to revere. (When Johnson was subsequently dismissed from the school, Regy, then a Cambridge undergraduate, took a term off to stay with and console him; and in 1923 he published a biography of him.) Under the great tutor's indulgent eye, Regy had affairs with several other boys in Johnson's charmed circle, including Francis Elliot, a future diplomat, and the Finch-Hatton brothers, sons of the Earl of Winchelsea. But his great love was Charles Williamson, a handsome Scot a year younger than himself, known as 'Chat'. In his diary for October 1868 the sixteen-year-old Brett records the following (probably not untypical) Sunday evening scene at Johnson's lodgings:

> Elliot and I lay together on the long morocco sofa. He put his dear strong arms round me & his face against mine. W. J[ohnson] in the big red chair close to our sofa. We kept calling for Chat, & finally he was lifted on to us, nestling in between Elliot and me. My arms were around him, & Elliot's were round him and me.

At this time Chat, who had other suitors, showed himself reluctant to abandon himself to Regy, but the following year they began a passionate affair, partly carried on during school holidays at Johnson's house in Devon. They remained lovers until 1875, when Chat, who had been deeply affected by the death of another Eton contemporary, decided to become a Catholic priest. Regy then transferred his romantic attention to two others: Ernlé Johnson (no relation of William), an emotionally susceptible fifteen-year-old schoolboy with Fauntleroy looks, with whom he began a friendship mostly carried on by correspondence, and probably platonic; and the magnificently handsome and devil-may-care Lord Binning, an Etonian four years younger than himself, with whom his relations were probably non-platonic. Brett was notably loyal to friends, and would stay in touch with Chat, Ernlé and Binning for the rest of their lives and help them out of various sorts of trouble.

In 1879, the twenty-seven-year-old Regy married a girl of seventeen, Eleanor ('Nellie') van de Weyer, whom he had met four years earlier through her cousins the Sturgis brothers, a pair of rich Americans (the younger of whom was homosexual) who had been at Eton with Regy and become great friends. Nellie was the youngest of six children of Baron Sylvain van de Weyer, an eminent Belgian who had served for long years as his country's diplomatic representative in London, and his wife, a Boston heiress. The marriage in some ways resembled that of Rosebery the previous year to Hannah de Rothschild, for Nellie was rich (at least sufficiently so to give Regy financial independence), worshipped her husband, and was happy to stay at home while he flitted about in political and social circles. From Regy's point of view she possessed two other advantages. Her parents had been friends of Queen Victoria; and although they had both recently died, her sister was one of the Queen's ladies-in-waiting, while her brother lived on an estate next to Windsor Great Park where he was frequently visited by the sovereign. (Eager to profit from this connection, Regy bought some of his brother-in-law's land, on which he built a house of his own, Orchard Lea.) And Nellie seems not only to have been aware of Regy's homosexual interests, but untroubled by them: indeed, she was generally happy to welcome both his former and current *amours*. Like Hannah, she bore her husband two sons and two daughters; like Rosebery, Regy concentrated his affections on the younger son.

Following his marriage, Brett guarded himself against writing letters and keeping diaries testifying to his secret life; but as he later wrote that he could not recollect the day when he had not cared passionately for a male friend, presumably there was a succession of young favourites. The next of these of whom we know was a blond Eton 'barbarian' of fifteen called Teddie Seymour for whom Regy fell in 1892, to the extent that he dedicated to him his first book which appeared that year, *Footprints of Statesmen*. Though interested in girls, Teddie enjoyed the attentions of his forty-year-old suitor and revelled in his power over him. He dropped in to see him at Orchard Lea whenever he pleased, and accepted Regy's presents and flattery as his due. When Regy announced that he was going abroad, Teddie objected – 'just think how I would get on; no talks, no advice, no nothing' – so Regy remained in England, and invited Teddie to join him on a holiday in the Isle of Wight. The relationship was to some extent 'protected' as Teddie's mother (sister of the Sturgis brothers) was Nellie's cousin, and Nellie was indeed happy to treat the boy as one of the family; but it nevertheless raised eyebrows both at Eton, where Regy constantly visited Teddie, and among statesmen such as Balfour who may have been surprised to find Teddie included in a luncheon designed to exchange political gossip. It may not have been entirely platonic – Regy wrote to Chat that they took baths together, that he enjoyed stroking the boy's hair, that Teddie was in the engaging habit of throwing off his clothes on ensconcing himself in Regy's study. He remained under Teddie's thrall until the youth left Eton aged eighteen, when Regy, attempting to get him into the army (he finally placed him in a regiment going out to South Africa), was shocked to discover that he had contracted syphilis from a prostitute.*

---

* As Major Edward Seymour, Teddie (doubtless through Regy's influence) later became an equerry to Queen Alexandra, eventually being knighted for services to the royal family. He married a daughter of Marquis Conyngham, was awarded a DSO during the First World War, and died in 1948.

The next object of Regy's passion was strange. He had always had a mutually mistrustful relationship with his elder son Oliver, a clever but unsentimental boy, while doting on his younger son Maurice, who was dim and pliable. From the moment of Teddie's departure, Regy began bombarding Maurice with frank love letters, addressing him as 'Molly': Maurice responded awkwardly, but was in awe of his father and tried to please him. Although the physical side of the relationship seems to have been confined to some fairly innocent petting,* Regy, with a view to recapturing his own adolescent passions, encouraged the boy (who was podgy and not very attractive) to have affairs with his Eton contemporaries and to write to him about these (he even put his room at Windsor Castle at Maurice's disposal for this purpose): Maurice did his best to satisfy his father in this regard, though it must have been hard work as he was mainly interested in actresses. Perhaps the oddest aspect of the affair was that Regy sent the boy, whose interest in current affairs was limited, almost daily descriptions of his dealings with politicians and royalty: of far greater interest to future historians than to their original addressee, these later formed the backbone of the first two volumes of Esher's *Journals and Letters* which Maurice edited after Regy's death:† even in their expurgated state they make clear Regy's fondness for Maurice, which he claimed to have discussed with Queen Victoria, the Prince of Wales, the Duke of Cambridge and Lord Rosebery (the last of whom, according to Regy, seemed particularly interested, perhaps because

---

* In 1901 Regy wrote to Maurice, then aged nineteen: 'I was almost certainly the first human being who kissed you at all, and quite certainly the first who kissed you passionately.'

† The final two volumes were edited by his elder brother Oliver, the 3rd Viscount, after the overweight Maurice had died of a heart attack while grouse-shooting at the age of fifty-two.

he harboured not dissimilar feelings for his own younger son Neil who was with Maurice at Eton).

When Maurice reached adulthood, Esher continued for some years to send him letters in which protestations of passion were mixed with details of royal confidences and political intrigues. His aspiration to live vicariously through his son was demonstrated when Maurice fell in love with the actress Zena Dare: after she had rebuffed Maurice's advances, Esher himself set out to fascinate and seduce her, eventually persuading her to marry the twenty-eight-year-old Maurice in 1911. Following the marriage, Esher transferred his affections to Laurence 'Thrushy' Burgin, a handsome, lower-middle-class youth of nineteen whom he appointed his secretary and who served him faithfully for the rest of his life. (Like most of her husband's male attachments, Laurence was accepted by Nellie, who became very fond of him.) And there seems to have been no shortage of other young men who tugged on Esher's heart-strings during his later years. He developed a 'crush' on Edward, Prince of Wales (the future Edward VIII and Duke of Windsor), whose mother, Queen Mary, innocently asked him to befriend and keep an eye on the wayward heir to the throne. During the First World War he was taken with the androgynous young millionaire MP and aesthete Sir Philip Sassoon, obtaining for him the job of private secretary to the British commander Sir Douglas Haig (who himself owed his career to Esher's favour). A final favourite was Maurice's son Tony, who inherited his mother's glamorous looks and was seventeen at the time of his grandfather's death.

Esher's closest friendships reflected his tastes. Apart from his male love of the moment, his chief soul-mates were his ex-lover Chat Williamson, who eventually left the priesthood to live with a succession of gondoliers, and his wife's cousin Howard Sturgis, author of discreetly homosexual novels. His most intimate friends in politics were Rosebery, Balfour and Loulou Harcourt. After the Liberals took power in 1905 he also established a close relationship with the War Secretary Richard Haldane, a rotund Scottish bachelor whose high-pitched voice and effeminate mannerisms earned him the nickname 'Priscilla' among his colleagues. He chose Arthur Benson, a romantic homosexual, to co-edit Queen Victoria's letters.

Esher's public and private lives were closely linked. Always taking care to remain behind the scenes, he proved a brilliantly effective operator in the realms of both clandestine romance and political intrigue. In both areas he showed a mastery of secretiveness and seductiveness. (In this respect, Esher comes across as more French than English, a product of his Gallic maternal heritage.) In both his political and his romantic endeavours he also exercised constant tact and caution – a lack of which qualities would be the undoing of the next subject of this chapter.

Though his viscountcy was earned rather than inherited, Lewis ('Loulou') Vernon Harcourt (1863–1922), 1st Viscount Harcourt, prided himself on an impressive genealogy. The Harcourts descend from the heirs of Odo, Bishop of Bayeux, half-brother of William the Conqueror, who after the Conquest (which inspired him to commission the Bayeux Tapestry) was granted the manor of Stanton (later Stanton Harcourt) to the west of Oxford, still held by Loulou's granddaughter today. They distinguished themselves as soldiers, statesmen, clergymen and lawyers, and married into some of the greatest families in the land. In the eighteenth century they became earls, and acquired another Oxfordshire estate, Nuneham Courtenay to the south of the city, where they resited a village to build a Palladian palace; when the earldom died out in 1830, the Harcourt estates were inherited by Edward Vernon, Archbishop of York, whose mother was a daughter of the 1st Earl, and who adopted the Harcourt name. Loulou's father Sir William Harcourt (1827–1904) was a grandson of the Archbishop, though as a younger son he had to make his way in the world. A Falstaffian figure, huge and energetic, clever and combative, he had a brilliant career as a lawyer and journalist before entering the House of Commons as a Liberal at the age of forty. Soon recognised as an outstanding parliamentary debater, he served in Gladstone's first government as Solicitor-General, in his second as Home Secretary, in his third and fourth as Chancellor of the Exchequer. As we have seen, he was expected to succeed Gladstone as Prime Minister in 1894, but the prize went to Rosebery, to Sir William's regret and Loulou's fury.

William Harcourt had been devoted to his wife Thérèse, whom he married in 1858, and whose stepfather, the Liberal statesman Sir George Cornewall Lewis,* became Harcourt's political mentor and great friend. She bore him a son who died; she herself then died giving birth to a second son; and soon afterwards Cornewall Lewis died, in whose memory Harcourt named the surviving child. Having lost his first son, wife and father-figure in short order, the grieving Harcourt became passionately attached to little Lewis, whom he idolised and spoiled: it was he who coined the rather soppy sobriquet 'Loulou' after the baby's attempts to pronounce his own name. He could not bear to be parted from the boy, and even took him to the political salons he frequented: by the time Harcourt

---

* Sir George Cornewall Lewis, 2nd Bt (1805–63), was successively Chancellor of the Exchequer, Home Secretary and War Secretary under Palmerston, whom he was widely expected to succeed as Prime Minister – though he died, aged fifty-seven, while Palmerston was still in office.

entered the government, Loulou, then aged ten, had become (to quote Sir William's biographer) 'the petted associate of half the public men of the time'. Having been steeped in political culture from the cradle, it is perhaps unsurprising that, on leaving Eton, Loulou decided not to go to Cambridge (where Sir William had been a brilliant scholar), but to become private secretary to his father, whose adulation he reciprocated and who had just been appointed Home Secretary in Gladstone's second government. A partnership was thus created which would last more than twenty years. They made a contrasting pair: Sir William fat, impulsive and boisterous; Loulou slender and calculating, a discreet, soft-spoken youth who observed and listened from the shadows.

Loulou's career in the 1880s and 90s had much in common with that of Regy Brett (the future Lord Esher), who was eleven years his senior and a close friend. (Their fathers, both top barristers who served as solicitor-general, were friends.) Both could have had successful careers in front-line politics, but preferred to operate behind the scenes; both were cunning intriguers who knew how to charm and manipulate the people who mattered. The difference between them was that, whereas the patriotic Regy concerned himself with the future of monarchy, army and empire, Loulou at this stage of his career had just one aim in view – to ensure that his beloved father always showed himself at his best, that he was a success in office, and that he eventually rose to the greatest office in the land. Over a dozen years he set out to befriend all the senior Liberals, to notch up favours among them (he assisted several of them over private-life problems), and to secure their agreement to support Sir William's bid for the premiership when the time came. The problem was that, while most of them liked the son, they found the father, with his overbearing manner, increasingly insufferable: indeed, several ministers who promised Loulou their support while in opposition changed their minds when the Liberals returned to office and Sir William, as Chancellor, subjected them to merciless bullying. When, despite hectic last-minute manoeuvres by Loulou, the premiership went to Rosebery, Loulou became extremely vindictive. He not only schemed, with notable success, to ensure the failure of Rosebery's administration, but he continued his plots after the Liberals had lost office, exacerbating the split between imperialists and radicals which kept the party out of power for a decade. Left to himself, Sir William would not have behaved like this, but he was in the habit of indulging his son in all things: indeed, his decision, against Loulou's advice, to accept office under Rosebery was one of the few occasions when he declined to let him have his way.

Following Sir William's brief spell (1896–8) leading the Liberals in opposition, Loulou, while continuing to act as his father's chief confidant and adviser, began to develop a life of his own. In 1899, aged thirty-six, he married an American heiress, Mary ('May') Burns: her mother was the sister of the great banker J. Pierpont Morgan and her (recently deceased) father had run the London branch of the Morgan banking empire. (The match was probably set up by Loulou's American stepmother, Sir William having taken as his second wife the widow of a former United States Minister to London.) There was a generous marriage settlement (of which Esher was a trustee), which enabled the couple to live and entertain in sumptuous style. She bore him three daughters and a son. In 1904, Loulou, who could have had a parliamentary seat for the asking at any time during the previous twenty years, finally became a Liberal MP at a by-election, being introduced to the House of Commons (whose precincts he had haunted since childhood) by his proud father. Around the same time, Sir William experienced a strange twist of fate. When, in his budget a decade earlier, he had introduced death duties, he imagined that, as a younger son, he himself would never be called upon to pay them. However, on the unexpected death of his nephew in 1904 he inherited Stanton Harcourt and Nuneham Courtenay: the shock of becoming responsible for these great properties and having to pay the tax on them may have contributed to his own death before the end of the year.

When the Liberals returned to power in 1905 Loulou, who was not popular with the party chiefs owing to his petulant and destructive behaviour of a decade earlier, was offered the somewhat lowly position of First Commissioner of Works, outside the cabinet. This, however, was a job which suited Loulou, an aesthete and art collector who was already busy restoring Stanton and Nuneham with his wife's money. Among his achievements during his five years in the post were the improvement of the London parks and the refurbishment of the Houses of Parliament. His political experience made him a valuable member of the government, and he was admitted to the cabinet in 1907 and promoted to Colonial Secretary in 1910. This was a time of imperial consolidation; colonial tensions with France and Russia had been defused by the 'ententes' of 1904 and 1907, and Loulou hoped to forge a similar agreement with Germany through his friendship with the counsellor at the German Embassy (and future wartime foreign minister), Richard von Kühlmann. Loulou got on well with Asquith, who enjoyed being entertained at the Harcourt residences,* but was mistrusted by colleagues who found him

---

* In 1912 the Asquiths acquired a country house at Sutton Courtenay, just across the Thames from Loulou's at Nuneham Courtenay: it seems likely that Loulou facilitated the purchase, which was made possible by a gift to the premier of £3000 from his wife's uncle, J. Pierpont Morgan.

devious and secretive: at cabinet meetings he would contrive to sit next to the Prime Minister and talk to him in undertones rather than participate in general discussion. Loulou's decade in government was notable in two other ways. He led the opposition in cabinet to 'votes for women', and was hated by the suffragettes, who tried to set fire both to Nuneham and to his house in Berkeley Square. And (like Beauchamp, his successor as First Commissioner) he belonged to the cabinet faction opposed to Britain's going to war with Germany in August 1914 – though he withdrew his threat of resignation after the Germans had invaded Belgium. Loulou was demoted to his old job at the Office of Works when the wartime coalition was formed in May 1915, and left the government altogether when Lloyd George succeeded Asquith in December 1916. (A year earlier he had refused the viceroyalty of India, doubtless feeling, like Esher, that his role as a 'wire-puller' required him to stay in London.) He was consoled for loss of office with elevation to the peerage as Viscount Harcourt (a title first created for his great-great-great-great-grandfather, Queen Anne's Lord Chancellor, in 1711). Another consolation was that, on the death of his mother-in-law, his wife inherited a palatial residence in Brook Street, Mayfair (now the Savile Club), where she and the new Viscount went to live.

Alongside his career and his marriage, Loulou, who was physically unattractive, pursued a clandestine sex life which consisted of forcing his attentions on young (in some cases, very young) people of both sexes. At Eton he was (to quote the diaries of his friend Sir Charles Dilke) 'caught misbehaving with two other boys': he avoided disgrace and expulsion, but was quietly removed from the school (which did not stop him revisiting it frequently in search of new objects for his passions). In adult life he remained close to his Eton schoolfriend

George 'Gogo' Maquay, scion of a family of Irish bankers in Florence, and they prowled together in search of youths for sex: this rather shocked Regy Brett, who was deeply romantic and believed that physical lovemaking should only take place in the context of an emotional bond: he referred disapprovingly to homosexual pouncers as 'harpies of the Loulou–Gogo type'. Regy became all too familiar with Loulou's tendencies, as the latter tried to seduce all four of Regy's children during their adolescence. (One wonders how Loulou later behaved with his own children.) In 1908, Regy confided to his son Maurice that his daughter Dorothy, then twenty-four and making a reputation as an artist, had again been pounced upon by Loulou, but that she had fought him off. 'These were his old games,' added Regy, 'played out with both sexes for years.' The worldly Regy, whose own private life was not exactly spotless, did not allow these episodes to affect his friendship with Loulou, but he was concerned that the latter should run such risks now that he was a married man and a cabinet minister. (He does not seem to have been overly concerned about the effect on his children: Dorothy claimed to have been permanently traumatised by Loulou's earlier assault on her during her girlhood.) A keen amateur photographer, Loulou also possessed a collection of pictures of naked youths, which he enjoyed showing to his homosexual friends: apart from Regy, these included Arthur Benson and the German diplomat Kühlmann. (He had also associated with Oscar Wilde in the 1880s, though distanced himself as Wilde became disreputable.)*

---

* Loulou played a small role in Wilde's libel case by ensuring (through his father) that Queensberry was not awarded the full costs of his defence on the grounds that these mostly consisted of 'bribes to blackmailers'. See Patrick Jackson (ed.), *Loulou: Selected Extracts from the Journals of Lewis Harcourt* (Fairleigh Dickinson University Press, 2006), pp. 259–61.

Shortly before Christmas 1921 the Harcourts gave a house party at Nuneham at which the guests included Mrs Willie James, a rich widow and society hostess, and her son Edward, aged thirteen, an Eton contemporary of the Harcourts' son Bill. James (who was himself homosexual in adult life) wrote in his memoirs that he spent the weekend trying to elude the attentions of the fifty-eight-year-old Lord Harcourt, who kept attempting to 'grope' him. As mother and son prepared to leave on Monday morning, Mrs James told Edward to say goodbye to their host. James recalled that he came into a long room at the end of which Loulou lay in bed. '[Harcourt] said, "Come nearer, child!" So I came a little nearer and made my speech. "Mummy wants me to thank you for a lovely weekend etc." And then suddenly he threw back the bedclothes revealing a large and hideous erection. He looked like an old goat with his large drooping beard and I ran out of the room.' James related the incident to his mother, a woman not noted for her reticence, and soon it was the talk of London. On the morning of 24 February 1922, Loulou was found dead by his valet in his bedroom at 69 Brook Street,* an empty bottle of bromide sleeping draught by his side. As the safe dose was a few drops in a glass of water, the obvious assumption was that he had taken his life. However, the family organised a cover-up. The inquest took place not in London but in Oxford, where the Harcourts had great local influence; it concluded that 'there was not the slightest motive for suicide', and returned a verdict of death by misadventure. The truth was nevertheless known throughout society, Sir Philip Sassoon writing to Esher that 'London is convulsed by the sordid tragedy'. (Interestingly, in the *Oxford Dictionary of National Biography*, the entry on Loulou, by a friend of his granddaughter, insists that he did

* Now the dining room of the Flyfishers' Club.

not commit suicide, while the entry on his son Bill, the 2nd and last Viscount, states categorically that he did.)

Loulou's tragedy was that he grew up in an unnaturally close relationship with his father, who smothered him with affection and who was probably the only person towards whom he ever felt a strong sense of emotional attachment. Through some obscure psychological process, this emotional background seems to have impelled him towards both his career as a devious political operator and the abusive sexual habits which came to obsess him. He was a Jekyll-and-Hyde character, regarded by some as a monster of depravity and a sinister intriguer, by others as generous, helpful and kind. Thus while Dorothy Brett claimed that he had ruined her life, her sister Sylvia (who was invited to honeymoon at Nuneham following her marriage to Vyner Brooke, future Rajah of Sarawak) wrote in her memoirs that he was the greatest charmer she had known. His redeeming features doubtless explain why his behaviour did not bring about his ruin sooner than it did.

Like Loulou Harcourt, with whom he served in the Liberal government of 1905–15, William Lygon, 7th Earl Beauchamp (1872–1938), took pride in the fact that his family had held its principal estate – Madresfield near Malvern, Worcestershire – in unbroken descent since the Norman conquest. The Lygons were less distinguished than the Harcourts, though they had often supplied the local MP. They had been ennobled quite recently when William's great-grandfather, a minor politician with an ambitious wife who had inherited a huge fortune from a distant kinsman, bought first a barony and then an earldom from a cash-strapped government during the Napoleonic Wars. William's father, the 6th Earl, a notorious prig, was a leading High Anglican and supporter of the Oxford

Movement, responsible for founding Keble College, Oxford; a Tory in politics, he held minor office in Conservative administrations of the 1880s. William's mother, a first cousin of Lord Rosebery, died soon after his birth, and the person to whom he felt closest was his older sister Mary, an accomplished woman who became a friend of the composer Edward Elgar (inspiring one of the Enigma Variations) and a lady-in-waiting to the future Queen Mary. William was an eighteen-year-old Oxford undergraduate when he succeeded to the earldom on his father's death in 1891. Having left the university under a cloud, he entered public life as Mayor of Worcester and a member of the London Schools Board, showing himself to be a man of progressive views. In 1899, aged twenty-seven, he was appointed Governor of New South Wales, probably through his sister's royal connections and much to the general surprise.* Beauchamp, who lived and entertained at Government House, Sydney in the grandest proconsular style, was at first treated by his colonial subjects as rather a joke, but won their respect through his concern for their welfare and the conscientious discharge of his duties – though he resigned the post after only eighteen months, ostensibly on account of the death of his younger brother in the Boer War. In 1902, soon after his return to England, he married Lady Lettice Grosvenor, sister of Hugh Grosvenor ('Bendor'), 2nd Duke of Westminster, reputedly the richest man in Europe; she was a pretty if somewhat simple-minded woman, and brought an immense dowry. The same year he broke with family tradition by joining the Liberal Party, he and

---

* Hence Hilaire Belloc's satirical lines on the young Lord Lundy:

> We had intended you to be
> The next Prime Minister but three ...
> But as it is – my language fails –
> Go out and govern New South Wales!

his wife dispensing lavish political hospitality at Halkyn House, their mansion in Belgravia.

Beauchamp was not intellectually outstanding, but until he became fat in his forties he was extremely handsome and distinguished-looking, somewhat resembling Hugh Bonneville playing the Earl of Grantham in *Downton Abbey*. After the Liberals came to power in 1905 he served for some years in middle-ranking government posts which combined political and ceremonial functions – first as Captain of the Gentlemen at Arms (who acted as government chief whip in the House of Lords), then as Lord Steward of the Household (who was then both a senior courtier and a government spokesman – Beauchamp's father had served as Lord Steward in the 1870s, and been responsible for answering Home Office questions in the upper house). He looked splendid in court uniform, was invited to carry the Sword of State at the coronation of George V, and at an unusually young age was awarded two of the greatest honours in the land when he was made Lord Warden of the Cinque Ports (1913) and a Knight of the Garter (1914). Asquith took a dim view of his abilities, but nevertheless promoted him to the cabinet in 1910 as Lord President of the Council, another post combining ceremonial and political duties. A few months later he succeeded Loulou Harcourt as First Commissioner of Works – a job which suited him as it had his predecessor, for he was a great aesthete and art collector, who spent much of his time and fortune improving his sprawling ancestral pile at Madresfield. Like Loulou, Beauchamp was a man of pacifist sentiments, appalled at the prospect of Britain declaring war on Germany in August 1914 – both men contemplated resigning from the government, but decided not to do so after Germany had invaded Belgium. (Ironically, it was Beauchamp, redesignated Lord President, who presided at the Privy Council meeting at which the King formally declared war.) However, when Asquith formed a coalition with the Conservatives the following May, he sacrificed Beauchamp (who had been under consideration as the next Viceroy of India)* to make way for Tory ministers. Although Beauchamp was never again to hold government office, he continued to play important roles in public life. As Lord Warden he hosted top-level Anglo-French conferences during and after the war at his official residence, Walmer Castle. In 1924 he became Liberal leader in the House of Lords, using his fortune to help the ailing party and his influence to resolve the feud between the followers of Asquith and Lloyd George. In 1929 he succeeded his cousin Lord Rosebery as Chancellor of London University.

Beauchamp seems to have been devoted to his wife, who bore him three sons and four daughters between 1903 and 1916. Perhaps these serial pregnancies affected her health, for she became increasingly 'vague' and gradually withdrew from active life into a world of religious obsessions, while losing such charms as she had once possessed. She showed little interest in her children, who regarded her as an unloving and rather frightening figure. On the other hand, they both adored and were adored by their father who, unusually for an aristocratic parent of the period, spent much time with them, supervising their upbringing and showing affectionate interest in all their doings. Once they had grown up, he became somewhat distant from his eldest son William, Viscount Elmley (born 1903), a priggish youth who was elected a Liberal MP in 1929, while

* Either Beauchamp, who was not finally offered the viceroyalty, or Loulou Harcourt, who refused it, would have been preferable to Frederick Thesiger, 3rd Baron Chelmsford, a mediocrity who like Beauchamp had served as Governor of New South Wales, and who was appointed mainly for the geographical reason that he happened to be present in India when the position had to be filled in 1916.

remaining close to his second son Hugh ('Hughie', born 1904), who was handsome, charming, dreamy and homosexual. (It will be recalled that both Rosebery and Esher were also infatuated with their second sons.) One characteristic which sat rather oddly with Beauchamp's roles as a radical politician and a loving father was a love of pomp and formality: even in the intimacy of his family circle, he addressed his children by their titles, and wore his Garter ribbon at mealtimes.

Beauchamp is a rare and fascinating case of a man who was simultaneously an important public figure, a devoted husband and father, and an active homosexual who, as time went on, barely troubled to conceal his proclivities from the world at large. (There may have been a 'gay gene' in the family as his uncle the 5th Earl, a restless character who never married and spent much of his life abroad, was generally known to be homosexual.) Unfortunately the diaries he kept all his life, which might have shed detailed light on his romantic history, were destroyed after his death by his eldest son. However, the abrupt termination of both his university career and his colonial governorship suggests that it was thought desirable that he should quickly move on; and there were several instances in his early adulthood of his suddenly going abroad on health grounds ('it sounds a very curious sort of illness', his sister wrote to him during one of these episodes). At Government House, Sydney, it did not escape the notice of visitors that he employed strikingly handsome footmen, and he clearly had an erotic fetish for personable male servants, especially footmen and grooms; he personally engaged these for his three residences, seeking youths who were not just good-looking but had well-shaped buttocks and thighs (over which he would run his hands during job interviews). Even among government colleagues he seems to have had a reputation: Asquith nicknamed him 'Sweetheart', while his wife Margot wrote in the Madresfield visitors book in 1909: 'They say – what say they? Let them say.' Many of his friends outside politics were homosexual, including the writer Edmund Gosse, the arts-and-crafts architect C. R. Ashbee (who carried out extensive work at Madresfield), the portrait artist William Ranken (who painted the family), and the Irish consul and humanitarian Sir Roger Casement (eventually hanged for treason). At Madresfield, where he lived with his wife, he seems to have been reasonably circumspect (though male friends of his children were warned to lock their bedroom doors at night); but at Walmer, where Lady Beauchamp rarely accompanied him, he seems to have abandoned restraint: he hired local youths and fishermen for the delectation of himself and his guests; and Sir William Jowitt and Lady Aberconway, who came to call, were surprised to meet the actor Ernest Thesiger stripped to the waist and wearing a string of pearls, and a young man who introduced himself as the tennis professional but did not seem to know how to hold a racquet. Nor did he confine his frolics to the privacy of his own properties: the (homosexual) novelist Hugh Walpole told Virginia Woolf that, visiting the public steam baths at Elephant and Castle, he had seen 'Ld Beauchamp in the act with a boy'.

Amazingly, Beauchamp appears to have enjoyed this hazardous hedonistic life for forty years without encountering any serious or lasting trouble, while occupying some of the greatest positions in the land. No one seems to have complained (or if they did, they were persuaded to remain silent); and the police, if aware of his activities, turned a blind eye. And he might have continued in this way indefinitely were it not for a vendetta by a single powerful and rancorous individual. The career of Beauchamp's brother-in-law, 'Bendor', Duke of Westminster, had been as undistinguished as Beauchamp's had been distinguished. He had failed to launch himself into politics, held no public offices of note, and owing to his two divorces was *persona non grata* at court. He was consumed with envy at Beauchamp's apparently effortless success in accumulating offices and honours. What enraged him most of all was that Beauchamp, despite his homosexuality, had, through his marriage to Westminster's sister, produced three sons, while Westminster himself, though three times married, had only managed to sire a single male heir, who had died aged four. The final straw was that Westminster believed, rightly or wrongly, that Beauchamp had inspired an article disparaging his morals (which were indeed deplorable, though his weakness was for girls rather than boys) in the *Church Times*. By 1930 Westminster had resolved to use his limitless riches to expose the homosexuality of his 'bugger-in-law', as he referred to him, and ruin him in a scandal of Wildean proportions: as a right-wing Conservative (who later became an admirer of Hitler), he hoped this would also finish off the ailing Liberal Party.

In the summer of 1930 Beauchamp, accompanied by Robert Bernays, a former President of the Oxford Union and an aspiring Liberal MP of homosexual tastes, and George Roberts, a particularly handsome footman from Madresfield, embarked on a world tour, whose ostensible purpose was to exchange views, as Chancellor of London University, with the holders of similar offices in Australia and America. As soon as he had left the country, Westminster's detectives got to work, and soon had a substantial dossier of signed statements from present and former staff at Beauchamp's three residences, testifying (either as witnesses or participants) to his homosexual activities. While abroad, Beauchamp seems to have done his best to add further material to the file: in Sydney he lived openly with Roberts as his lover, a matter which received

official notice when the federal authorities in Canberra felt
obliged to request that he should not bring Roberts with him
to the reception they were giving in his honour. When
Beauchamp returned to England in February 1931,
Westminster struck. He first summoned his sister and presented her with the evidence of her husband's proclivities: for
years Lady Beauchamp had been in a fragile emotional state,
and the shock of these revelations caused a breakdown.
(Though vaguely aware of her husband's propensities, she did
not really know what homosexuality was, telling friends that
'Beauchamp was a bugler'.) Bullied by her brother, she then left
her husband, began divorce proceedings against him, and
retired to Saighton Grange, a Grosvenor property in Cheshire,
where she spent the remainder of her life as a depressed
invalid. Westminster next approached the Beauchamps' children and demanded that they testify against their father,
which they indignantly refused to do. Finally Westminster
brought his discoveries to the notice of the King. George V
(whose first reaction was allegedly to remark, 'I thought men
like that shot themselves') was horrified at the thought of a
public scandal involving a distinguished courtier, who had
served as his Lord Steward and officiated at his coronation;
moreover, his family was implicated, as his two younger sons,
Prince Henry and Prince George (both of whom had bisexual
reputations), were friends of Beauchamp's elder sons and had
often visited Madresfield, leading to speculation that Prince
George hoped to marry Beauchamp's pretty daughter Mary
('Maimie'). The King therefore brokered a deal, whereby
Westminster would not press for a prosecution provided
Beauchamp undertook to resign all his offices and leave
England immediately and for good. This proposal was put to
Beauchamp on the King's behalf in June 1931 by a deputation
headed by Lord Stanmore, Liberal Chief Whip in the House

of Lords (and himself a homosexual bachelor);* Beauchamp immediately complied, leaving the country within twenty-four hours, and giving up most of his offices during the following months. (He delayed over resigning the Lord Wardenship, presumably to give time for the removal from Walmer of papers and other possessions.)

To Westminster's annoyance and the King's relief, there was no open scandal: the press magnate Lord Beaverbrook, who was the lover of Beauchamp's daughter Sibell, ensured that no mention of the affair appeared in the newspapers. The official story was that Lord Beauchamp had relinquished his duties and gone abroad on account of his health. Nevertheless, his disgrace soon became common knowledge throughout society, by which he was henceforth shunned. Those few worthies who continued to associate with him incurred Westminster's wrath: even the Conservative leader Baldwin, who despite their political differences had always been friendly with Beauchamp, a Worcestershire neighbour, was attacked by the Duke for having accepted an invitation to Madresfield shortly before the Earl's departure. Westminster also saw to it that Beauchamp's children suffered ostracism: he had not forgiven them for their refusal to join their mother in collaborating in his vengeful scheme. At the time of Beauchamp's exile, only one of them was married – the eldest daughter, to a landowning baronet: the others were effectively unable to find suitable spouses from their own class, or continue the social life

---

* George Hamilton-Gordon, 2nd and last Baron Stanmore (1871–1957), was the son of a colonial governor and a grandson of the Liberal Prime Minister Lord Aberdeen. He began his career in 1892 as private secretary to his childless uncle George Shaw-Lefevre, First Commissioner of Works in Gladstone's last government. After succeeding to his peerage in 1912 he served as a government whip in the House of Lords until 1918, then as Liberal Chief Whip there from 1923 to 1944 (for seven of which years Beauchamp was Liberal leader in the Lords). He was a close friend of the bachelor diplomat Sir Louis Mallet (see Chapter 5), and a lover of Italian gardens.

(revolving around 'the county' and the London Season) to
which they had been accustomed. Nor was much political
favour shown to Viscount Elmley MP, though his party, the
Liberal Nationals, featured prominently in the National
Government which held office from August 1931. (In the
event, he served for seven years as parliamentary private secretary to the party's rising star in the government, Leslie
Hore-Belisha, to be considered in Chapter 10.) Despite having
suffered from his disgrace, the three unmarried daughters, and
Hughie, stood loyally by their father: fearful that he might
commit suicide, they resolved that at least one of them should
accompany him wherever in the world he happened to be.

Beauchamp, who remained a rich man, embarked on a
comfortable but rootless life of exile, travelling between the
homosexual Meccas of Paris, Rome, Venice, San Francisco and
Sydney. He rarely stayed more than three weeks at any of his
European pleasure-grounds (for Westminster's detectives were
still on the prowl); but he made a long annual visit to Sydney
from November to February, where he felt at home and seems
to have been popular. He bought a house there, and met a
young Australian, David Smythe, whom he appointed his secretary and who became his inseparable companion for the rest
of his life: David was cautiously accepted by the family, representing Beauchamp in 1935 at Elmley's marriage (deplored
by all) to a middle-aged Danish widow. After George V's death
in January 1936, Beauchamp hoped to return home, but
Westminster remained implacable: when Lady Beauchamp
died in July that year, it was made clear to him that he risked
arrest if he tried to attend her funeral. The following month
Hughie, who was still adored by his father despite his having
'taken to the bottle', was fatally injured in an accident while
motoring in Germany: chartering an aeroplane, the stricken
Earl rushed to his side, arriving in time to see him die. He was

determined to bring Hughie's body back to Madresfield for burial, no longer caring what happened to him. In the event, his visit was not interfered with, though he was advised to stay no more than a few days. However, a year later, he learned that he could safely return to England without fear of arrest: this development may have owed something to the new Home Secretary, Sir Samuel Hoare, married to Beauchamp's half-sister Maud and himself probably a clandestine homosexual (see Chapter 5). Beauchamp ended his enforced exile on 19 July 1937, returning to Madresfield after six years' absence. He did not stay long: without public duties to absorb him, and unable to show his face in society, he was soon off again with David, first to Venice, then to Australia at the end of the year. He was visiting New York when he died in November 1938, aged sixty-six.

During Beauchamp's exile his unmarried daughters had continued to live at Madresfield, where they were often visited by their friend Evelyn Waugh: they cheered each other up at a time when the sisters were still reeling from their father's disgrace and Waugh was depressed in the interval between his two marriages. Waugh had known Elmley and Hughie at Oxford, where they had all belonged to the Hypocrites, a heavy-drinking dining club with homosexual overtones, and Waugh and Hughie had been lovers for a time. In the summer of 1932 Waugh accompanied the sisters to stay with their father in Rome: he was struck by Lord Beauchamp's dignity in adversity, his old-fashioned manners, his Byronic air. Waugh later immortalised Beauchamp, his house and his family in *Brideshead Revisited* (1945). Brideshead is based on Madresfield, lived in by the same family for almost a thousand years, a glorious architectural hotchpotch which almost seems to grow out of the landscape. Its owner Lord Marchmain is based on Lord Beauchamp, the great aristocrat obliged to live abroad. (Marchmain's misdemeanours are not specified; but the outrageous aesthete Anthony Blanche refers to him as 'the last historic, authentic case of someone being hounded out of society'.) The pious and destructive Lady Marchmain is based on Lady Beauchamp (with a touch of her frightful brother). The priggish heir, Lord Brideshead, is based on Lord Elmley (both marry unsuitable widows). The beautiful younger son Sebastian Flyte, whose early promise evaporates in a haze of alcohol, is based on Hughie Lygon; the statuesque elder daughter Julia is based on 'Maimie' Lygon: just as Charles Ryder, the novel's narrator, falls in love first with Sebastian and later with Julia, so Waugh loved Hughie in the 1920s and Maimie in the 1930s. The main story of the novel ends with Lord Marchmain's return from exile to die at Brideshead following the death of his wife. The irony is that, had 'Bendor' not taken the action that he did, Beauchamp would now be quite forgotten, for he had few real achievements to his name despite all his offices and honours; but as it is, he will always be remembered for having inspired this famous work.

It is interesting to compare Beauchamp with his cousin Rosebery (who was twenty-five years Beauchamp's senior, and died two years before his disgrace). Both lost one parent early in life and did not get on with the other; both inherited earldoms while Oxford undergraduates; both owed their success in part to handsome looks; both married immensely rich heiresses; both were loving fathers (particularly of their second sons); both joined the government aged thirty-three and the cabinet aged thirty-seven; both possessed radical sentiments, and favoured House of Lords reform; both served in local as well as national government; both became Chancellor of London University; and both were persecuted by vindictive fellow noblemen who claimed to have proof of their homosexual activities. It will probably never be known for certain whether Queensberry really possessed the evidence of Rosebery's transgressions which he threatened to publicise unless Wilde was convicted (or whether, indeed, such evidence existed); but Rosebery seems to have been terrified of the rumours and threats. Beauchamp, having got away with indulging his forbidden pleasures for so long, became insouciant and incautious, and paid the price.

# 2

# THE MYSTERY OF
# EDWIN MONTAGU

Before leaving the Liberals (who gradually fizzled out as a serious political force after 1922, though they would provide the great homosexual scandal in British politics in the final quarter of the century), one must examine the strange case of Edwin Montagu (1879–1924), who as Secretary of State for India from 1917 to 1922 (generally considered to have been one of the outstanding holders of that office) introduced the legislation which put 'the Raj' on the path to self-government. It may seem odd to include him here, as the great known fact of his private life was his professed adulation of Venetia Stanley, who eventually consented to marry him. However, the marriage seems to have been unconsummated; and there is much about Montagu which speaks of ambiguous and repressed sexuality.

He was the seventh of ten children of Samuel Montagu, a rich Jewish banker who served as Liberal MP for Whitechapel from 1885 to 1900 and was raised to the peerage in 1907 as Baron Swaythling. Edwin adored his mother but hated his father, a domineering figure who insisted on strict Jewish observance and kept his children on a tight financial rein. He was sent to Clifton, a public school with a Jewish house, but was miserable there, and completed his secondary education as a day boy at City of London School. He was also sent round the world with his Hebrew tutor, who saw to it that he adhered to Jewish ritual even in distant lands: of all the countries they visited, it was India, with its exoticism and contrasts, which most fascinated him. At nineteen he went to Cambridge to read natural sciences with the vague intention of becoming a doctor, his father having made it clear that he would have to make his way in the world. His academic career was undistinguished, but he proved to have great talent as a debater, becoming President of both the University Liberal Club and the Cambridge Union. Though Montagu had by now developed much charm and capacity for friendship, he was a tortured personality. He possessed a manic-depressive nature, veering between elation and melancholy; he was (like Rosebery) a self-pitying hypochondriac, forever complaining of headaches and other ailments which seem to have been largely psychosomatic; conscious of being ugly and ungainly, he suffered from a streak of self-loathing, along with a desperate desire to be loved. He had turned against the religion of his ancestors, protesting that he could not accept the tenets of Orthodox Judaism intellectually and considered it his duty as a Jew to assimilate himself into English society: his father responded by threatening to deny him further support unless he remained outwardly observant. Apart from politics, his great passion was ornithology.

Two close friendships of his early adulthood are worthy of note. The first was with John Maynard Keynes (1883–1946), then actively homosexual and making little secret of it to his friends, who came up to Cambridge in Montagu's last year. Montagu seems to have been immensely taken with him, grooming him for office at the Liberal Club and the Union (in both of which Keynes eventually succeeded him as President). After they had both left Cambridge, Montagu continued to do all he could to further Keynes's career: as Undersecretary for India in 1913, he appointed him to the Royal Commission on Indian Currency, on which the young economist made his name; two years later, as Financial Secretary to the Treasury, he secured for Keynes a senior Treasury post; in 1919 he arranged for him to be included in the British delegation to the Paris Peace Conference. After Montagu's death, Keynes wrote of him to Lydia Lopokova (his own future wife): 'Although he was extraordinarily hideous, I (unlike many) never found him physically repulsive.' The other friendship was with Auberon Herbert (1876–1916), a dashing young Liberal aristocrat who had lost a leg in the Boer War and whom Montagu accompanied to Canada in 1903 on a mission to discover whether the Canadians wanted the 'imperial preference' then being advocated by Joseph Chamberlain: having ascertained that this was not the case, they published a book together on their return, to which Lord Rosebery contributed a preface. ('To know him was to delight in him', wrote another of Herbert's admirers, Winston Churchill. 'His open, gay, responsive nature, his witty, ironical but never unchivalrous tongue, his pleasing presence, his compulsive smile, made him much courted by his friends.') In 1905 Herbert inherited a peerage from his childless maternal uncle, becoming the 8th Baron Lucas, and for most of the next decade he was Montagu's colleague in the Liberal government: after losing office on the formation of the wartime coalition in 1915, he volunteered for service in the Royal Flying Corps, in which, aged forty and unmarried, he lost his life the following year. In 1917 Montagu told Lady Desborough (Lucas's cousin) that, apart from Venetia, 'Bron' was the person he had loved most.

Montagu owed his political career to two fortunate circumstances. As an undergraduate politician, he impressed Asquith, then a leading opposition figure,* with his zeal and debating style; and in the 'Liberal landslide' of 1906 he unexpectedly found himself elected to parliament for the normally Conservative seat of West Cambridgeshire. The result was that, aged just twenty-six, he was appointed by Asquith, now Chancellor of the Exchequer, to be his parliamentary private secretary, a job he retained when Asquith became Prime Minister in 1908. Montagu proved an invaluable PPS owing to his love of gossip: he always seemed to know what was going on. ('I never knew a male person of big mind like his who was more addicted to gossip than Edwin Montagu', wrote Keynes. 'He could not bear to be out of things.') During the 1906–10 parliament, Montagu spent most of his time with the Asquiths, who treated him as one of the family: he was now estranged from his own family, though he wrote to his mother daily, while his father begrudgingly allowed him a modest (and in Edwin's view scandalously inadequate) £500 a year in return for his equally begrudging presence in synagogue on Jewish festivals. After the two general elections of 1910, in which Montagu narrowly retained his seat, he enjoyed rapid promotion, becoming Undersecretary for India from 1910 to 1914, Financial Secretary to the Treasury (which involved sorting out the financial complications arising from Britain's going to war) in early 1914, finally entering the cabinet in February 1915, aged thirty-five, as Chancellor of the Duchy of Lancaster. Meanwhile, his father had died in 1911, bequeathing him a considerable fortune (assuring him an income of more than £10,000 a year) on condition that he did not marry outside the Jewish faith.

For some years Venetia Stanley (1887–1948), a close friend of Asquith's daughter Violet, had been a visitor to the Asquith

---

* And, like Montagu, an 'old boy' of City of London School.

household. Venetia was the daughter of Edward Stanley, 4th Baron Stanley of Alderley, an eccentric aristocrat and former Liberal MP of radical views, and had inherited her father's independence of mind and interest in politics. She was handsome rather than beautiful, indeed considered rather 'masculine' in her appearance and tastes. In January 1912, Asquith and Montagu visited Sicily, where they were joined by Violet and Venetia. During this winter holiday, Asquith (aged fifty-nine) established an amorous friendship with Venetia (aged twenty-four), based to some extent on their common teasing of Montagu, who was in one of his melancholy moods. Opinions differ as to whether they went on to have a physical affair (the capricious Venetia later gave different accounts to different people); but it is clear that Asquith became increasingly infatuated with her, bombarding her with letters in which protestations of love were mixed up with outrageous indiscretions about matters of state, until by the end of 1913 he hardly wished to take any serious decision without consulting her, a situation which she found flattering but also rather frightening. Meanwhile, following their Sicilian encounter, Montagu decided that he too was in love with Venetia: he wrote her letters rather different from Asquith's, full of pleading and self-abnegation. He twice proposed to her and was rejected, she making it clear that she found him physically unappealing. However, soon after joining the cabinet in 1915 he proposed a third time, and was accepted. She did not love him, but regarded the marriage as a means of escape from her entanglement with the Prime Minister, by which she now felt overwhelmed; she also saw advantages in being the wife of a rich cabinet minister who was already spoken of as a possible future Liberal leader. In order that Edwin should hang on to his inheritance, she agreed to convert to Judaism; in return, she insisted (and he readily accepted) that, while being free to pursue extramarital love affairs, she should be under no obligation to fulfil her conjugal responsibilities. Asquith knew of Montagu's advances to Venetia but refused to take them seriously; he was devastated by the news of the engagement, which may have contributed to his sudden capitulation to Conservative pressure to form a coalition government (in which Montagu was demoted to his old job of Financial Secretary and dropped from the cabinet, to return to it a year later as Minister of Munitions).

The marriage, which took place in July 1915, was a predictable disaster. Not only did Venetia, while declining to sleep with her husband, become the talk of London through her love affairs (notably with Lord Beaverbrook), but such was her extravagance that the formerly wealthy Edwin soon found himself in debt. With the passing years she became increasingly indifferent towards him, though they remained together, he continued to assure her of his devotion, and they became fashionable hosts at their town house in Queen Anne's Gate and their moated manor in Norfolk (where they entertained Venetia's circle of bohemian young patricians known as 'the coterie'). It has been suggested that Edwin may have been 'a closet homosexual' who married Venetia to 'cover his sexuality'. Certainly he never showed much romantic interest in other women,* while the Jewesses that his family had wished him to marry (mostly his own relations) he regarded with positive loathing. Asquith's son Raymond (killed in action in

---

* There are two possible indications to the contrary. In 1908 he befriended Lady Dorothy Howard, daughter of the Duke of Norfolk, who shared his interest in bird-watching: when she married in 1913, Montagu wrote to his mother regretting that he had been unable to propose to her himself owing to their difference in religion. And in a letter to Lord Reading of October 1921, Montagu remarked that 'Pearl has just given me a little daughter and we are very happy about it'. Naomi Levine, in the exhaustive research for her 850-page biography of Montagu, discovered no further trace of either 'Pearl' or the daughter (*Politics, Religion and Love*, pp. 652–5). Possibly there is an error as to date, and the reference is to Judith's arrival in 1923; or Montagu's remark was a coded reference to something else.

1916) wrote to his friend Conrad Russell that 'the Stanley–Montagu match' was 'a marriage of convenience', adding that he 'wouldn't like to go to bed with Edwin'. A daughter, Judith, was born to Venetia in 1923; while Edwin was officially acknowledged as the father, and indeed wrote to all and sundry of his delight at becoming a parent, there is no reason to doubt Venetia's claim to her friends (and eventually to Judith herself) that the child in fact resulted from her affair with Viscount Ednam, later 3rd Earl of Dudley.

Montagu meanwhile buried himself in his career, experiencing triumph and tragedy. He was dropped from the government after Lloyd George displaced Asquith as Prime Minister in December 1916, but returned to it in July 1917 in the role he had long coveted – Secretary of State for India. In October of that year he embarked on a six-month tour of India to study political conditions there, the first time a serving Secretary of State had visited the subcontinent (and not, one might have thought, the preferred act of a man devotedly in love with a recently married young wife he would be leaving behind). The result was the Montagu–Chelmsford Report, recommending a substantial measure of Indian self-government at the provincial level, which became enshrined in the Government of India Act of December 1919. However, by then the war had ended, a general election had taken place, and although the coalition government continued in office under Lloyd George, it depended overwhelmingly on Conservative parliamentary votes. And right-wing Conservatives and their press allies were increasingly hostile to Montagu, with his sympathy for Indian nationalist aspirations and his unwillingness to employ ruthless force to suppress the disturbances sweeping the subcontinent. While their opposition was to the policies rather than the man, their attacks on him contained more than a hint of anti-semitism, especially after the appointment of another Jew, Rufus Isaacs, Lord Reading, as Viceroy of India in 1921: this was galling to Montagu, who had ceased to observe Judaism and longed to be accepted as an ordinary Englishman, to the extent that he ardently opposed Zionism (and the Balfour Declaration of November 1917 in which the British government expressed its support for a Jewish homeland in Palestine) on the grounds that it was unpatriotic. Early in 1922 Lloyd George bowed to Conservative pressure and dismissed Montagu from the government; in the general election held eight months later, Montagu (after a campaign marked by extraordinary unpleasantness, in which he had received little support from his wife) was humiliatingly defeated in his Cambridgeshire seat, being beaten into third place.

Following these experiences, and disillusioned by his empty marriage, Montagu became profoundly depressed and seems to have lost the will to live. For some years he had predicted for himself an early death, and almost seemed to look forward to it. He soon fell ill with a variety of maladies and expired in November 1924, aged forty-five.

# 3

# MR B. AND MR C.

Arthur (later Earl) Balfour (1848–1930) and Winston (later Sir Winston) Churchill (1874–1965) share the distinction of having enjoyed two of the longest careers of modern British political history. Both were elected to parliament aged twenty-six; both still held public office aged eighty. Both became Conservative Prime Minister, Balfour in his fifties (1902–5), Churchill in his sixties and seventies (1940–5 and 1951–5). Both re-emerged into the political limelight after a period of disgrace, thanks to war: a decade after his premiership had ended ignominiously, Balfour resumed office as an elder statesman during the First World War; a decade after he had seemed irredeemably discredited following a long, chequered career as the *enfant terrible* of first Liberal and then Conservative governments, Churchill led his country to victory in the Second World War. One thing which united them (and distinguished them from other contemporary statesmen) was their championship of Zionism (though Balfour, unlike Churchill, did not particularly like Jews, and may have conceived his 'Declaration' of November 1917, expressing the

British government's sympathy for a 'Jewish national home' in Palestine, partly with to a view to getting them out of the way).

In other respects they were as different as could be imagined. Churchill was as hot-blooded as Balfour was cold-blooded. Churchill was a supremely decisive character, the ultimate man of action; Balfour (though capable of ruthlessness) was one of nature's ditherers. ('If you wanted nothing done', wrote Churchill of Balfour, his cabinet colleague from 1917 to 1929, 'A.J.B. was undoubtedly the best man for the task. There was no one to equal him.') Churchill was totally absorbed in politics, war, and the writing of his books (which mostly concerned politics, war, and himself and his family); Balfour was a rare example of a statesman who puts politics out of his mind during his leisure moments, mostly spent among the circle of patrician aesthetes known as 'the Souls'. Churchill was a man of passionate convictions; Balfour, a cynic who saw this life as a mere prelude to the afterlife, believed that 'nothing matters very much'. Churchill was an intensely physical presence; Balfour was intensely cerebral, not quite of this world. Churchill, with his military background and swashbuckling personality, seemed the embodiment of manly virtues; Balfour (despite his prowess on the tennis court) came across as a feline, effeminate dandy. Churchill was apparently happily married for more than fifty years to his 'Clemmie', who bore him five children; Balfour was a lifelong bachelor, the only unmarried Prime Minister to take office from Pitt the Younger to Edward Heath.

In fact both men had a low sex-drive, and put their passion (such as in Balfour's case it was) into politics. However, while both seem to have had limited interest in the physical act of sex, they did possess romantic feelings. Paradoxically, Balfour, regarded by not a few contemporaries as homosexual, seems to have been romantically interested mainly in women; while

Churchill, the uxorious bulldog, generally disliked women, and was inspired by personable young men.

Balfour was the eldest son of seven children, and his parents' favourite. His father died when he was a boy and he became closely attached to his mother, a strong-willed and rather puritanical woman. 'Why do I love you so much?', he asked her when he was six – the first recorded of the speculative questions for which he would become renowned. As a child he was considered delicate, so that during his schooldays he was excused games (though he later became an enthusiastic tennis player and golfer). At Eton, like Rosebery and Esher, he fell strongly under the influence of William Johnson, who encouraged intimate relationships among his protégés. (For some reason Balfour never got on with Rosebery, his contemporary; but he became a lifelong friend of Esher, his junior by four years.) At Cambridge, where he wore velvet and collected blue china, he acquired a reputation as an art-loving dandy, being nicknamed 'Miss Balfour' and 'Pretty Fanny'.

After coming down from Cambridge with a second-class degree, and coming into a fortune at twenty-one, Balfour, who combined a languid manner with a sharp, cynical intellect, seemed destined for the life of a pleasure-loving bachelor-aesthete drifting from one country house party to another, like Lord Henry Wootton in *The Picture of Dorian Gray*. In 1874 he was elected MP for Hertford, a borough 'in the pocket' of his uncle, the Conservative statesman Lord Salisbury; but after two years he had not got round to making his maiden speech, and was regarded in the House of Commons as something of a joke: further nicknames he acquired included 'Clara', 'Niminy Piminy' and 'Daddy Long-Legs' (a reference to his habit of falling asleep on the parliamentary benches while sprawling on the base of his spine). During the 1880s, however, he showed himself to be a wily politician with a taste for plotting and intrigue, rather in the mould of Loulou Harcourt. As Salisbury in the Lords and Northcote in the Commons became rivals to succeed Disraeli as Conservative leader, Balfour allied himself with Northcote's great enemy, the firebrand Lord Randolph Churchill, to ensure his uncle's succession; he then deftly distanced himself from Churchill, who overreached himself and fell to his political doom soon after the Conservatives returned to office in 1886. The following year, Salisbury caused surprise by appointing his nephew, not yet forty, to the cabinet as Chief Secretary for Ireland (hence the quip 'Bob's your uncle', implying nepotism). Apart from being dangerous (five years earlier, the incumbent had been murdered by the Fenians), the post was considered a bed of nails, as Ireland's main political movement, Parnell's Home Rulers, refused to cooperate with the Chief Secretary's schemes and took delight in baiting him in parliament – they had driven Balfour's predecessor to a nervous breakdown, and looked forward to making quick work of Balfour himself, whom they contemptuously dubbed 'the scented popinjay'. However, Balfour's polished and 'delicate' exterior turned out to conceal a core of steel, and in office he proved himself to be both unflappable and ruthless, parrying the taunts of the Irish parliamentarians with icy repartee, while pursuing a twin policy of brutally crushing dissent and offering limited concessions. After four years, 'artful Arthur' (as Gladstone called him) was judged to have made a success of the job, and was promoted to be Leader of the House of Commons – effectively becoming deputy to his uncle, whom he succeeded as Prime Minister a decade later.

Given Balfour's reputation as a mother's boy, a narcissistic dandy and a sly political manipulator, it is not altogether surprising that contemporaries such as Rudyard Kipling (a homophobe who was not a complete stranger to homosexual feelings himself, having married the sister of a deceased friend with whom he had been infatuated) considered his sexuality to be suspect. However, unlike the twentieth century's only other bachelor premier, Ted Heath, Balfour was no misogynist. He enjoyed the company of pretty, intelligent women, was attractive to them, and basked in their admiration. On the other hand, he never seems to have had any serious desire to marry or even to make love to any of them. Soon after the death of his mother in 1872, he attached himself to a red-headed beauty named May Lyttelton. When, three years later, May died of typhoid, he affected to be devastated; he gave the world to understand that, having lost her, he found it difficult to contemplate marriage to anyone else; he made a cult of her memory, to the point of dabbling in spiritualism with a view to communicating with her. Balfour's most recent biographer argues that there is something decidedly unconvincing about this story: if (as Balfour later suggested) he was unofficially engaged to her, she never mentioned the fact in her many surviving letters to her other intimates; and during the ten weeks that she lay gravely ill, he did not once visit her. It seems likely that Balfour seized upon her death as an excuse to explain away his lack of appetite for matrimony. During the 1880s he befriended three beautiful and clever women a decade or so younger than himself, all of whom would have liked to marry him – Ettie Fane, Mary Wyndham and Margot Tennant; but having waited in vain for him to propose, they married others – Ettie, the banker William Grenfell (whom Balfour later had raised to the peerage as Baron Desborough); Mary, the Scottish laird Lord Elcho (later 11th Earl of Wemyss), who owned an estate in Lothian near Balfour's; Margot, another future prime minister, H. H. Asquith. He continued to see much of them, as they were at the heart of 'the Souls', the aristocratic circle devoted to intellectual conversation and the appreciation of beauty, of which he was the great ornament (his nickname among them being 'the gazelle'). Margot Asquith once remarked reproachfully to Balfour that, though he was no doubt fond of the three of them, she believed he 'would not mind terribly' if they all died. He replied: 'I should mind if you all died on the same day.'

However, he seems to have developed quite a close relationship with Mary Elcho, and to have loved her in so far as he loved any woman after the death of his mother – though he could never quite bring himself to say so in his letters to her. (The nearest he came was to write, in 1893: 'Think what you would like best to hear, and have faith that it is what I should like to speak.') It is unlikely that they were ever lovers in the conventional sense; but thinly veiled references in their correspondence indicate that they developed a sado-masochistic relationship, in which Balfour took the submissive role: a St Valentine's letter she sent him in 1907, celebrating twenty years of this relationship, mentions 'a birch rod, a brush and a tin of squirting grease' (these objects being illustrated by humorous drawings in the margins); other letters refer to 'gear-changing' and 'our finishing-school'. It would seem that, about to go to Ireland as Chief Secretary in 1887, with the risk that he might be murdered like his predecessor, he wished to experiment with fantasies which had long been obsessing him (possibly originating with early treatment from his adoring but stern mother): Lady Elcho was happy to oblige, and carried on obliging for the next forty years. A year before his death she wrote to him teasingly reminding him of the original experience, adding that 'you won't describe this incident in your Memoirs, important tho' it was . . . ' Balfour seems, indeed, to have displayed masochistic feelings in other respects: when, at the January 1906 general election, his party suffered a landslide defeat in which he himself lost his parliamentary seat, he confided to Lady Salisbury that he experienced 'a kind of exhilaration at the catastrophe'.

For all his narcissism, there is not much evidence that Balfour yielded to homosexual urges. He was amused by Oscar Wilde, whom he met at Ettie Grenfell's before Wilde's disgrace; he was also close to Esher and presumably knew about his inclinations, lunching *à trois* with Regy and Teddie Seymour, the Eton boy with whom Esher was infatuated: but such associations surely indicate not that he shared their tastes but that he tolerated them. Nor was Balfour, unlike Rosebery and Churchill, known for surrounding himself with handsome young assistants – with one notable exception. When, in 1880, Balfour, aged thirty-one, first met Mary Wyndham (later Elcho), then seventeen, he also met her sixteen-year-old brother George (1863–1913), a boy of exceptional beauty who showed promise both as a poet and a sportsman. On leaving Eton, George Wyndham pursued a military career, covering himself with glory in Egyptian campaigns; but in the mid-1880s he left the Army and asked Balfour to help launch him into politics, which Balfour (who had just begun his ministerial career) was happy to do, appointing Wyndham his private secretary, and later securing his candidature for the safe Conservative seat of Dover. However, the reciprocal admiration which undoubtedly existed seems to have been stronger on Wyndham's side than Balfour's: he worshipped Balfour and looked up to him as a role-model, imitating his dandyism and mannerisms. In 1900, aged thirty-seven, he followed in Balfour's footsteps when he was appointed Chief Secretary for Ireland. But Wyndham lacked his hero's icy detachment: an impulsive, romantic character, who at heart sympathised with the Irish nationalists and despised the Ulster Protestants, he ultimately proved a disaster in the job, the stresses of which drove him to alcoholism, a nervous breakdown, and his resignation from the government early in 1905. 'Tell Arthur I love him' were his final words on leaving office – though Balfour had been careful to distance himself from Wyndham as he observed him going downhill. Wyndham married a rich and beautiful widow, Sibell Grosvenor,* by whom he had one son, and is known to have conducted affairs with other women;† but he also possessed homosexual tendencies – it has been suggested that his death in Paris at the age of forty-nine, commonly supposed to have occurred in the arms of his mistress Lady Plymouth, in fact took place in a male brothel. As with his hero Balfour, he was perceived by contemporaries as a narcissist with feminine characteristics. Lord Curzon (his rival for the hand of Sibell) wrote that he combined 'the physical beauty of a statue and the tenderness of a woman'. Observing Wyndham's parliamentary manner, one crusty Tory MP exclaimed, 'Damn the fellow, he pirouettes like a dancing-master.'

Following the death of their mother, when he was twenty-four, Balfour's unmarried sister Alice lived with him for the rest of his life, and acted as his housekeeper. (She was two years younger than Arthur, and survived him by six years.) A somewhat neurotic character, she usually acted as his hostess only on family occasions, and rarely accompanied him to official functions; but he seems to have been devoted to her.

Some have suggested that Balfour was devoid of sexual feelings altogether. Admiral Fisher described him as 'a soul

* Mother, by her first marriage to Earl Grosvenor, of 'Bendor', 2nd Duke of Westminster, who was to be the undoing of Lord Beauchamp.

† Wyndham was rumoured to be the natural father of Anthony Eden, whose mother was thought to have been one of his mistresses. Eden did extraordinarily resemble Wyndham, as well as sharing his narcissistic and neurotic nature, and he himself did not rule out the possibility of such paternity. However, Eden's biographer D. R. Thorpe has pointed out that Wyndham was visiting South Africa at the probable time of Eden's conception.

without a testicle', while Lord Beaverbrook insinuated that he was 'a hermaphrodite – no one ever saw him naked'.* This is probably an exaggeration – both men harboured grudges against Balfour, who seems to have derived 'kicks' from the admiration of women, not to mention his games with Mary Elcho, even if his sexual fires burned low and he was too fastidious to engage in conventional sexual activity. But he was certainly the coldest of fishes, in contrast to the torrent of emotion that was Winston Churchill – though Churchill's affections tended to focus on the male sex.

There is nothing to show that, in adulthood,† Churchill ever engaged in physical homosexuality, save for one curious episode at the outset of his career. Around the time of his twenty-first birthday, one A. C. Bruce, a fellow subaltern in the Fourth Hussars, accused him of having 'participated in acts of gross immorality of the Oscar Wilde type' while they had been cadets at Sandhurst a couple of years earlier. Bruce had just resigned from the regiment, claiming that Churchill and others had hounded him out of the Army on snobbish grounds: his 'case' was taken up by the journal *Truth*, owned and edited by the radical firebrand Henry Labouchere MP, instigator of the notorious 'amendment' of 1885. Wary of libel, *Truth* did not refer directly to the homosexual allegations; but Bruce's father mentioned them in February 1896 in a letter to another officer who was buying his son's military gear. Less than a year after the Wilde trial, this was the most serious imaginable slur, and

* This curious statement (is it normal to see cabinet ministers naked?) is apparently contradicted by an official who had attended upon him in his bathroom at a moment of crisis (see R. F. Mackay, *Balfour: Intellectual Statesman* [OUP, 1985], p. 8).

† He may of course have had some encounter with the phenomenon at Harrow, which had one of the more homosexual reputations among the major public schools.

on being shown the letter Churchill issued a writ for libel. Unable to prove the truth of what he had written, Bruce *père* settled the matter by issuing an apology and paying Churchill £500 (more than four times his annual army pay of £120).

From boyhood onwards, Churchill was consumed with ambition, determined to make a swift military reputation from which to launch a brilliant political career. Had he possessed homosexual inclinations, the allegations (whether true or not) of Bruce, supported as he was by the homophobic Labouchere, are likely to have given him a serious fright and determined him to keep such feelings firmly under control. Certainly there were elements in his make-up which might have aroused suspicions of homosexuality. He was intensely narcissistic and exhibition-istic; he had an emotional personality, being easily moved to tears; he was a sybarite, with a passion for silk underwear; he felt self-conscious about his short and hairless body, seeking to compensate for it with daring feats of endurance. And there were elements in his background which might have tended to nurture a homosexual outlook: in boyhood he worshipped his beautiful mother and his beloved nanny while seeing little of his father, the maverick politician Lord Randolph Churchill, whose general attitude towards him was of snubbing disapproval. Moreover, during his teens he was profoundly affected by his father's rapid physical and mental decline, rumoured to be the result of syphilis: some historians have questioned whether Lord Randolph in fact suffered from this disease, but it was what most well-informed people, including Churchill himself, believed when Lord Randolph died in 1895, aged forty-five. This may have instilled in Churchill a generalised suspicion of womankind, and possibly explains why, unusually for a dashing cavalry officer, he seems to have had no significant physical experience of women before marrying in his mid-thirties. In the official biography, his son Randolph makes the most of his admiration of the beautiful Pamela Plowden, whom he met in India, and his stage-door infatuation for the actress Ethel Barrymore; but the available evidence does not suggest that these relationships were seriously pursued (Miss Plowden wrote to him that she considered him 'incapable of love'). In his only novel *Savrola*, published in 1899, the (obviously autobiographical) hero has a purely chaste relationship with the heroine (obviously based on Churchill's mother).*

In 1900 Churchill, now a war hero after his (greatly self-publicised) exploits in India, the Sudan and South Africa, entered the House of Commons as a Conservative. For the next three years his closest friends were four other rebellious young Tory MPs, of whom one was outstandingly handsome and the other three were confirmed bachelors.† They called themselves 'the Hughligans' after Lord Hugh Cecil, youngest son of the Prime Minister Lord Salisbury and oldest member of the group, and regarded as their mentor Lord Rosebery, who following his brief spell as Liberal premier in the 1890s had distanced himself from his party and become a politically independent figure, while continuing to delight in the company of young men.‡ Around this time Churchill acquired a

---

* Towards the end of the First World War, Churchill's mother, then aged sixty-four, married Montagu Porch, a colonial civil servant aged forty, who is said to have reminded her of Winston (who was two years older). Porch seems to have had homosexual interests: he faced a criminal charge in Nigeria for having allegedly had sexual relations with one of his male servants, though the charge was eventually dropped – possibly through the influence of his stepson, who was Colonial Secretary, 1921–2. (Information from Anne Sebba.)

† The stunner was the Canadian-born Ian Malcolm, who later married the daughter of Lily Langtry; the bachelors were Lord Hugh Cecil, Arthur Stanley and Earl Percy (the last of whom, the eldest son and heir of the Duke of Northumberland, died mysteriously in a Paris hotel in 1909).

‡ In 1903 Rosebery asked Churchill to help him find a new private secretary – Churchill (a close friend of Rosebery's adored son Neil) would not have needed to be told that youth and good looks were qualifications required for this post.

reputation (which he would never lose) as a misogynist who could be notoriously rude to the women he was seated next to at dinner parties. When he met his future wife for the first time in 1904 (their mothers were friends), he characteristically began by lecturing her about himself, and finally ignored her altogether. In fact, the only woman to whom he seems to have paid much attention as a bachelor MP was Violet Asquith, the sharp-witted daughter of the leading Liberal politician H. H. Asquith: she was clearly in love with him, but Churchill, who 'crossed the floor' to join the Liberals in 1904, did not reciprocate her feelings, and his attentiveness appears to have been prompted by the assumption that her father would soon be in a position to offer him important favours. This assumption proved correct: upon becoming Prime Minister in 1908 Asquith appointed Churchill, still only thirty-three, to the cabinet as President of the Board of Trade. Violet was consternated when, a few months later, Churchill proposed marriage not to her but to Clementine Hozier (though she consoled herself with the reflection that 'his wife could never be more to him than an ornamental sideboard').

Churchill's marriage to Clementine (with Hugh Cecil as best man) is usually regarded as a love-match (he himself concludes the memoirs of his early life with the bald statement that they 'lived happily ever afterwards'), but seems in reality to have been rather cold-blooded. Having become a privy counsellor and cabinet minister, and wishing, with his strong dynastic sense, to have descendants, he clearly felt it was time he married; and Clementine, with her 'virginal' beauty and upright character, seemed the best of the candidates on offer. (His first choice had been the vivacious Lady 'Goonie' Bertie, daughter of the Earl of Abingdon, who turned him down in favour of his brother Jack.) Churchill resolved to propose to her in the romantic surroundings of Blenheim Palace, his birthplace and ancestral home, but managed to oversleep on the morning in question. Jock Colville, the future private secretary of Churchill's premierships, wrote that Churchill looked to his wife to provide him with 'a well-run household, ambrosial food, children, and a loyal heart'. She certainly supplied all this, along with a salutary corrective to his more extravagant enthusiasms, but he seems to have taken her contribution for granted; he thought nothing of taking such an important step as buying Chartwell, his country house in Kent, without consulting her, or of abandoning her for months on end, often to stay with one of the many friends she disapproved of. Between the wars she became increasingly exasperated by his emotional unresponsiveness and constant demands, and on several occasions considered leaving him. On the other hand, there is nothing to suggest that he was ever unfaithful to her (though a number of sirens, such as Venetia Stanley and Daisy Fellowes, tried their best to seduce him).

Almost as important as his relationship with 'Clemmie' was his bond with 'Eddie' Marsh. Upon being appointed Undersecretary for the Colonies in the new Liberal government of 1905, Churchill caused surprise by demanding to have this minor official, whom he had recently met at a party, as his private secretary. Marsh, two years older than Churchill, was good-looking in a rather prim way; he had a high-pitched voice and effeminate mannerisms, and was already known for his 'crushes' on handsome young writers and actors. (He was rumoured to be impotent but was in fact a foot-fetishist, who got a kick out of pulling off the boots of young men returning from hunting at country house parties.) Marsh was reluctant to accept the private secretarial job, which meant stepping off the ladder of promotion; but having been persuaded to take it he became slavishly devoted to his master, whom he continued to serve in the same relatively humble capacity in every ministerial post Churchill occupied for the next quarter of a century. 'Few people have been as lucky as me', wrote Churchill to Marsh in 1908, 'as to find in the dull & grimy recesses of the Colonial Office a friend whom I shall cherish & hold on to all my life.' Marsh for his part wrote that he saw himself as 'Ruth to Winston's Naomi'.* When Churchill resigned from the cabinet in 1915, both men were in tears; but as soon as he returned to it two years later Marsh was there to resume his devoted service, remaining at Churchill's side until he relinquished office as Chancellor of the Exchequer in 1929. Down the years, Churchill was introduced by Marsh to various queer theatrical personalities such as Ivor Novello and Noël Coward, in whose company he seems to have been at ease. In 1914 he also met Marsh's literary protégé Rupert Brooke, and arranged for 'England's handsomest poet' to be commissioned into a unit under his control, the Royal Naval Regiment. When Brooke died early the following year it was Churchill who wrote the fulsome eulogy in *The Times* – 'joyous, fearless, versatile, deeply instructed, with classic symmetry of mind and body, all that one would wish England's noblest sons to be' – which led to the creation of such a legend around this in fact rather neurotic character.

Churchill's association with Brooke was brief, but there was another youth of almost equally angelic beauty whom he met shortly before the First World War and with whom he established a close and mutually dependent relationship lasting a decade. This was Sir Archibald Sinclair (1890–1970), a Scottish baronet and cavalry officer who looked up to Churchill as a father-figure (his own father, like Churchill's, having died of syphilis). Sinclair hoped to become a Liberal

---

* ' ... whither thou goest, I will go; and where thou lodgest, I will lodge: thy people shall be my people, and thy God my God ... ' (Ruth 1:16)

MP and Churchill offered to launch his career, though Sinclair's looks were not matched by much in the way of brains. When war broke out Churchill was determined to 'keep Archie safe', securing for him the appointment of ADC to his friend Jack Seely, the former Secretary of State for War, now a general. In 1916, when Churchill himself, having resigned from the government in the wake of the Dardanelles fiasco, went to command a battalion on the Western Front, he pleaded, successfully, to have Sinclair appointed his second-in-command. Much of their early correspondence seems to have been lost, but what survives shows a mutual affection which verges on the amorous (though Sinclair's devotion to Churchill did not prevent him embarking on a marriage which, while not entirely happy, produced four children). When Churchill became Minister of War in 1919 he appointed Sinclair his 'military secretary'; and when Churchill transferred to the Colonial Office in 1921 he again insisted on taking Sinclair with him in an 'undefined role ... as assistant, confidant and Man Friday'. (During his spell as Colonial Secretary Churchill also established an intimate friendship with T. E. Lawrence, to whom he remained close for the remainder of that homosexual adventurer's life.) Sinclair was subsequently elected to parliament as the Liberal member for Caithness, much of which he owned. In 1935, after all the more talented Liberals had lost their seats, he unexpectedly found himself leader of the Liberal Party, in which role he gave staunch support to Churchill in his campaign for rearmament. In 1940 Churchill appointed him Air Minister in his coalition government, but (aware of his limited abilities) without a seat in the War Cabinet; his subservience to the Prime Minister earned him the nickname 'the head-boy's fag'.

Another handsome Scot for whom Churchill fell was Robert 'Bob' Boothby (1900–86), a charismatic bisexual rake who was elected for East Aberdeenshire in 1924 as the youngest Tory MP (and who will be further considered in Chapter 6). The manner in which their association began was curious. Boothby, whose youth was matched by a bumptious self-confidence, was a convert to the economic theories of Keynes, and wrote to Churchill, then Chancellor of the Exchequer, criticising his decision to restore the gold standard. Churchill responded to this impertinence by sacking his parliamentary private secretary and offering the position to Boothby. Though Boothby felt unable to refuse (it was almost unknown for an MP in his mid-twenties to be offered such a position by a senior member of the government), he continued to disagree with many of Churchill's decisions and on several occasions asked to resign, but Churchill would not hear of this and kept Boothby as his aide until he left office in 1929. During the 1930s Boothby, like Sinclair, was a key parliamentary supporter of Churchill in the latter's 'wilderness years'; he was appointed Parliamentary Secretary to the Ministry of Food in 1940 but soon got into trouble owing to some financial impropriety and Churchill, by now both aware of Boothby's dodginess and exasperated by his continuing outspoken criticisms, made no attempt to save his ministerial career – though on becoming premier again in the 1950s he tossed Boothby a knighthood (Sinclair got a viscountcy).

Sinclair and Boothby (both Old Etonians), as well as Marsh (a great-grandson of the Prime Minister Spencer Perceval), came from backgrounds not altogether unlike Churchill's own. The same could not be said of Brendan Bracken (1901–58), a wild youth of completely unknown origin who was not yet twenty-two when he met Churchill early in 1923 and swept the forty-eight-year-old off his feet. He was in fact a con-man on the make: he claimed (among other tall stories) to be an Australian orphan educated at an English public school; he was in fact from Tipperary, the self-educated son of an Irish stonemason of republican sympathies, and had managed to bluff his way into spending one term at Sedbergh aged nineteen, pretending to be fifteen. Though not exactly handsome, he had a striking appearance, tall and perky with a shock of flaming red hair; his assets included quick wit, a remarkable memory (he is said to have memorised the whole of *Who's Who* at the age of twenty), and boundless audacity. In his early twenties – while serving first as a flogging prep school master, then as a junior employee of a publishing firm – he gatecrashed smart parties in London and boldly introduced himself to well-known personalities, many of whom were astonished that he seemed to know so much about their careers and some of whom were sufficiently impressed to ask him to dinner. One such was J. L. Garvin, editor of the *Observer*, at whose table he met Churchill, who was seeking to re-enter parliament having recently been defeated in his Dundee constituency at the general election of November 1922. Churchill was immediately smitten by Bracken. 'Who is this extraordinary young friend you've been hiding away?', he asked Garvin. 'I would like to see him again.' He did not have long to wait, for within days Bracken found an excuse to visit Churchill at his London house in Sussex Square, where he again worked his magic. As Bracken's biographer Andrew Boyle writes:

No doubt Bracken's spontaneous offer to place himself unreservedly at Churchill's disposal, and do all within his power to restore him to the high position in politics that was rightfully his, touched the soft heart of the older man; but the vitality, the charm, the boldness and the infectious wit of this red-headed ball of fire who hailed, so he said, from Australia struck responsive chords in Churchill ...

The only obstacle ... was the antagonistic attitude of Mrs Churchill. She could not understand why Winston liked him.

The two men remained close for eighteen months, during which Bracken ran Churchill's spirited but unsuccessful campaigns in two parliamentary by-elections. Owing to Mrs Churchill's hostility they ceased to meet in Sussex Square; but during 1923 Churchill moved into Chartwell, where Bracken was a constant visitor – as Clementine acidly remarked, 'Mr Bracken arrived with the furniture, and he never left'. She was not alone in being mystified by her husband's passion for this strange, pushy youth, and the (ludicrous but widely believed) rumour arose that Bracken was Churchill's illegitimate son – which Bracken did nothing to deny, and which merely seemed to amuse Churchill, though it caused great offence to his wife and his genuine son Randolph. By the time Churchill returned to parliament and to office in October 1924 a temporary coolness had entered into his relations with Bracken, who had presumed too far when he purloined some notes of Churchill, wrote them up into an article, and published them under Churchill's name in a journal he was editing, all without a word of consent. Bracken spent the next few years (during which Churchill's need for a sympathetic young male companion was satisfied by Boothby) making a fortune and cultivating his contacts, and managed to get elected as Conservative MP for North Paddington at the general election of 1929. He immediately resumed his close relationship with Churchill, becoming his devoted fixer and henchman during his 'decade in the wilderness'; and when war came, Churchill – as First Lord of the Admiralty, then Prime Minister – kept Bracken as his parliamentary private secretary and right-hand man. Bracken entered the cabinet in 1941 as Minister for

Information, a role to which this great fantasist and fixer was ideally suited; he continued to have the Prime Minister's ear and performed a curious variety of other roles (for example, having memorised *Crockford's Clerical Directory* in his twenties, this Catholic-born Irishman delighted in exercising on Churchill's behalf the prime ministerial right to appoint Anglican bishops). Churchill appointed him First Lord of the Admiralty in his caretaker administration of 1945, and was dismayed when Bracken, whose health was deteriorating, declined to serve under him again in 1951 ('I want you beside me, my dear'). On hearing of Bracken's early death in 1958, his eyes filled with tears.

Bracken, whose pushiness was complemented by a streak of prudishness, never married, and is not known to have consummated any heterosexual affairs. He claimed to be infatuated with a number of titled women, and proposed to at least one of them, but they did not take his advances seriously and turned him down. (This aspect of Bracken is satirised by Evelyn Waugh in the character of Rex Mottram in *Brideshead Revisited*, who is uninterested in women but wants an aristocratic wife for reasons of social prestige.) There is some evidence that he was a closet homosexual. At the age of twenty he was a notoriously sadistic master at a boys school, and a diary later kept by the housekeeper at a property he rented in Scotland hinted at goings-on involving boy scouts. Among the friends who helped him up the ladder, lending him large sums of money, were two rakish homosexual heirs to fortunes and peerages, Gavin Henderson (later 2nd Baron Faringdon) and Evan Morgan (later 2nd Viscount Tredegar). Two handsome (and heterosexual) assistants who worked for him down the years, Robert Lutyens, son of the architect, and Garrett Moore, later 11th Earl of Drogheda, both believed him to have been in love with them; and he was a regular attender at parties given by Moore's louche bisexual brother-in-law, Sir Paul Latham MP. His biographers, however, have dismissed this evidence, pointing out that all the others they interviewed who had known him in politics and journalism believed him not to be homosexual, merely wedded to his work. But Bracken was a brilliant concealer, who throughout his adult life managed to ensure that almost nobody was aware of his true background. (Beaverbrook was one of the few who knew, but liked Bracken and kept the secret to himself.) Had he wished to lead a secret life as a practising homosexual, he would have known how to go about it. By his instructions, all his private papers were destroyed on his death.

Bracken was one of what Colville describes as 'the three horsemen of the apocalypse' who were Churchill's devoted henchmen in the 1930s and later became his close advisers as wartime Prime Minister, the other two (both befriended by Churchill as young men during the First World War) being the intelligence officer Desmond Morton and the Oxford physics professor Frederick Lindemann (later Viscount Cherwell). Like Bracken, Morton and Lindemann were bachelors; and Morton (who also arranged for his papers to be posthumously destroyed) was reputed to be homosexual. Rumours to this effect also circulated with regard to Lindemann, though his latest biographer insists that these were baseless and that the Professor was devastated when the attractive daughter of an earl whom he had hoped to marry suddenly died in 1937. Certainly 'the Prof' was gallant towards women, and (unlike many of Churchill's friends) popular with Clementine, though he was otherwise an odd friend for Churchill to have, being a vegetarian, a non-smoker, a teetotaller, a howling snob, a sadist and an anti-semite.

Another youth for whom Churchill harboured romantic feelings was his only son Randolph (1911–68). (It will be recalled that Rosebery, Esher and Beauchamp were each in love with one of their sons.) As an Eton schoolboy and Oxford undergraduate Randolph was both clever and seraphically handsome, and Winston doted on him, lavishing upon him the passionate love which he failed to show his wife, who seems to have loathed the boy from birth: indeed, Churchill's adoration of their son was one of the chief causes of Clementine's exasperation with her husband which brought her close to leaving him.* In honour of Randolph's twenty-first birthday in May 1932 Churchill commissioned a ravishing idealised portrait of him from Philip de Laszlo, and gave a huge stag dinner at Claridge's for 'great men and their sons'. However, as the 1930s progressed and Randolph became a coarse womaniser, whose looks soon deteriorated owing to excessive drinking, his father's feelings for him cooled: his love for Randolph was to some extent transferred to his illustrious ancestor John Churchill, 1st Duke of Marlborough, whose biography he wrote during these years, in which he dwelt rhapsodically on the handsome looks and sexual prowess of his young forebear. Indeed, as demonstrated by his feelings for Sinclair and Bracken, Churchill had a need to lavish affection on a 'son-figure'; at different times such sentiments were directed towards his debonair political 'heir' Anthony Eden and his dashing sons-in-law Duncan Sandys and Christopher Soames, all of whom were disliked by Randolph (who also had something of a love–hate relationship with Bracken, accepting frequent help from him but referring to him sneeringly in public as 'my brother').

There is no shortage of other examples of Churchill taking

---

* In his memoir *Twenty-One* (Weidenfeld, 1965), pp. 24–5, Randolph writes that he was once 'interfered with' by a master at his prep school, and that his father was beside himself with rage when he later heard about this ('I don't think I've ever seen him so angry'), immediately making a journey of more than 100 miles to the school to demand the master's dismissal, only to find he had already been sacked.

a fancy to young men. His favourite cabinet colleague in 1914 was the dashing and unmarried 'Bron' Lucas (his eulogy of whom is quoted in Chapter 2). He was known for his 'fatherly' interest in attractive Conservative MPs, including such homosexuals (to be considered later) as Victor Cazalet, Alan Lennox-Boyd, Jack Macnamara (a great favourite whom he promoted to important military roles during the Second World War) and Ronnie Cartland. He liked Somerset Maugham's queer nephew Robin Maugham, whom he encouraged (fortunately unsuccessfully in both cases) to enter politics and seek the hand of his youngest daughter Mary. At the time of Munich he even warmed to the raffish Soviet agent Guy Burgess, then a twenty-seven-year-old BBC talks producer, whom he invited to Chartwell, presented with a signed copy of his speeches, and offered to employ in the event of war. He became fond of his personable young wartime private secretary Jock Colville, whom he recalled to his service in the 1950s, and of another handsome civil servant, Anthony Montague Browne, whom he asked to serve him in his retirement. (Colville and Browne were both married and presumably heterosexual, though the former has written frankly of Churchill's indifference to women.) He was taken with Eden's handsome private secretary Valentine Lawford (later the lover of the photographer Horst), whom he often 'borrowed', notably as an aide during the Yalta Conference. He was devoted to his wartime stenographer Patrick Kinna (1913–2009), whom he begged (unsuccessfully) to stay with him after 1945 (and who is still fondly remembered in Brighton's gay community). His bodyguards included the beautiful Alex Beattie of the Coldstream Guards (later the lover of Alan Lennox-Boyd). One of his favourite wartime commanders (though Churchill later refused to speak to him after he had 'given away' India) was the handsome and sexually ambiguous Lord Louis Mountbatten, whom he appointed Chief of Combined Operations at forty-one and Supreme Commander South-East Asia at forty-three. He became infatuated with André de Staercke, a seductive young Belgian diplomat who served from 1942 to 1944 as secretary to his country's government-in-exile in London, who frequently found himself summoned by the great man to late night tête-à-tête drinking sessions. (Staercke too he regarded as a possible suitor for Mary: the poor girl had some lucky escapes.)* In the 1950s he took a liking to the youngish Conservative whip Edward Heath and often invited him to Chartwell (which Heath's biographer Philip Ziegler finds slightly puzzling, given his subject's gauche and unclubbable nature). It is possible that his quixotic and unavailing attempt to help Edward VIII save his throne in 1936, made against the advice of his friends and at some cost to his career, owed something to that sovereign's Prince Charming looks.

Apart from a few relations of his wife or himself with whom he liked playing cards, and his younger daughters Sarah and Mary (he never cared much for his firstborn Diana), the only females whose company Churchill enjoyed were pretty young women who flattered and made a fuss of him, such as Diana Cooper in the 1920s, his daughter-in-law Pamela (later Harriman) in the 1940s, and Wendy Reeves, the luscious wife of his literary agent with whom he often stayed in the South of France (and who later vehemently denied that she had been his mistress), in the 1950s. He also harboured romantic feelings for the Queen, who came to the throne aged twenty-five just a few weeks after Churchill had returned to the premiership aged

---

* Staercke, who never married, was the lover of Fernand Spaak, diplomat son of the Belgian statesman Paul-Henri Spaak, who was later murdered by his wife after she had learnt of his infidelities with both sexes. (Information from Professor John Rogister.)

seventy-seven. With the possible exception of Violet Bonham Carter, he had a particular dislike of women in public life, such as Lady Astor. (Along with Loulou Harcourt, Churchill had been the member of the Asquith government most vehemently opposed to the suffragettes.)

Churchill felt relaxed in the company of homosexuals (Somerset Maugham was a lifelong friend), and regarded their activities as a subject for good-natured ribaldry. When the louche Tom Driberg, who had irked him as an MP critical of his wartime policies, caused surprise in 1951 by marrying an unattractive woman, Churchill quipped that 'buggers can't be choosers'.* Learning in November 1958 that the Foreign Office minister Ian Harvey (who as an Oxford undergraduate in 1936 had met Churchill with Lindemann) had been caught with a guardsman in St James's Park, he commented: 'On the coldest night of the year? It makes you proud to be British.' He summarised the traditions of the Royal Navy as 'rum, sodomy and the lash.' Churchill was in the last year of his premiership when, in 1954, the proposal came before cabinet to set up a body to review the law relating to homosexuality in response to the debate then taking place in the press: his first reaction (which surely contained an element of jocularity, though he seems mainly to have been concerned that the introduction of such a controversial matter might imperil the government with its small majority) was to suggest a change in the law to prevent the press mentioning the subject. His view of the Wolfenden Report when it was published three years later is not recorded; but as Churchill's earliest public act, as a Sandhurst cadet in 1894, had been to campaign, on libertarian grounds, against an

---

* I am aware that the phrase had already been used by Bob Boothby some years earlier, to describe a matrimonial project (which came to nothing) of Maurice Bowra. (See Richard Davenport-Hines [ed.], *Hugh Trevor-Roper: The Wartime Journals* [I. B. Tauris, 2012].)

attempt by 'the purity brigade' to close the Empire Theatre, a notorious haunt of prostitutes of both sexes, it is hard to believe that he would have been troubled by its recommendations. (In a letter dated 18 October 1894 published in the *Westminster Gazette*, Churchill had written: 'State intervention ... in the form of statute ... will never eradicate evil. It may make it more dangerous for the evildoer. But such a policy, while not decreasing immorality, only increases its ill effects ... The state should protect [its citizens] from harm, and must govern men as they are and not as they ought to be.')

In old age (they were born and died in the same years), Maugham is said to have asked Churchill whether he had ever had a homosexual experience, and allegedly received the reply: 'I once went to bed with Ivor Novello: it was very musical.' If such an event took place (or, indeed, horseplay with fellow cadets at Sandhurst) we may assume that it was incidental, and Churchill was surely a virtual stranger to physical homosexuality: for that matter, he seems to have had a low sex drive and is unlikely to have engaged in much serious cohabitation with his wife except as was needed to produce their offspring. Yet emotionally, he was clearly drawn to men rather than women, a fact which needs to be borne in mind when assessing his complex personality: the closest relationships of his life were with members of his own sex, even if they stopped short of the physical.

# 4

# IMPERIALISTS

It is perhaps no coincidence that Churchill, the admirer of young men, was an ardent imperialist. He began his career as a dashing soldier in and chronicler of imperial campaigns; he gloried in the role of imperial warlord in both world wars; as Undersecretary for the Colonies (1905–8) and Colonial Secretary (1921–2) he worked to consolidate and extend imperial rule; in the 1930s he fought against the granting of self-government to India; indeed, his whole swashbuckling life-story reads like something out of the *Boy's Own Paper*, or a novel by Henty. As Jan Morris writes in her great trilogy on the history of the British Empire, 'love between men, generally platonic but often profound, was an essential strain of the imperial ethic'. The Empire was a rugged, male-bonding world; its rulers came from the public schools, at which intense (often sexual) friendships were common, and boys were encouraged to obsess themselves with muscular development through sport and the study of classical civilisations with their bisexual cultures; exotic distant territories provided a means of escape from the sexual restrictions and prudery of the mother country.* This chapter will consider six notable imperialists who were also politicians – Curzon, Kitchener, Rhodes, Milner, Lothian and Lloyd. They were all ambitious men, who would never have allowed their private lives to put their careers at risk, and it must be said that (as with Churchill himself) there is little evidence that any of them (with the possible exception of Kitchener and Lloyd during the oriental wanderings of their youth) ever led an overtly homosexual life: indeed, two of them, Curzon and Milner, had thoroughly heterosexual reputations, Curzon also being something of an obsessive 'homophobe'. Yet none of them was a stranger to the notion of 'love between men'; and in each case it is possible to see their endeavours as fuelled by a degree of repressed homosexuality.

Proud, handsome, authoritarian, hard-working and intellectually outstanding, George Nathaniel Curzon, first and last Marquess Curzon of Kedleston (1859–1925), is often thought of as the archetypal Edwardian imperialist. He came from an ancient but dim line of Derbyshire squires whose sole distinction had been to commission Robert Adam to design their magnificent Palladian seat, Kedleston Hall, the building of which in the 1760s almost bankrupted them. Determined to achieve the greatness which had eluded his ancestors, Curzon won all the prizes at Eton and Balliol, was elected to parliament at twenty-six and became a member of Salisbury's Conservative government at thirty-two. His early reputation as aloof and disdainful (reflected in the ditty 'My name is George Nathaniel Curzon,/ I am a most superior person') was not entirely deserved: he was in constant pain owing to

---

* Thanks to the activities of the 'purity brigade', this became progressively less true from the 1880s onwards, but as late as the Second World War India and Egypt provided opportunities to homosexuals which were unheard-of in England.

curvature of the spine and wore a brace to correct this, giving him a deceptively 'stiff' appearance. Although he never suffered fools gladly, he was a charming and popular figure in the London society of the 1880s and 90s, known for his good fellowship and brilliant conversation; along with Arthur Balfour and George Wyndham, he was one of the leading lights of 'the Souls'. But there can be no doubt of his consuming ambition: from his mid-twenties he was determined to become Viceroy of India, a role for which he prepared himself through extensive travels in Central Asia and writings on the political problems of the region, notably Britain's rivalry with Russia. Curzon achieved his great wish when he was appointed to the viceroyalty in 1898, some months before his fortieth birthday. By then, singlemindedness and overwork had altered his personality, his formerly warm, approachable nature having given way to something in the nature of cold fanaticism.

Curzon was an outstanding administrator, who overhauled the Indian bureaucracy and introduced salutary reforms. Although he believed that the British were in India to stay, and consistently blocked measures to give Indians a greater role in running their country, he was determined that British rule should be seen by all to benefit the subcontinent: he was ferocious towards lazy or incompetent British officials who failed in their duty to provide good government, and once disciplined an entire regiment after horseplay by some officers had led to the death of an Indian cook. There can be no doubt of his love of Indian culture, manifested by his devoted efforts to conserve and repair the subcontinent's great monuments. His principal failings were, first, his belief that the Indians who mattered were the princely families who ruled the native states, rather than the rising, liberal (and increasingly nationalist) middle class produced by decades of British education; and secondly, his tendency to ride roughshod over anyone who disagreed with his views. Though Curzon was generally in the right, he caused offence by his high-handed and tactless behaviour, both in India and in London. These resentments proved fatal to him when, in 1904–5 (having meanwhile been appointed to a second term as Viceroy), he quarrelled with the new Commander-in-Chief, Kitchener, over control of the Indian Army. Although Curzon was right as usual (the army which Kitchener proceeded to organise without viceregal control went on to suffer disaster in Mesopotamia a decade later), Kitchener had no difficulty in finding allies to support him in the dispute; enraged at failing to get his way, Curzon resigned in a huff at the end of 1905, returning to England just in time to see his party swept from power. He endured a decade in the political wilderness until the First World War brought him back into government (as it did other glamorous figures from the past such as Balfour, Milner, and indeed Kitchener himself). Curzon went on to become Foreign Secretary from 1919 to 1924; when the mortally ill Bonar Law resigned as Conservative Prime Minister in 1923 Curzon expected (and was generally expected) to succeed him, and was devastated when (largely owing to Balfour's feline influence) the premiership instead went to Stanley Baldwin – a man of inferior talent and experience, if better suited to the times. Worn out by disappointment and overwork, Curzon died in 1925 at the age of sixty-six.

Although, like many imperialists, he went through periods of self-enforced chastity while he dedicated himself to the achievement of his goals, Curzon was a great admirer of women, most of whom found him very attractive. He married twice, in both cases rich Americans, having three daughters by his first marriage (it bitterly disappointed him that his second marriage failed to provide him with a son and heir); and while he lacked warmth as a suitor and husband, he became devotedly fond of his first wife, by whose early death in 1906 he was devastated. He also had two long, well-documented affairs, with Sibell Grosvenor (future wife of George Wyndham) in his twenties and the romantic novelist Elinor Glyn in his fifties. Indeed, his philandering almost cost him his career: as a rising politician in his thirties, he narrowly avoided being cited as a co-respondent in a divorce case, and also had to cope with a former mistress who tried to blackmail him. Yet he was also a man with many feminine characteristics. He took no interest in sport (except for tiger-hunting, part of the 'show' of viceroyalty), but loved old buildings and interior decoration. He was childishly vain and narcissistic, and adored dressing up and participating in lavish ceremonies. His touchiness and petulance had an epicene quality. As a young man he was given to forming intense platonic friendships with members of his own sex, including Balfour and Wyndham – a whole book has been written about these relationships – though in bitter middle age he succeeded in quarrelling with most of these former soulmates. Encountering bisexual cultures during his youthful travels, he showed himself responsive to male beauty, writing of Syrian boys as 'fine, stalwart bronzed figures ... handsome enough to satisfy even the ancient Greeks'. While he is unlikely to have engaged in physical homosexuality as an adult, he certainly enjoyed close romantic relationships with a number of boys at Eton (notably Alfred Lyttelton, Gladstone's nephew and a future Colonial Secretary), and it is difficult to believe that none of these strayed into the realms of sensuality. (His papers contain several letters from older boys who were clearly in love with him, and who claimed to be concerned to 'protect' him, as a pretty boy, from the gross physical attentions of other boys.) Moreover, while at the school Curzon formed a close attachment to a housemaster, the avuncular and inspirational Oscar Browning; their relationship caused much disquiet to the Eton authorities, especially as Browning was not Curzon's own housemaster, and largely on account of it Browning was forced to leave the school. Although Browning's obsession with teenage boys was well known (when he later became a Cambridge don it was an open secret that he frolicked with young soldiers and sailors), Curzon remained devoted to him after his disgrace, often accompanying him on continental holidays, and later having him to stay as a viceregal guest in Calcutta and Simla.

Curzon might therefore have been expected to take a relatively tolerant view of homosexuality. However, as Viceroy he was bizarrely obsessed with the prevalence of what he called 'abominable practices' among the princely rulers of the native states, which he regarded it as his mission to stamp out. This topic took up an inordinate amount of space in his correspondence with the Secretary of State for India, Lord George Hamilton, a broadminded man who was frankly puzzled by Curzon's obsession. When Curzon opined that the cause of this 'horrible taint' was the custom of early marriage – 'a boy gets tired of women at an early age, and wants the stimulus of some more novel or exciting sensation' – Hamilton dared to suggest a simpler explanation: that what Curzon regarded as 'unnatural vice' was 'for the Indian upper orders, a natural pleasure'. He warned Curzon against treating the princes like 'a set of unruly, ignorant and undisciplined schoolboys'. But Curzon was not to be deflected from his moral crusade. When the Maharajah of Ulwar, despite being 'an active youth and splendid polo player', was found to be 'infected with this virus', he was deprived of power in his state and 'placed in the hands of a British officer under a strict system of discipline and control'. When the Maharajah of Jodhpur was found to be indulging in 'dissolute orgies at the palace ... a carnival of unnatural vice', Curzon decreed that 'he be treated like a confirmed drunkard or madman', writing to Hamilton that 'far the best thing is that the boy should die'. Similar sanctions were taken against the rulers of Bhurtpore, 'a confirmed sodomite', and Bharatpur, who was suspected of having murdered the objecting father of one of his 'catamites'. When Queen Victoria expressed her fondness for the Maharajah of Holkar, who sent her charming telegrams on her birthday, the Viceroy hastened to disillusion his octogenarian sovereign with the news that this ruler was 'addicted to horrible vices'. Curzon's naive solution to this 'problem' was to set up a Cadet Corps to train young native princes to serve as his bodyguard. When he first inspected the Corps at their headquarters at Dehra Dun in 1902 he was delighted. 'Its tone and spirit [writes his latest biographer] seemed admirable, and he believed its well-born apprentices were as enthusiastic ... as if they had been English public schoolboys. Unfortunately it soon transpired that the Corps shared another trait popularly associated with public schoolboys.' It was fortunate that the inevitable scandal did not break until after the Delhi Durbar of 1903 in which the Corps had played a prominent role. Richard Davenport-Hines, noting that Curzon's descriptions of the 'depravities' of the princes contain a mixture of 'effulgent disgust and prurient relish', sees his behaviour as an attempt to 'overcome his own femininity' through 'fury at the sexual ambivalence of others ... There were no open and honest memories of Eton; no realisation that what he feared most were the feminine traits in himself.'

Curzon showed a similar attitude to the case of Sir Hector Macdonald, a Scottish hero who had risen from the ranks to become the general commanding the army in Ceylon, and who in 1903 was accused by white settlers of indulging in orgies with 'temple boys': after returning to London to explain himself to the military authorities, he committed suicide in a

Paris hotel room (leading to George V's remark at the time of the Beauchamp affair that he 'thought men like that shot themselves'). Curzon wrote to the new Secretary of State St John Brodrick (one of the boys to whom he had been close at Eton) that he had 'so little sympathy with the vice under discussion' that he did not waste 'a drop of regret' at the tragedy, adding that 'such a brute is best kept out of the way'. On this episode at least, Kitchener expressed similar views to Curzon ('this horrible thing'): Macdonald had been one of Kitchener's subordinate commanders in the Sudan, and is said to have aroused his jealousy owing to his popularity with the troops. However, when it came to sexual emotions Kitchener was a very different being to Curzon: indeed, Peter King, author of a book on the Curzon–Kitchener feud, *The Viceroy's Fall* (1986), sees it as a battle of wills between an essential heterosexual with a streak of masochism (Curzon) and an essential homosexual with a streak of sadism (Kitchener).

Like Curzon, Herbert, 1st Earl Kitchener (1850–1916) was intensely ambitious and narcissistic, with a monstrous ego, and devoted himself singlemindedly to the achievement of his goals. The son of a cavalry colonel, he was closely attached in childhood to his mother, by whose death when he was sixteen he was devastated. (When in 1898 he became 'Baron Kitchener of Khartoum' he added the territorial designation 'of Aspall in the County of Suffolk' – her birthplace.) As a boy and young man he was blessed with pretty, rather feminine looks, which by his late twenties he had hidden behind the famous bushy moustache. Like that other Victorian military hero of ambiguous sexuality, General Gordon, Kitchener began as an officer of the Royal Engineers, considered to be the 'cleverest' branch of the armed services, but owed his rapid promotion more to a talent for intrigue and self-publicity, allied to a magnificent appearance and good luck, than to any brilliance. He was adulated by the British public and showered with honours as the supposed architect of two great imperial victories, in the Sudan (1896–8) and South Africa (1899–1902). Most military historians now take a jaundiced view of these achievements: the Sudan was conquered as a result of a slow, methodical campaign which left nothing to chance, and culminated in the unheroic massacre of dervishes armed with rifles by troops using the latest machine guns; while in the Boer War Kitchener, who was responsible for several early blunders (notably the bloody engagement at Paardeberg), took the credit for a transformation in British fortunes which was mostly the work of Lord Roberts. In both campaigns he won a reputation for callousness: Winston Churchill, present in the Sudan as a war correspondent, attacked him both for his bestial treatment of the enemy and his unconcern for the British wounded; in South Africa, he achieved final victory by herding the Boer population into concentration camps at a cost of untold suffering. Owing to his vanity and conceit Kitchener got on badly with most senior figures, but was a problem for the government as he could not be sidelined owing to his public popularity. After serving as Commander-in-Chief in India he hoped to be appointed Viceroy, but was instead sent to rule Egypt. When the European conflict broke out in 1914, Kitchener, who had just been raised to an earldom, was appointed to the cabinet as Secretary for War: the Liberal government hoped to use him as an inspirational figurehead, hence his arresting appearance on the celebrated recruiting poster (never in fact printed except as a magazine cover) 'Your Country Needs You!'. Kitchener was one of the few to realise from the outset that Britain was in for a long war, and he did his best to prepare her for it. Otherwise he was a nightmare for the authorities, as he aspired to run the entire war on his own, and quarrelled both with the commander in the field, Sir John

French, and the politicians. (Interestingly, one of the few
people he got on with was Lord Esher, who helped smooth
over the troubled relationships.) His cabinet colleagues were
at their wits' end as to how to get rid of him, when Kitchener
solved the problem (and sealed his own heroic reputation) by
perishing at sea in June 1916, after the warship *Hampshire*
taking him to military talks in Russia sank after hitting a
German mine.

Unlike Curzon, who adored the company of women,
Kitchener had a reputation as a confirmed misogynist. On the
whole he was bored and irritated by women, and rarely
remembered who they were on meeting them a second time.
He never chose married officers to serve on his staff. In his
mid-thirties he was said to be devoted to the teenage daughter of his friend Valentine Baker, a swashbuckling British
general in the Egyptian Army; after her sudden death, it was
rumoured that they had been unofficially engaged; but both
his sister and his cousin Edith thought it improbable that he
would have married her had she lived. In his forties he was
advised to marry by his friend the Duke of York (the future
King George V), whereupon he proposed to a daughter of
Lord Londonderry, who had the good sense to refuse him. On
the other hand, Kitchener, with his handsome looks and cold,
intense personality, exercised a great fascination on some
women, a fact which he exploited to win allies among influential women in London society in order to advance his
career – notably Lady Cranborne, daughter-in-law of the
Prime Minister, Lord Salisbury. He even directed his steely
charms towards Curzon's wife Mary (though when they saw
each other for the last time before the Curzons' departure
from India, he cut her dead). Queen Victoria said of him:
'They tell me he dislikes women, but I can only say he has
always been very nice to me.'

The only time the almost machine-like Kitchener seems to have shown much human warmth was in his relationships with various young officers. At Woolwich Military Academy he became attached to a fellow cadet named Clive Conder; after graduating, they both went to Palestine where for a couple of years they led a fraternal existence combining map-making, archaeology and espionage, living in close proximity to the Bedouin, the 'blood brothers of the desert'. Later, as Sirdar of the Egyptian Army, he was devoted to several of his staff officers, to whom he gave affectionate nicknames such as 'Brookie', 'Hammy', 'Birdie', 'Conk' and 'the Brat', as well as to a team of young, handpicked sappers who built the railways which facilitated the Sudan campaign, who became known as 'Kitchener's band of boys'. From 1907 until his death he was inseparable from his aide-de-camp Captain Oswald Fitzgerald ('Fitz'), who lived with him at Broome Park, the Jacobean house in Kent which he bought in 1911, and who eventually perished with him on the *Hampshire*. As Ronald Hyam notes, he also 'worshipped General Gordon, cultivated great interest in the Boy Scout movement, took a passing fancy to the son of General Botha and the sons of Lord Desborough, and embellished his rose garden with four pairs of sculptured bronze boys'.

Kitchener's most recent biographer John Pollock, an Anglican clergyman, devotes an appendix of his book to examining the rumours that Kitchener may have been homo-sexual, and concludes that there is no evidence for this. As with Rosebery's biographer McKinstry, one wonders what evidence he was expecting to find: Kitchener was notorious for his 'oriental' secrecy, and during his sea journey to India in 1902 destroyed most of his private papers by tipping them into the ocean. Certainly there were widespread rumours during his lifetime not only that there was a romantic element in his

attachment to young officers but that, during his long years in
the Near East, he had developed a penchant for buggering
shapely-bottomed young people of both sexes. Wearne,
Reuters' representative in Egypt during the Sudan campaign,
later told colleagues that Kitchener possessed 'that failing
acquired by most of the Egyptian officers, a taste for buggery',
a suggestion echoed in the memoirs of St John Brodrick.
Diana Cooper told A. N. Wilson that, when she complained
that Asquith had 'groped' her at dinner, her mother told her
that she was lucky 'K.' had not been a member of the party, as
he was known to steal into the bedrooms of the young guests
with a view to buggering them. Such stories were also believed
by the family of Detmar Blow, the architect who restored
Broome Park, whom Kitchener befriended to the point of
becoming godfather to Blow's son. When Peter King was writing *The Viceroy's Fall* he met a very old lady who told him that
she had been unable to marry the love of her life in the 1920s
because, as he explained to her, the experience of being
sodomised by Lord Kitchener had left him incapable of relations with women. King suggests that, irrespective of whether
Kitchener's homosexuality was repressed or active, it provides
the key to understanding his strange, inscrutable, devious personality. Of Kitchener's other biographers, two who were
themselves homosexual, Lord Esher and Philip Magnus (the
former of whom had had close personal dealings with him
over twenty years), had little doubt that Kitchener shared their
tastes.

Cecil Rhodes (1853–1902) had an astonishing career: in
little more than a decade, starting in his early thirties, he
became one of the richest men on the planet, founded what is
still one of the world's leading mining companies, served for
six years as Prime Minister of Cape Colony, founded two
other British colonies (which would bear his name for the next

seventy years), was responsible for three wars, and established the modern fruit and wine export industries of South Africa. All this implies immense energy and drive: but in fact Rhodes suffered throughout life from chronic chest ailments which would kill him before he was fifty; indeed, it was because of fears that he would not survive another English winter that his father, a Hertfordshire parson, sent him to South Africa when he was seventeen, to join an older brother working there as a cotton planter. Rhodes soon drifted to the recently discovered diamond mines at Kimberley; over a period of fifteen years, with a mixture of skill, luck and daring (and financial backing from the Rothschilds), he succeeded in amalgamating the Kimberley mining interests into the great conglomerate of De Beers. In the midst of this hectic business career he managed to read for a degree at Oxford, and get elected to the Cape Parliament. What drove Rhodes above all was a passionate belief in the superiority of the British race and the destiny of the British Empire. He declared that 'the more of the world we inhabit, the better for the human race'; that he 'would annex the planets if I could'; that to be born British was 'to win first prize in the lottery of life'. (His vision had some bizarre inconsistencies: he believed in 'racial purity', but all his main business associates were Jews; he combined an almost religious attachment to the Empire with both support of Irish nationalism and admiration for Britain's main commercial and geopolitical rival, Germany.) During the 1890s, now Premier of Cape Colony, he put into practice his dream of extending the British Empire when his British South Africa Company exploited the territories north of the Zambesi, finally, after much devious dealing with local chieftains and two bloody wars, establishing the string of protectorates which later became the colonies of Northern and Southern Rhodesia. However, Rhodes overreached himself in 1895–6 when he incited his close friend Dr Leander Starr Jameson to invade the Transvaal with an armed column of six hundred men, hoping to bring that territory into the British Empire and its goldfields into Rhodes's business empire: the 'raid' was a fiasco, and led to the end of Rhodes's public career (though his behind-the-scenes machinations contributed four years later to the outbreak of the Boer War, which after much suffering and turmoil brought the Boer Republics under British control). In his will, Rhodes bequeathed much of his fortune to a trust (which survives to this day) designed to provide an Oxford education to men from the Commonwealth, the United States and Germany.

Rhodes claimed to be too busy to interest himself in women, and had little to do with them. (At the end of his life an adventuress, one Princess Radziwill, tried to blackmail him, claiming that he had been her lover and had promised to marry her; but it has never been seriously believed that there was any substance to these allegations.) On the other hand, there is ample evidence that he was infatuated with young men, especially if they were well-built, fair-haired and good-looking (i.e., perfect specimens of 'the master race'). Certainly the closest relationship of his life (perhaps the only true love relationship, for he was notoriously aloof in his social dealings) was with the handsome and exuberant Neville Pickering, another parson's son, four years Rhodes's junior, whom he appointed secretary to his company in 1881, with whom he shared a house in Kimberley for the next five years, and who was the sole beneficiary of a will which (the already rich) Rhodes made in 1882. Unfortunately a riding accident in 1884 reduced Pickering to an invalid, and he died in 1886: during his last weeks, Rhodes nursed him lovingly, neglecting his business; at the funeral he burst into hysterical sobbing. After that, there were further handsome secretaries, but none of them engaged his affections as had Pickering, and he acrimoniously dispensed with their services if they married. He was also close to Jameson, another confirmed bachelor, who as a medical man had attended upon the dying Pickering; Jameson later nursed Rhodes through his own last illness, became the residuary beneficiary of his estate, and was eventually buried alongside him. No doubt most of these friendships were platonic, and there has been some debate as to whether Rhodes engaged in physical homosexuality: some of his biographers believe him to have been sexually incapable (like Haldane and Marsh, he had a startlingly high-pitched voice), while Ronald Hyam cites 'circumstantial evidence' that 'his hearty horseplay with blue-eyed valets may have been sexually expressed on occasion', also noting his 'openly displayed collection of phallic cult carvings'.

Alfred, 1st and last Viscount Milner (1854–1925), whose career intersected with those of Curzon, Kitchener and Rhodes (none of whom he particularly esteemed), was born in Darmstadt of mixed English and German parentage. After a brilliant career at Oxford, he distinguished himself successively as a journalist, private secretary to the Chancellor of the Exchequer, a civil servant overseeing the Egyptian economy, and head of the Inland Revenue, earning a reputation as an outstanding administrator. He was admired by both political parties, combining as he did an interest in social reform with a belief (reminiscent of Rhodes's) that the British race, through its Empire, was destined to dominate the globe. In 1897 he was sent to govern South Africa, where a serious crisis was brewing owing to the refusal of the Boer Republics to grant civic rights to the large population of recent British settlers attracted by the fortunes to be made from the goldfields. As an arch-imperialist Milner refused to compromise in the dispute, thus attracting some of the blame for the outbreak of the Boer War in 1899, with its initial military humiliation of the British and its devastation of large parts of South Africa. However, following the British victory Milner oversaw the reconstruction of the enlarged British South Africa with his usual skill. Milner retired from public service in 1905 to pursue a business career, but was invited to join the war cabinet by Lloyd George in 1916, where his experience as a wartime administrator proved invaluable in helping Britain survive the difficult last two years of the Great War. He ended his career as Colonial Secretary from 1919 to 1921.

A workaholic who regarded women as a distraction from his great tasks, Milner spent much of his life under a regime of self-enforced chastity. His great love was Violet Cecil (*née* Maxse), a woman of strong personality who at the time of their first meeting in 1899 was married to the youngest son of the Prime Minister Lord Salisbury, and whom Milner himself married twenty-two years later following the death of her first husband. However, another aspect of Milner's life was that, ruling South Africa as a virtual dictator from 1900 to 1905, he surrounded himself with a coterie of talented and personable Oxford-educated young bachelors, many of them destined to have brilliant future careers, whom he imbued with his imperialist creed and who came to be known as his 'Kindergarten'. They included (amongst others) the future novelist John Buchan, the future editor of *The Times* Geoffrey Dawson, the future journalist and statesman Philip Kerr (considered below), the future theorist of the Commonwealth Lionel Curtis, the future city financier Robert Brand, and the future Governor-General of South Africa Patrick Duncan. Some (such as the American conspiracy theorist Carroll Quigley) have seen the Kindergarten as a sinister secret society, with overtones of Rhodes's concept of rule by a racial and intellectual elite whom he called 'the elect'.

Certainly they all kept in close touch long after they had left South Africa and even after Milner's death; and they exercised influence behind the scenes of British politics, playing a role not just in 'imperial' developments but in such matters as Asquith's replacement by Lloyd George as Prime Minister in 1916 (and Milner's simultaneous projection into the war cabinet), and the policy of 'appeasing' Nazi Germany in the 1930s. While it is unlikely that any of the Kindergarten were practising homosexuals,* there was a strong socratic bond between them and their father-figure, Milner; they were all unmarried at the time they served him, and subsequently married late in life (like Milner himself), or not at all.

One member of the Kindergarten who remained a lifelong bachelor was Philip Kerr (1882–1940), who succeeded his cousin as 11th Marquess of Lothian in 1930. Lothian is reminiscent of that other unmarried Scottish statesman Arthur Balfour – both were handsome, androgynous, narcissistic (Lothian was derisively nicknamed 'Narcissus' by his enemies), intellectual, charming but aloof, keen on golf but otherwise lacking in manly virtues (Lothian avoided service in the First World War), and admiring of and admired by women while showing no desire to marry or make love to them. Both were in thrall to powerful and religious mothers – though whereas Balfour's mother, sister of Lord Salisbury, was ardently Protestant, Lothian's, sister of the Duke of Norfolk, was fervently Catholic. After a brilliant career at Oxford, Kerr became one of Milner's last recruits before his retirement in 1905, serving as secretary to various committees. In 1907 his Kindergarten colleagues persuaded him to leave public service to edit a journal advocating their goal of unifying the four South African colonies as a self-governing dominion; once

---

* Though some have detected a homoerotic strain in Buchan's novels and stories.

this aim was accomplished in 1910, he was appointed editor of *The Round Table*, a new London quarterly sponsored by the Kindergarten advocating imperial federation. *The Round Table* proved influential – though Kerr suffered a nervous breakdown in 1912, after which he came increasingly to believe that the Empire (including India) should be prepared for self-government, and gradually abandoned his Catholic beliefs to become a Christian Scientist. As a journalist and member of the Kindergarten, Kerr was active in the intrigues which led to Lloyd George replacing Asquith as Prime Minister in December 1916, after which 'L.G.' employed him as his private secretary and unofficial adviser until 1921, being considerably influenced by him particularly during the Paris Peace Conference which remade the world in 1919. During the 1920s Kerr became a pundit expressing liberal and internationalist views, and secretary of the Rhodes Trust in Oxford. On his succession to the marquessate he took the Liberal whip in the House of Lords, and in 1931–2 served as a minister in the National Government coalition, his main contribution being to advance India's progress to self-rule. During the 1930s Lothian, as a member of the 'Cliveden set' presided over by his fellow Christian Scientist Lady Astor, was a noted advocate of 'appeasing' Hitler; but he recanted his beliefs in view of Nazi aggression and in 1939, months before the outbreak of war, was appointed by his fellow ex-appeaser, the Foreign Secretary Lord Halifax, to be British Ambassador to Washington. Popular with Americans (of whom he had much experience through the Rhodes Trust), Lothian proved ideal for the task at a critical juncture in Anglo-American relations, but suddenly died in December 1940, aged fifty-eight, of a treatable infection for which, as a Christian Scientist, he had refused to seek medical help. Though affable and generally liked, Lothian seems to have had no close male friends; his greatest intimates

The 5th Earl of Rosebery (*above*),
Liberal Prime Minister 1894–5,
and the 7th Earl Beauchamp
(*left*), Liberal cabinet minister
1910–15 (and model for Lord
Marchmain in *Brideshead
Revisited*), were cousins through
their mothers, and partly owed
their success to handsome looks.
Both were hounded by vindictive
fellow noblemen who claimed to
have proof of their homosexual
activities.

Reginald 'Regy' Bret
2nd Viscount Esher
(*above*), and Lewis
'Loulou' Harcourt, 1
Viscount Harcourt
(*left*) – intriguers in
realms of both politi
and forbidden love.

George Wyndham (*left*) worshipped his political mentor Arthur Balfour (*above*), but lacked his icy ruthlessness, and died a broken man.

Winston Churchill (*far left*) with fellow Sandhurst cade[ts] the 1890s: he later won a li[bel] action after allegations tha[t] he had engaged with them [in] 'acts of gross immorality o[f] Oscar Wilde type'.

Churchill as Undersecretary for the Colonies (*right*) with his private secretary 'Eddie' Marsh (*left*), whom he described as 'a friend I shall cherish and hold on to all my life'.

Churchill, aged forty-two, as a battalion commander of the Royal Scots Fusiliers in 1916 with his second-in-command and beloved protégé 'Archie' Sinclair, aged twenty-five.

Churchill with his son Randolph, his adoration of whom almost led to a rift with his wife.

Three homosexual imperialists: Lord Kitchener (*above left*), who surrounded himself with handsome young officers a was described as possessing 'a taste for buggery'; Cecil Rhodes (*above right*), wl was devastated by the death of the intim friend with whom he lived; and George Lloyd (*left*), seen here enrobed as Gover of Bombay in the 1920s, whose struggle with his proclivities inspired a novel.

amuel Hoare ('Slippery Sam')
ates on thin ice, while his wife
Lady Maud looks on.

Sir Philip Sassoon – MP,
millionaire aesthete, and admirer
of airmen.

Two rakes and risk-takers
fresh-faced Bob Boothby (
after his election to parliar
in 1924 as the 'Baby of the
House', and a raddled Tom
Driberg (*below*) in 1953: t
long survival in politics w;
tribute to their sharp wits.

were his mother, his sisters, Lady Astor, and his devoted secretary Muriel O'Sullivan (who wrote that 'having been
brought up in a religion which makes a woman the Queen of
Heaven, he became a convert to a religion founded by a
woman [Mary Baker Eddy, founder of Christian Science]').

George Lloyd, 1st Baron Lloyd of Dolobran (1879–1941),
admired Curzon and sought to follow in his footsteps, though
being twenty years younger than his hero he found that impe-
rialism had become less in tune with the spirit of the times. He
was a member of the Quaker banking dynasty (though his
grandparents' generation had embraced Anglicanism, and he
himself became a devout Anglo-Catholic); his ancestry was
largely Welsh, his dark looks and fiery temperament giving him
a foreign air among the English. His early life was marked by
two formative factors: his love for 'Sam' Pepys Cockerell, whom
he met at Eton and to whom he remained passionately attached
until Cockerell's death in action in 1915; and the sudden death
of both his parents within a few weeks of each other in 1899.
Lloyd, then a Cambridge undergraduate, left the university
without taking a degree, and used his ample private means to
embark on a decade of travel in the East, becoming fascinated
by the Turks and Arabs and their languages. Like Curzon, he
saw these journeys (which resulted in useful reports for the
British government) as preparation for a future proconsular
role. In 1910, aged thirty, he was elected to parliament as an
advocate of 'imperial protection'. Lloyd spent most of the First
World War doing intelligence work in Cairo, where he
befriended four sexually ambiguous colleagues – the civil servant Ronald Storrs, the novelist Compton ('Monty')
Mackenzie, and the swashbuckling adventurers T. E.
Lawrence ('Lawrence of Arabia') and Aubrey Herbert (the
model for John Buchan's 'Greenmantle'). At the end of the war,
aged thirty-nine (the age Curzon had been on receiving the

viceroyalty), Lloyd was appointed Governor of Bombay; after completing his term there, and being elevated to the peerage, he served from 1925 to 1929 as High Commissioner in Egypt. Hard-working and effective in the Curzon tradition, Lloyd was a diehard imperialist who had little time for nationalists seeking greater self-determination: in Bombay he oversaw the arrest and imprisonment of Gandhi, while in Cairo he constantly reminded the Egyptians (sometimes by summoning a gunboat) of the limits of the partial independence they had been granted in 1922. The coming to power in 1929 of a Labour government which was out of sympathy with his views brought his proconsular career to an end. During the 1930s Lloyd was a leading Conservative right-winger in the House of Lords, in violent opposition both to the granting of further self-government to India and to the 'appeasement' of Hitler, stances which enhanced his already close friendship with Winston Churchill. In 1937 he became chairman of the British Council, which he moulded into an effective instrument of cultural propaganda. On becoming Prime Minister in May 1940, Churchill appointed him to the cabinet as Colonial Secretary and Leader of the House of Lords. But Lloyd lasted less than a year in these posts: worn out by a restless life of overwork, he died of a blood infection in February 1941, aged sixty-one.

Lloyd was an unashamed misogynist (he was appalled at the idea of women getting the vote), and given to establishing close romantic relationships with other men. His friendship with Sam Cockerell was, as he wrote after the latter's death, 'the deepest possible'. It is not clear whether they were lovers (Cockerell never married), but it seems likely that, during his oriental wanderings in his twenties, Lloyd gave some physical expression to the homosexuality which for the rest of his life he kept firmly bottled up. In 1911 he caused surprise among his friends by marrying Blanche Lascelles, sister of his friend Alan

('Tommy') Lascelles, another married homosexual who later became private secretary to King George VI; they had one son. During the 1920s and 1930s Lloyd surrounded himself with handsome secretaries and ADCs, one of whom (in India) had to be sent away when Lloyd felt unable to master his feelings for him. Another, James Lees-Milne (later famous as a diarist and an architectural conservationist), who served him for three years in the 1930s, was aware of Lloyd's sexual interest in him, though conscious that such feelings were kept under control. Many of Lloyd's friends were homosexual: apart from Storrs, Mackenzie, Lawrence and Lascelles these included Harold Nicolson and Noël Coward. Always slim and well-groomed, Lloyd prided himself on retaining boyish looks into middle age. With the passing years, however, he became increasingly nervous and restless, always on the move, always pacing the room. He threw himself ever more manically into his many spheres of work, and suffered from insomnia. The strain of sexual repression may have contributed to his early death.

Fifteen years after Lloyd's death, his old Cairo intelligence colleague Compton Mackenzie published a novel based on his life, *Thin Ice*, perhaps the most fascinating work of English literature to be inspired by the closet-queen phenomenon. (Though Mackenzie [1883–1972] had three childless marriages, many of his novels have homosexual overtones, and he lived for several years on Capri, where his friends included Norman Douglas, Somerset Maugham and Axel Munthe; certainly the young men who met him at the Savile Club in the 1950s thought him homosexual.)* *Thin Ice* deals with the career of Henry Fortescue, which is largely identical to Lloyd's.

---

* In 1938 Mackenzie published a spirited defence of Edward VIII's conduct in the Abdication crisis, *Windsor Tapestry*. The ex-King at first encouraged him in the project, but broke off all contact after being informed by his adviser Walter Monckton that Mackenzie had a homosexual reputation.

He is born in 1879 and dies in 1941; he is a passionate imperialist; he travels in the East, and admires the Turks and the Arabs; he is elected to parliament before the First World War, during which he does intelligence work in Cairo; in the 1920s he holds public office, then falls out of favour; with the coming of the Second World War he returns to high office in the intelligence world. Fortescue has a bosom friend from Eton, Edward Carstairs, to whom he remains close in his twenties; but the narrator of his story is another friend and confidant, George Gaymer, whom Fortescue meets at university, and who is heterosexual and conventional. Gaymer is aware that Fortescue has no time for women, but is nevertheless shocked to discover, accompanying Fortescue on holiday to Morocco, that the latter has homosexual inclinations which he freely indulges when travelling abroad. However, a few years later Fortescue tells Gaymer that, ambitious for a brilliant career in politics, he has decided to repress these inclinations and lead a celibate life. Fortescue holds to this vow for eighteen years; but when, after losing office in the 1920s, he feels that his political career is finished, he decides once again to taste the pleasures of which he has deprived himself for so long. He meets an attractive young man whom he appoints his secretary, with whom he has an affair lasting three years. After this lover leaves him, and he returns from a further long spell in the East during which he has no difficulty in gratifying his desires, he starts cruising London's streets in search of 'rough trade'. This involves appalling risks, which he seems to enjoy, and he shows skill in extricating himself from 'tight corners'. The war is now under way and Fortescue is doing work vital for his country's survival, but he continues to engage in hairraising escapades. The police are starting to take an interest in his activities, and he narrowly avoids exposure at the hands of a blackmailer (who is paid off by Gaymer); but before further scandal can bring about his ruin, Fortescue is killed in a bombing raid.

The main differences between Lloyd and Fortescue are that Lloyd married and Fortescue does not (though he ends up living with a widowed sister-in-law who is understanding about his tastes); and that Lloyd maintained his iron repression until his death, which Fortescue does not. During their time together in Cairo, Mackenzie evidently became aware that Lloyd had powerful homosexual urges which he had indulged in the past but resolved to repress in future; observing Lloyd (whom he admired) over the next twenty-five years, he wondered what might have happened had Lloyd let himself go. *Thin Ice* was published in 1956, while the Wolfenden Committee was deliberating; it shows considerable familiarity with the homosexual world of the time, and Mackenzie admitted in his memoirs that it cost him a greater effort to write than any of his other books. On the face of it, Gaymer's narrative laments that his brilliant friend's life should have been marred by such uncontrollable weaknesses; but the novelist seems to invite the reader to conclude that Fortescue only truly came alive when he surrendered to his inmost desires.

# 5

# SAM AND PHIL

The 1920s were a crucial decade for British aviation. The RAF became firmly established (and generously funded) as the third of the fighting services, despite attempts by both the Army and the Navy to absorb it. With air routes linking the mother country with far-flung territories of empire, Britain pioneered long-distance civil aviation. Flying, once regarded as the pursuit of cranks, became a glamorous activity patronised by the royal family and aristocracy, as well as becoming a popular sport through flying clubs. These developments, which were to have momentous consequences for the future, were largely the work of two Conservative politicians who had been elected to parliament in their twenties before the First World War – Sir Samuel ('Sam') Hoare, 2nd Baronet (1880–1959), who served (except for a few months of Labour government) as Secretary of State for Air from 1922 to 1929, and Sir Philip Sassoon, 3rd Baronet (1888–1939), who was Undersecretary for Air from 1924 to 1929, and again from 1931 to 1937.

At first sight these two men could not have been more different. Hoare came from an old-established English family which had been famous in banking since the early eighteenth century; they had been prominent Quakers (the Quaker social reformer Elizabeth Fry was Hoare's great-great-aunt), though in the nineteenth century they had embraced Anglicanism. Sassoon came from a family of Baghdadi Jews which had moved to British India in the 1830s and there made a colossal fortune: his grandfather had only settled in England in the 1870s. Hoare came across as an uncharismatic, cold-blooded Englishman, Sassoon as an exotic bloom of the East. Hoare was thick-skinned, Sassoon hypersensitive. Hoare was dedicated to politics and intensely ambitious for high office, going on to serve as Foreign Secretary and Home Secretary. Sassoon was an unashamed dilettante, who combined politics with his vocations as a host, gardener and art collector at his three sumptuous houses; his ambitions were satisfied by the ministerial post (outside the cabinet) of First Commissioner of Works, responsible for the nation's buildings and parks, which he held during the last two years of his life.

Yet they did have something in common – apart from the obvious facts that they came from rich families, and inherited baronetcies. Although they had sporting achievements to their names (both were good tennis players; Hoare was a crack shot and an accomplished figure-skater; Sassoon was an ardent aviator), both struck contemporaries as being somewhat deficient in masculinity. Both served (admittedly with distinction) in non-combatant roles during the First World War. Hoare was full of prissy mannerisms, with a voice 'like an anxious curate'; Sassoon, who was immensely affected in both speech and deportment, seemed not just foreign and exotic, but almost hermaphroditic. Both were nervous, fastidious, hypochondriacal, inscrutable. In fact both were indubitably homosexual in outlook, though it seems unlikely that they ever gave much physical expression to that side of their natures.

\*

Hoare was the eldest son of a retired banker who served without great distinction as Conservative MP for North Norfolk for more than twenty years, but who inculcated in his heir a burning desire to get on in politics. Educated at Harrow and Oxford, he served on the London County Council before being elected MP for Chelsea just before his thirtieth birthday in 1910. During the First World War he combined his parliamentary role with secret service work in Russia and Italy, becoming imbued with the conspiratorial spirit. Subsequently he won a reputation as a crafty schemer and manipulator, known as 'Slippery Sam': he played a key role in both the Conservative backbench rebellion which led to the downfall of the Lloyd George coalition in 1922, and the negotiations which led to the formation of the next coalition, the National Government of 1931–40. His great ally was that other artful dodger Lord Beaverbrook, who supported him through his press empire. However, Hoare was not just a cunning party manager but also a highly effective departmental minister. As Air Secretary in the 1920s (a post he was offered with the warning that it might soon be abolished), he ensured Britain's future in both military and civil aviation. As Secretary of State for India from 1931 to 1935 he managed, despite fierce resistance from right-wing backbenchers of his own party led by Winston Churchill, to steer legislation through parliament which paved the way for Indian self-government. As Home Secretary from 1937 to 1939, he put in place the civil defence system which enabled Britain to survive the coming war. Baldwin and Chamberlain admired his considerable gifts, as did most of those who worked closely with him; but on the whole he was not popular with fellow MPs, who found him charmless, aloof, shifty and nakedly ambitious.

Hoare's only notable failure was as Foreign Secretary under

Baldwin during the second half of 1935. Faced with Mussolini's invasion of Ethiopia, and under pressure to find a solution which would keep Italy on the side of the Western democracies and out of the arms of Hitler, he devised a compromise with the French premier Laval which would have partitioned Ethiopia between its native Emperor and the Italians. The so-called 'Hoare–Laval Pact' was accepted by the British cabinet; but it provoked an outcry from liberal public opinion, as a result of which the 'Pact' was abandoned and Hoare, having been made a scapegoat, resigned. However, just six months later he was back in the cabinet as First Lord of the Admiralty. Together with Chamberlain, Halifax and Simon, Hoare was one of the quartet of senior ministers who promoted the policy of 'appeasing' Hitler with concessions in the late 1930s, culminating in the Munich Agreement of September 1938 which led to the dismemberment of Czechoslovakia (a state which, ironically, Hoare had played a significant role in setting up in 1918–19). During the 'Phoney War' Hoare was a member of Chamberlain's War Cabinet; but Churchill, on becoming Prime Minister in May 1940, sacked him from the government, while retaining the other three 'appeasers' – he had not forgiven Hoare for the India Bill, and seems to have felt an almost gut dislike of this devious and old-maidish character. However, just a few weeks later Hoare was sent to Madrid as British Ambassador, with the vital mission of keeping General Franco (who was naturally sympathetic to Hitler and Mussolini who had helped him to power) neutral in the war now that France had fallen to the Germans. It was perhaps there that 'Slippery Sam' did his greatest service to his country: using all his cunning and guile, along with much bluster and bribery, he succeeded in his mission against all the odds, finally retiring from his ambassadorship and public life in 1944, when he was raised to the peerage as Viscount Templewood.

In 1909 Hoare married Lady Maud Lygon, daughter of the 6th Earl Beauchamp – a somewhat masculine woman, 'big and gauche' as James Lees-Milne described her. It was an advantageous political alliance with the old Tory establishment, and Lady Maud dedicated herself to advancing her husband's career in a manner almost reminiscent of Lady Macbeth; but Hoare's biographer writes that 'it would probably be more appropriate to describe it … as a *mariage de convenance* rather than a love match … outsiders considered it to be a relationship somewhat lacking in warmth and in a very developed sense of fun'. They had no children; but Hoare grew devotedly fond of one of his nephews, Paul Paget (1901–85), son of a bishop, who served as his private secretary in the mid-1920s. Paget later became a distinguished architect, in partnership with John Seely who was also his lover; Hoare commissioned him to build Templewood (completed in 1937), the country house in Norfolk from which he took his title, and made him his heir. Though widely suspected of having homosexual tendencies himself (a cousin interviewed in 2013 had no doubt of it), Hoare almost certainly led a celibate life – as in the case of George Lloyd, that other repressed, married homosexual, the element of sensuality in his life seems to have been provided by Anglo-Catholicism. At least twice, however, Hoare was confronted with the question of homosexuality. In 1931 (as described in Chapter 1), his brother-in-law, the 7th Earl Beauchamp, faced with the exposure of his (far from repressed) homosexuality by *his* brother-in-law Bendor, Duke of Westminster, was forced to resign his offices and flee abroad to avoid prosecution. Hoare and his wife must have been extremely nervous, and relieved that the episode gave rise to no public scandal. It is probably no coincidence that, just a few weeks after Hoare's appointment as Home Secretary in May 1937, the criminal charges pending against Beauchamp were finally dropped, enabling him to return to live at his beloved Madresfield for the last fifteen months of his life. And in 1954, Hoare, then Chancellor of Reading University, was asked by his Vice-Chancellor, John Wolfenden, whether he should accept the invitation to chair a committee to investigate the reform of the law relating to homosexuality: Hoare (to quote the Committee's latest historian) 'persuaded Wolfenden of the importance of the work which had been entrusted to him' and unhesitatingly advised him to accept (though he refrained from participating in the House of Lords debate on the Wolfenden Report in December 1957).

Philip Sassoon was just twenty-three when, on the death of his father in 1912, he inherited a baronetcy, a fortune, and properties which included a palatial town house in Park Lane and a Georgian country house in Middlesex. At a by-election a few months later he also succeeded his father as Conservative MP for Hythe in Kent, becoming 'the Baby of the House'. Yet fifty years earlier, hardly anyone in England had heard of the Sassoons. They were prominent Jews of Baghdad, where they had allegedly lived since the Babylonian exile. During an outbreak of Ottoman anti-semitism in the 1820s they decided to move on, first to Persia and then to British India: in Bombay, where they settled in 1832, they became vastly rich within a few decades, first by cornering the trade in Indian opium when the government relinquished its monopoly, then by exporting Indian cotton when the American product became unavailable during the Civil War. Though Philip's great-grandfather David Sassoon, founder of the family trading firm, wore oriental dress and spoke no English, they ingratiated themselves with the British rulers, using their wealth to endow schools, hospitals and other amenities. Six of David's eight sons eventually settled in England, starting with Sassoon

Sassoon (Siegfried Sassoon's grandfather) in 1858. The eldest
son, Philip's grandfather, who was born Abdullah but angli-
cised his name to Albert, received an Indian knighthood in
1872 for his public benefactions, and was still based in
Bombay three years later when he lavishly entertained the
Prince of Wales on his visit to the city. Soon afterwards he too
moved to England, where he continued to associate with the
heir to the throne, as did his brothers Arthur and Reuben: as
well as being his generous hosts, they showered the Prince
with gifts, advanced him money, and became his racing com-
panions. In 1890, in recognition of his help in entertaining the
Shah of Persia on a state visit, Albert was made a baronet. The
Sassoons also became close to the 'royalty' of European Jewry,
the Rothschilds; in 1886 Albert's only son Edward married
Aline de Rothschild, daughter of Baron Gustave who co-
directed the Paris Rothschild bank. Edward inherited both the
chairmanship of the family firm and the baronetcy on his
father's death in 1896, and three years later was elected MP for
Hythe, largely through the influence of the Rothschilds, who
owned extensive property there. Meanwhile Aline had borne
him two children, Philip and Sybil.

Philip Sassoon was born at his maternal grandparents' Paris
mansion and spent much of his childhood there, raised bilin-
gually and acquiring an early connoisseurship of art through
proximity to the fabulous Rothschild collection of pictures and
furniture. His father, preoccupied by business and politics, was
a remote figure, but he was close to his mother, a pretty
woman with aesthetic interests whose admirers included
Bernard Berenson and John Singer Sargent. At thirteen, he
went to Eton, where his exoticism ('dark face, heavily lidded
eyes, French accent and something of a lisp') made him an
object of fascination to some and derision to others; Osbert
Sitwell, who became his fag, remembered him as 'very grown-

up for his age, at times exuberant, at times melancholy, but always unlike anyone else – which he remained all his life'. From there he proceeded to Christ Church, Oxford, where he began his lifelong practice of dispensing lavish hospitality and giving expensive presents to anyone he liked or wished to please. But in his early twenties, his life was traumatically affected by a series of deaths. His beloved mother died of cancer in 1909; his Rothschild grandparents then both died; his father followed in 1912. Barely of age, the new baronet and MP found himself a solitary figure. The people to whom he felt closest were his younger sister Sybil, who a year later married an English aristocrat, the Earl of Rocksavage (later 5th Marquess of Cholmondeley), and his older cousin Hannah Gubbay, a wise and maternal figure married to another cousin who ran the Sassoon firm. These were the women in his life, who would act as hostesses at his entertainments and eventually inherit what remained of his fortune: he never contemplated marriage. A cartoon by Max Beerbohm shows him looking isolated and out of place in the House of Commons, a tiny, refined, foreign figure surrounded by coarse, fat, baying Tory MPs.

From his lonely position, Sassoon devoted himself to beautifying the two great houses he had inherited, the Park Lane mansion and Trent Park, Middlesex, and filling them with the treasures collected by his Rothschild grandparents. He also built a new house in his constituency, Port Lympne, on a spectacular site between Romney Marsh and the English Channel, begun by the 'architect of empire' Herbert Baker and finished by the fashionable (and homosexual) young Philip Tilden, in a style which combined Cape Dutch and Moorish elements; its interiors displayed *avant-garde* decoration and the last word in luxury. While these projects were under way the First World War broke out, during which Sassoon's bilingual accomplishments made him valuable as a staff officer in France. His Rothschild relations owned several châteaux behind the British lines which they put at the disposal of the generals, and it was partly through their influence and partly through the patronage of his new admirer Reginald, Viscount Esher (with whom he exchanged letters full of gossip, teasing and sexual innuendo) that Sassoon secured the appointment of private secretary to the new British Commander-in-Chief Sir Douglas Haig (another protégé of Esher) in December 1915, a job which he held until 1919 and which enabled him to meet and get to know most of the Allies' leading military and political figures. Philip saw little of the slaughter of the trenches which inspired the poetry of his cousin Siegfried, and the sight of him mincing about in immaculately tailored uniforms aroused resentment among young officers going to the front; but he did his job well, proving particularly skilful at managing the difficult relations between Haig and the press. He was also surprisingly popular with his chief, who while sending tens of thousands to their deaths seems to have been cheered by the presence of this lively, witty, androgynous figure (though he was disliked by Lady Haig).

Sassoon was not yet thirty when the war ended, and for the next twenty years he became a legendary giver of fabulous parties at Port Lympne, Trent Park and Park Lane, where his guests included politicians and soldiers, writers and artists, socialites and sportsmen. What impelled him to devote himself (and sacrifice much of his fortune) to this endless round of lavish entertainment? He was above all an artist, who derived aesthetic pleasure from dispensing perfect hospitality in perfect settings. He also longed for the world's praise. (In this regard he achieved mixed results: some of his guests mocked him as an ostentatious Jew; others were captivated not just by his hospitality but by his quirky intelligence and charm.) He also hoped that pandering to the great would help advance him in public life. In the immediate postwar years he successfully ingratiated himself with two exalted personages, Edward, Prince of Wales (whose grandfather had been entertained by Sassoon's grandfather), and the Prime Minister Lloyd George, inviting them to visit his houses whenever they wished together with their respective mistresses, Freda Dudley Ward and Frances Stevenson. Sassoon hoped that Lloyd George would appoint him to a junior post in the government, but instead, in February 1920, he made Sassoon his own parliamentary private secretary, attracted by the prospect of using the Sassoon houses as venues for political and diplomatic meetings – thus in 1920 Lloyd George twice commandeered Port Lympne for conferences with the French to discuss the peace terms to be offered to the Turks, and in the autumn of 1921 the Park Lane house discreetly hosted meetings with the delegates to the Irish Treaty negotiations. Though on the lowest rung of the governmental ladder, Sassoon revelled in his access to high-level gossip. It was also his job to keep his master informed about the humbler gossip of the House of Commons, and this he seems rather to have neglected – he was imperfectly aware of the disenchantment with Lloyd George among Conservative MPs which led to their ejecting him from power in October 1922.

Sassoon finally received government office in 1924 when Hoare invited him to become his Undersecretary at the Air Ministry. Hoare's hope was that Sassoon would help make flying fashionable; and during more than a decade in the job, he certainly contributed to this result. He used his friendship with the Prince of Wales to enlist royal support for aviation; he made the Auxiliary Air Force (in which he was an honorary commodore) a magnet for young aristocrats; he gave talks at public schools, encouraging their pupils to go into the RAF; he founded flying races and endowed their trophies; he travelled by air all over the Empire, popularising civil aviation and boosting morale at distant outposts of the RAF. Thanks largely to his efforts, by the mid-1930s it was almost as 'smart' for a school-leaver to go into the RAF as into a good regiment, or for a passenger to travel to a distant destination by air as by land and sea. He himself became a keen aviator, keeping a small fleet of planes at his private aerodrome at Port Lympne, including his favourite 'Gulf' monoplane with an interior finished in red leather. Port Lympne was also close to several RAF bases which Sassoon frequently visited, befriending the officers and inviting them back to his property to attend his parties or just enjoy the amenities (his photograph albums feature many decorative young airmen using the swimming pool); eventually there was an annual fortnight's 'summer camp' at Port Lympne for all ranks of the RAF.

Following an interlude of Labour government, Sassoon returned as Undersecretary for Air from 1931 to 1937, now with greater responsibilities, as the Secretaries of State during these years were peers and Sassoon had the task of getting the annual Air Estimates through the House of Commons. He thus oversaw the first stage of Britain's aerial rearmament (though he had a difficult relationship with Winston Churchill who pressed for more rapid rearmament, having loyally sided with Hoare in his row with Churchill over India). In May 1937, when Chamberlain succeeded to the premiership, Sassoon finally exchanged his undersecretaryship for the post he had long coveted of First Commissioner of Works – which had been held in their day by Rosebery, Harcourt and Beauchamp* (though unlike all of them, and

---

* And the Secretary of the Office of Works from 1895 to 1902 had been Esher, who later befriended Sassoon.

indeed his immediate predecessor and successor, Sassoon was not made a member of the cabinet, evidently being considered too lightweight). It was a job for which he was ideally suited, for 'he brought to bear on the property of the public the same trained taste and the same devotion to detail that he had lavished on his own houses'. Among the projects he supervised were the restoration of the Royal Naval College at Greenwich, the redesigning of Trafalgar Square, improvements to Downing Street and the Palace of Westminster, and the replacement of the ugly cast-iron public seating in the royal parks with oak benches. He was also able to indulge his taste for high camp: when the French President visited, he arranged for the footmen at the state banquet to be attired in eighteenth-century livery. The First Commissioner was traditionally the government minister in closest daily contact with the royal family, and Sassoon revelled in his access to the newly crowned King George VI and Queen Elizabeth, and the art-loving Queen Mary, to discuss the care of their collections and the refurbishment of their residences. (Sassoon had no trouble transferring his loyalty from Edward VIII, whom he had shamelessly flattered, to George VI, just as fifteen years earlier he had had no problem slavishly serving Lloyd George who had been on the worst terms with his former boss Haig.)

Sassoon had served at the Office of Works for two years, winning golden opinions, when he suddenly died on 3 June 1939 after a severe attack of influenza, aged just fifty. He had always believed that, like his parents, he would not live to see old age; and he had been in indifferent health since a botched minor operation a few years earlier. It was perhaps as well for him that he departed when he did. He would not have enjoyed the Second World War, when his properties were requisitioned and most of the airmen he had loved lost their lives, and it is unlikely that Churchill would have retained his services in the government. Also, twenty years of munificent hospitality had depleted his fortune: his will caused embarrassment as his estate, after deduction of death duties, turned out to be insufficient to meet all the bequests.

Sassoon's ancestry was wholly Jewish, and his family's links with England were extremely recent, but he studiously avoided drawing attention to his background. The fact of his being orphaned in his early twenties somehow gave him the air of an exotic creature who sprang from nowhere. He seems to have encouraged the absurd but widespread rumour that he was not a Jew but a Parsee (Bombay, where the family had made its fortune, being the main Parsee centre): Hermann Goering, whom he had the temerity to visit in 1933 to discuss Anglo-German aviation issues, believed him to be Parsee. Although he subscribed to Bevis Marks, the oldest synagogue in London, of which his father and grandfather had been generous supporters, he never went there. His admirer 'Chips' Channon (an American who hated Americans) described him as a Jew who hated Jews, and he certainly had little social contact with other Jews (other than close relations), whom he rarely invited to his parties. He even steered clear of his handsome, bisexual (and only half-Jewish) second cousin, the great war poet and chronicler of English country life Siegfried Sassoon (a fact which rather puzzled Esher, who admired them both). In 1928 he made a highly publicised air journey to India, designed to boost the civil aviation links between Britain and 'the Raj' and test the recently developed Iris flying boat. The trip resulted in his only book, *The Third Route*, in which he made no mention that his family had lived and made its fortune in India. (He avoided Bombay, where the Sassoon name was famous – though in Karachi, where his outward air journey ended, he did briefly visit the local office of the firm founded by his great-grandfather, of which he remained a nominal director.) The book also describes two lengthy stops in Iraq, then the main centre of British air power in the Middle East (partly spent with T. E. Lawrence who was stationed there), again without mentioning that, until their departure just a century earlier, the Sassoons had been among the leading Jews of Baghdad since time immemorial.

Given his secretiveness regarding his origins, it is unsurprising that Sassoon should have been even more guarded when it came to intimacy with his fellow human beings. After the deaths of his parents, the only people with whom he acknowledged closeness were his sister Sybil and cousin Hannah. He subsequently became attached to Esher. Another older man with whom he formed a close relationship was Sir Louis Mallet (1864–1936), a bachelor diplomat who had served as British Ambassador to Constantinople in 1914 (where he surrounded himself with queer young attachés such as Harold Nicolson, Gerald Tyrwhitt and Gerry Wellesley). Mallet teasingly called Sassoon 'Phil', apparently the only person so to do. After 1918, Sassoon encouraged Mallet to retire from the service, sell his house, and move into private apartments both in Sassoon's Park Lane mansion and at Port Lympne; the architect Tilden (himself an intimate of Mallet) who created these apartments wrote that 'Philip needed someone of experience near him as a dumping ground for confidences' – to which Sassoon's biographer adds that 'whatever these confidences may have been, they have not been preserved'. Sassoon destroyed most of his private papers, but among the few to survive are copies he kept of several undated letters he wrote to an unidentified friend named 'Jack', written in a characteristic flowery style reeking of sexual innuendo. ('So you waited all the day & all the evening to ring me up ... But I'll be even with you. I'll ring you up tomorrow morning – very early ... before even the rosy fingered dawn has caused your white pyjamas to blush ... I will wait until you are weak unwoken & at my mercy. You!') The dates of the letters are not clear, but this is probably the 'Jack' with whom Sassoon travelled to Spain and Morocco in 1922. Sassoon was devastated by the death, in a flying accident in the late 1920s, of a handsome airman: he displayed a photograph of the deceased at Port Lympne, poured out his heart about him to friends such as the (reputedly bisexual) American novelist Thornton Wilder, and approached another novelist, Mrs Belloc Lowndes, asking if she might arrange spiritualist seances with a view to communicating with him. In the 1930s he was infatuated with the attractive young bachelor MP Ronnie Cartland (to be considered in Chapter 9), whom he implored (unsuccessfully) to become his parliamentary private secretary.

Apart from Esher, Mallet, Tilden and Cartland, many of the people whose society Sassoon enjoyed were homosexual or bisexual – Cecil Beaton, Gerald Berners, Bob Boothby, Malcolm Bullock, Chips Channon, T. E. Lawrence, Harold Nicolson, Glyn Philpot, Osbert Sitwell, Rex Whistler. He clearly loved surrounding himself with dashing airmen. He also had some fairly close women friends of an older generation, to one of whom he explained that he could never marry as he was in love with his sister and 'she has set me too dizzying a standard'. With his aversion to matrimony, his liking for certain men, his outrageously camp mannerisms and his extravagant aesthetic taste, it seems to have been generally assumed that Sassoon was homosexual. Were he to have indulged in physical relationships he would certainly have gone to extraordinary lengths to ensure their secrecy; but it is quite possible that he expressed his nature through admiration, flirtation and gossip, and led a celibate life. Harold Nicolson found him 'removed from the ordinary passions' and 'the most unreal creature I have known', who seemed to regard even his friends as 'mere pieces of decoration to be put about the room'.

Though they were so different, and only worked together for a few years, Hoare and Sassoon developed a lasting bond which verged on the romantic. Hoare seems to have been another of those sexually ambiguous older men, like Esher and Mallet, who aroused emotional feelings in the fatherless Sassoon. (There was in fact less than a decade between them; but whereas Hoare was perpetually middle-aged, there was about Sassoon something of the eternal child.) Hoare chose Sassoon as his undersecretary in 1924 in the (justified) belief that this brilliant entertainer would glamorise aviation, but Hoare himself appears to have been seduced by both the entertainment and the man, Trent Park becoming the favourite retreat for his leisure moments throughout the 1920s and 30s. Sassoon worked hard and successfully to win his approval, and wrote (in one of the few fragments of his diary to have survived) that 'I prefer to work under Sam Hoare than anyone else'. When their ministerial partnership was ended by the defeat of the Conservative government at the 1929 election, Sassoon wrote to him: 'You know how happy I have been working with you & how much I appreciate all the unfailing kindness you have always shewn me. These last 4½ years have been among the happiest in my life & *I owe it all to you.* I hope that before long we shall be working together again ... Please use Trent as if it were your own.' When, a decade later, Sassoon died, Hoare wrote a fulsome appreciation of him in *The Times.*

There was no one in my lifetime like Philip Sassoon ...
Being so sensitive and volatile it is difficult for even those
who knew him best to describe his charm or define his
character ... He was not ostentatious at all. There was nothing coarse about him. Vulgarity of all kinds was entirely
repugnant to him ... His sensitivity was constantly apparent. I knew it to be no foolish nervousness, but a true
sensitivity of the head and the heart ... He could not bear
dullness, ugliness, delay or disappointment ... Such sensibility is too rare to be lightly forgotten.

# 6

# BOB AND TOM

B ob Boothby (1900–86) and Tom Driberg (1905–76) were a pair of brilliant rogues – both in terms of their morals, and in the sense of being completely 'one-off' originals. Boothby sat as a Conservative MP for more than thirty years, Driberg as a Labour one for almost as long, but both were really independent politicians (Driberg was originally elected to parliament as an independent) who were generally regarded as thorns in the sides of their respective parties – though Boothby held minor office in two governments, while Driberg served as chairman of the Labour Party (a largely honorific position) in 1957–8. They had much in common apart from their shared sexual tastes. They were both outrageous risk-takers (in Boothby's case an addicted gambler), with a talent for getting out of scrapes. Although both professed egalitarian principles, they were tremendous hedonists who gorged themselves on life's luxuries, spending much of their lives in debt. Nor did their principles prevent them from revelling in the peerages which they brazenly asked for and duly received, Boothby becoming Baron Boothby of Buchan and Rattray Head and Driberg, Baron Bradwell of

Bradwell-juxta-Mare. Towards the ends of their lives they both wrote fascinating autobiographies, Driberg's describing, in lurid detail, how he managed to combine a rackety queer sex life with successful careers in journalism and politics.

Their backgrounds, though rather different, were both upper-middle-class. Boothby was the son of a well-connected Edinburgh businessman. After Eton and Oxford he was at first destined for a legal career, but at twenty-four he was fortuitously adopted as Conservative candidate for the marginal seat of East Aberdeenshire, where he was returned with large majorities at eight general elections, becoming immensely popular with his constituents. He was too impetuous and outspoken to be a successful party politician, but he could later claim to have been right on two important subjects: he saw that Keynesian economics provided a route out of the Depression, and he was one of Churchill's steadfast supporters in his campaign for rearmament in the 1930s. As we have seen, Churchill, as Chancellor in the 1920s, had taken a fancy to him and appointed him his PPS; but though supporting Churchill politically Boothby did not warm to him personally. Certainly Churchill showed him little gratitude: after Boothby had played a key role in helping Churchill become premier in 1940 he was rewarded with a minor post as deputy to Lord Woolton at the Ministry of Food; and when, a few months later, he was embroiled in the so-called 'Czech Assets affair' (in which he failed to declare an interest when asking a parliamentary question), Churchill threw him to the wolves. Boothby's biographer Robert Rhodes James argues that he paid a heavy price for a minor transgression, but clearly Boothby did not hesitate to cut corners in his business dealings. The stigma of the affair disqualified him from future government office – though after the war he became a huge celebrity on radio and television with his swaggering personality, arresting appearance, and forthright opinions delivered in a gruff voice. Opinion polls suggested that he was the nation's favourite politician, and his name was mooted (by his friend Patrick Gordon Walker, Shadow Foreign Secretary in the early 1960s) as a possible future Ambassador to France.*

Boothby, who as a young man was extremely good-looking and all his life possessed legendary seductive charm, had a powerful libido and seems to have been sexually omnivorous. Rhodes James insists that he was predominantly heterosexual; but a more recent biographer, John Pearson, maintains that his preference was always for teenage boys and young men. There was an incident in 1959, reported in the press, when a seventeen-year-old constituent who had been visiting him in London was arrested in possession of his gold watch and chain. Boothby's heterosexual reputation rests largely on his affair with Lady Dorothy Macmillan, wife of his fellow Tory MP Harold Macmillan, which began in 1929 and continued (eventually assuming a platonic character) until her death in 1966. It was she who seduced Boothby and made the running throughout the affair. Boothby, while finding her passion exhausting, was undoubtedly fond of her: a rather masculine woman, she reminded him (as he confided to another raffish Tory politician, Tony Lambton) of a caddie he had once seduced on the golf links at St Andrews. Pearson suggests that the affair (which was common knowledge at Westminster) suited both Boothby and Macmillan: for Boothby, it was a convenient smokescreen for his homosexual activities, while Macmillan was relieved to see less of a demanding wife as he got on with his political career, which culminated in his attaining the premiership in 1957. Certainly (after some initial distress on Macmillan's part) the personal relations between the two men remained good,

---

* In the event, Harold Wilson appointed another charismatic Tory politician to this post – Winston Churchill's son-in-law Christopher Soames.

and Macmillan as Prime Minister was happy to nominate Boothby for the peerage he craved. Boothby married twice. His first wife, Diana Cavendish, was Dorothy Macmillan's cousin. According to Rhodes James, he proposed to her when drunk and got such cold feet at the prospect of marrying her that he spent the weeks before their wedding in 1935 in an alcoholic stupor. They lived together for barely a year before divorcing. His second wife, the Sardinian Wanda Senna, whom he married in 1967, was thirty-three years his junior, and fulfilled a role as companion and nursemaid during his later years. (The marriage led to the immediate departure of Boothby's long-standing homosexual butler and confidant, Goodfellow.) According to Rhodes James, there were several other women he proposed to and then jilted – apparently he enjoyed the idea of married life but shrank from the reality.

In his memoirs *Recollections of a Rebel*, published in 1978, Boothby writes about homosexuality as a subject in which he takes a sympathetic interest but which does not directly apply to him. He admits that he was presented with tempting opportunities both as an Oxford undergraduate after the First World War and as a visitor to Germany in the 1920s, but implies that he did not avail himself of these. He takes pride in the fact that, through speechmaking and lobbying in the early 1950s, he helped bring about the appointment of the Wolfenden Committee,* whose recommendations (including an age of consent of twenty-one) he considers 'wholly admirable ... I

---

* Boothby does himself a disservice – the idea of the Committee was almost entirely his own, and he fought what was virtually a one-man campaign to get it set up, personally lobbying the Home Secretary, Sir David Maxwell Fyfe, in public and in private for some months. (See Michael McManus, *Tory Pride and Prejudice: The Conservative Party and Homosexual Law Reform* [Biteback Publishing, 2011], Chapter 1.) Boothby had been an Oxford contemporary of Maxwell Fyfe, and possibly he knew of some means of putting pressure on him, for Maxwell Fyfe fought for the Committee in cabinet despite his declared belief that homosexuality was a scourge and the law should not be changed.

was thankful, and slightly surprised, when Parliament implemented them so quickly [after ten years].' He goes on to write:

> I have known many homosexuals in the course of my life, in
> this country and abroad; and some of them are my
> friends ... Down the centuries they have played a large part
> in the development of ... western civilisation. As artists they
> can depict and interpret emotion ... perhaps better than
> anyone else; but in their own lives they shrink from it. With
> rare exceptions they are by nature promiscuous. They like to
> pick each other up, casually, in bars, clubs and Turkish baths.
> They enjoy sex in its cruder manifestations; but the enjoy-
> ment is transient ... They don't believe in a past, or a future.
> They live for the day, and even for the hour. Many of them
> are attracted by the ritual of the Church, and by the per-
> sonality of Jesus – no nonsense about family life there; but
> few of them are religious in depth. They call themselves 'gay',
> and so they are, for they are nearly always good company;
> but basically they are not happy. Homosexuality is equally
> prevalent among what used to be called 'the higher and the
> lower orders'; and sometimes these are attracted to each
> other. This is known in homosexual circles as 'plain sewing.'*
> They are addicted to blackmail [*sic*] ... It is because they
> have played, and always will, an important part in shaping
> all our lives ... that I have done and written so much about
> them. The trouble is that, to a considerable extent, and much
> against my will, I share their general outlook on life.

As we shall see, Boothby was himself 'attracted to the lower
orders' and as a result had suffered from blackmail in the not

---

* Friends of the author who are familiar with the argot of yore assert that 'plain
sewing' usually referred to mutual masturbation rather than to relationships
between 'the higher and the lower orders'.

too distant past. It is certainly the case that Boothby had homosexual friends: his greatest intimates included his fellow MPs Harold Nicolson and Malcolm Bullock,* not to mention Driberg (an example of a homosexual 'attracted to the ritual of the Church'). The same year as he published his memoirs, Boothby showed letters he had received from Nicolson to James Lees-Milne, who was writing Nicolson's biography. Lees-Milne wrote in his diary: 'They disclosed that H.N. was homosexual, Lord Boothby remarked to me. I thought they disclosed that Boothby was too, or H.N. would not have written to him recommending a harbour in Greece where pretty sailors were to be seen drinking and smoking.'

Rhodes James goes along with Boothby's view of himself as an essentially heterosexual man, looking tolerantly down on the homosexual world.

> The frequent allegation that Boothby was a homosexual has been ridiculed by a considerable number of his friends, and particularly his women friends ... Certainly his eye for women was not in any way deterred by any deviations he may have had with men ... When he subsequently supported homosexual law reform, he was indignant that it was hinted that he had a personal interest to declare ... He was certainly not a 'congenital' homosexual, unlike several of his

---

* Nicolson will be considered in Chapter 8. Bullock (1890–1966) has already been encountered in a footnote to Chapter 1 as the close friend and comrade in arms of Neil Primrose who married Neil's widow, Lord Derby's daughter, after his death in action in 1917. Like Boothby, Bullock sat in the House of Commons from the 1920s to the 1950s, representing Lancashire constituencies. After the death of his wife in a hunting accident in 1927, he 'devoted his life to theatre, gossip and the company of young men' (to quote the biographer of the Australian novelist Patrick White, who as a youth in London in the 1930s was one of Bullock's protégés). He was also a noted balletomane who became chairman of Sadlers Wells, and a great favourite of royalty, including Queen Mary and Queen Elizabeth (consort of George VI).

friends, notably Harold Nicolson, Tom Driberg, Maurice Bowra, Noël Coward and Somerset Maugham ... But there was a homosexual strain as well, which surfaced from time to time, and which made him sensitive to the concerns and difficulties of what he cheerfully called 'the buggers'.

We have already encountered Rhodes James as the historian who, in his biography of Lord Rosebery, managed to say nothing about the widespread contemporary rumours that Rosebery was homosexual, and who also produced studies of other sexually ambiguous politicians while saying little or nothing about their 'queer' sides.

Driberg was the youngest son of a retired member of the Indian Civil Service. His whole life was a reaction against the stifling bourgeois gentility of his upbringing in Crowborough, Sussex. During his schooldays at Lancing, where he befriended Evelyn Waugh and was influenced by the inspiring (and homosexual) master J. F. Roxburgh (later headmaster of Stowe), he acquired his lifelong passions for literature, left-wing socialism, High Anglican ritual and homosexuality. At Oxford he was both an outrageous aesthete and dandy and an active member of the Communist Party, as well as becoming an acolyte of the satanist Aleister Crowley. Leaving the university without a degree, Driberg hoped to make a career as a poet, like his friend Auden. Although the samples of his verse quoted by his biographer do not suggest much talent in this direction, his enthusiasms won him the patronage of Edith Sitwell, through whose influence he obtained a job as a gossip columnist on the *Daily Express*, a métier for which he proved to have considerable flair. During the 1930s, as a protégé of the paper's impish proprietor Lord Beaverbrook, Driberg became famous through writing the subversive 'William Hickey' column. He was paid a large salary, which went on good living. He was also recruited to MI5 by a clandestine homosexual and fellow occultist named Maxwell Knight, whose brief was to keep an eye on extremists of both left and right; it is not clear whether Driberg's role was to help identify Nazi sympathisers or betray fellow communists, but when, in 1941, the 'comrades' discovered (probably through Anthony Blunt) his secret service affiliations, he was expelled from the party. The following year, when the war was going badly and the government was unpopular, Driberg was elected to parliament as an independent at a by-election at Maldon on the Essex coast; before the outbreak of hostilities he had bought a manor house in the constituency, Bradwell Lodge, where he aspired to live and entertain as an opulent squire. He subsequently joined the Labour Party, under whose colours he held Maldon until 1955 and another Essex seat, Barking, from 1959 to 1974. As a celebrity left-winger he was elected to the party's National Executive in 1949, on which he remained for twenty-three years; in 1957 it was his turn to serve as chairman, in which role he made 'fraternal' visits to Chairman Khrushchev. He seems to have maintained connections with both the British and Soviet security services, though it is doubtful whether he passed on much information of value in either direction. He kept up his career in journalism as a columnist on the left-wing Sunday newspaper *Reynold's News*, and had his great scoop in 1956 when he interviewed Guy Burgess in Moscow. While eloquently embracing left-wing causes (as well as the youth culture of the 1960s), Driberg revelled in Anglo-Catholic ritual, enjoyed the best food and drink, was snubbing to 'menials' (unless they were desirable young men), and was a howling snob (his seventieth birthday was notable for the presence of bishops and dukes). His notorious private life and radical views precluded him from public office (the job he most wanted, for which he begged Harold Wilson in vain, was that of Minister to the Vatican); but after retiring from the House of Commons he was overjoyed to receive (thanks to his friend Michael Foot) a life peerage, taking his title from the country house he had recently sold to clear his debts. Lord Bradwell lived for only nine months to enjoy the House of Lords, though during that time he managed to embarrass the Labour government by advocating withdrawal from Northern Ireland and other radical measures. At his funeral his coffin was draped with the red flag during a full requiem mass.

During his brief sojourn in the upper house, Driberg's fellow peers (particularly the not inconsiderable number who might be described as closet queens) were alarmed to hear that he was writing memoirs dealing frankly with his homosexuality. When these were published under the title *Ruling Passions* in 1977, a year after his death, it transpired that they were incomplete and had been heavily expurgated by lawyers. But enough remained to cause a sensation, for no autobiography of a public figure can ever have treated a raffish sex life so candidly, or with such relish. Driberg revealed that his homosexual career had begun at the age of three, when he inserted a finger into a hole in the trousers of his unsuspecting teenage brother, and experienced an instant thrill. In his last year at Lancing he was caught having an affair with a fellow pupil, and only avoided disgrace thanks to an indulgent headmaster. This, however, was a rare example of Driberg being romantically involved with a member of his own class; for already, on visits to Brighton, he had acquired a taste for sex with strangers in public lavatories, which establishments (including the 'gents' at the House of Commons) he was to haunt almost daily for his whole adult life. As he later told his friend Boothby, his ideal relationship was with a man he had never met before and would never meet again. His preference was for giving oral sex to handsome and basically heterosexual working-class youths. This of course involved great risks, but Driberg had a sixth sense for avoiding danger; he also became a master of the art of fellatio, giving his partners much pleasure irrespective of their orientation. He was especially popular with the young, sex-starved British servicemen he met in Cairo during the war, or reporting from Korea in the 1950s, or visiting Cyprus as a political observer in the 1960s: they positively queued up for his services. He was a fast operator: if he fancied a waiter on a train, or a sailor in a pub, it usually took him just a moment to connect and disappear with the object of his desire (as astonished witnesses to these disappearing acts later informed his biographer Francis Wheen). Sometimes the most unlikely people succumbed to his advances – such as the great Labour politician Aneurin Bevan when they were alone after a few drinks. Inevitably Driberg's activities sometimes landed him in 'tight spots', from which he showed skill in extricating himself: once during the war, when he was caught by a policeman fellating a Norwegian sailor in an air-raid shelter, he not only persuaded the officer to ignore the incident but subsequently had a friendly correspondence with him on literary subjects (an episode used by Compton Mackenzie in his novel *Thin Ice*). He was also 'an expert at bribing policemen' (as he assured Tony Crosland and Roy Jenkins, with whom he shared a regular illegal canasta game in the House of Commons in the late 1940s). Only once, in 1935, was he charged with indecent assault, after two Scottish coalminers he had invited to his house complained to the police: on that occasion he was saved by Beaverbrook, who paid the costs of his successful defence and ensured that no mention of the case appeared in the press.

Though Driberg's proclivities were notorious in the circles in which he moved, he was sufficiently mindful of his reputation to get married in 1951, much to the astonishment of all who knew him. (The humorist Osbert Lancaster wrote a

'Wedding Ode', in which the enquiry as to 'just impediment or cause' was 'followed by an awkward pause'.) His bride, Ena Binfield, was a Jewish divorcée two years older than himself and an active member of the Labour Party: she had fallen in love with him, knew about his inclinations, and seemed happy to marry him on the understanding that she would make no sexual demands. Presumably he acquired a wife for political reasons, to help him hang on to his marginal seat, and in the hope of office at a time when his party was still in power. The marriage was not a success: he conceived an intense loathing for her on their honeymoon and behaved to her with sadistic cruelty for the next twenty-five years, while contriving to see as little of her as possible (though they never divorced or formally separated). She was evidently a glutton for punishment, for despite this treatment she did all she could to support him, not just performing those duties expected of an MP's wife but attempting to manage his chaotic finances and slaving as his housekeeper at Bradwell Lodge.

During the 1960s, both Boothby and Driberg, no doubt feeling that they could get away with anything, indulged a taste for rough trade from the criminal underworld. Boothby had an affair with a pretty young cat burglar named Leslie Holt, sometimes letting him know which rich peers were away on holiday, whose residences Holt would then burgle, sharing the proceeds with Boothby. Driberg befriended an armed robber named Steve Raymond: once, when Raymond's gang were doing a big job, Raymond provided himself with an alibi by arranging to spend part of the evening at the Gay Hussar restaurant with Driberg, who was dining there with the Solicitor-General, his old friend Sir Dingle Foot. Early in 1964, the Government Chief Whip Martin Redmayne learnt from a reliable source that Boothby and Driberg had been seen together hobnobbing with young criminal types at the White

City dog track: public records released in 1995 show that this news, coming just months after the Conservative government had been rocked by the Profumo scandal, led to anxious consultations involving the Home Secretary and the Prime Minister. Meanwhile, Boothby and Driberg had made the acquaintance of the Kray twins, homosexual East End gangsters, as a result of visiting a West End gambling club the twins had acquired, Esmeralda's Barn. The Krays ran an escort service of handsome youths (mostly their own lovers) for the benefit of customers who might be useful to them, of which both Boothby and Driberg took advantage: it was thus that Boothby met Holt. Though the twins, at thirty-one, were too old to interest him sexually, Boothby seems to have enjoyed their company: he entertained them at the House of Lords and White's Club, and accepted their invitations to West End restaurants and their Walthamstow flat. It was not long before the twins were seeking favours from Boothby, asking if he would lend his name to a proposed business venture (in fact a scam) in West Africa; they visited him at his flat in Eaton Place to discuss the matter, where they were photographed with him.

Somehow the photograph fell into the hands of the *Sunday Mirror*, whose chairman, Cecil King, was out to curry favour with the Labour Party, which was expected to return to power at the general election due within a few months. In July 1964, the paper ran a sensational story to the effect that a well-known Tory peer was on intimate terms with gangsters who were being investigated by the police. Having been identified as the peer in the foreign press, Boothby at first contemplated suicide, but then learnt that the *Mirror* story was alarming not just to the Conservative government but also to the Labour opposition, as it risked leading to the public exposure of their ex-chairman, Tom Driberg MP. (Possibly Redmayne, having learnt some months previously that Boothby and Driberg hunted as a pair, had hinted to his Labour opposite number that, if Boothby 'came a cropper', Driberg would too.) Acting on the advice of Arnold Goodman, solicitor and friend of the Labour leader Harold Wilson, Boothby issued a public statement declaring that he had never been a homosexual and had never met the Krays except on business, and denouncing the *Mirror* story as 'a tissue of atrocious lies'. (The story was of course essentially true, while Boothby's statement was mostly lies.) He then began libel proceedings against the newspaper, which settled the case by offering Boothby an unqualified apology and paying him the enormous sum of £40,000 – equivalent to at least a million pounds in the values of fifty years later. The money may have been well spent: a Driberg scandal might have cost Wilson the election, which he won that October with a majority of just four seats. The episode, however, had a baleful effect on public life, as it encouraged politicians who had something to hide to believe that they could get away with anything if they stuck to stout denial. (It is interesting that a great friend of Boothby, who regarded him as a role model, was Jeremy Thorpe.) It also helped the Krays evade justice; for if Boothby had been exonerated by the *Mirror* apology, so to some extent had they. Moreover, they proceeded to blackmail Boothby: when, in 1966, they were tried at the Old Bailey for demanding money with menaces, they extracted funds from him which they used to pay the costs of their defence and of the bribery and intimidation of jurors and witnesses which secured their acquittal, enabling them to continue their increasingly violent criminal career for another two and a half years. Around the time of his second marriage in 1967 (which represented escape from a way of life that had become nightmarish and was intensifying his alcoholism), Boothby told Driberg that his libel windfall had all gone – 'which he was wise to say', Driberg remarked to a friend, 'otherwise I might have tapped him'.

When Boothby received his apology from the *Mirror* he was showered with congratulations, not just from political friends such as Michael Foot but from editors of other newspapers, who without any hint of irony wrote approvingly in their columns of the stand he had taken. His biographer Rhodes James also describes the episode as just reparation for a monstrous slur. If one compares this with the sceptical hilarity which greeted Driberg's marriage a decade earlier, one can see that, for all the similarity between the two men, there was an important difference – whereas Driberg's proclivities were common knowledge in the circles in which he moved, Boothby for the most part managed to keep his homosexual life secret from all but a few like-minded friends. Indeed, but for Boothby's reputation as a red-blooded heterosexual who was conducting an open affair with the wife of a cabinet minister, it is unlikely that he would have influenced the homophobic Maxwell Fyfe to set up the Wolfenden Committee in 1954. The fact that Boothby and Driberg survived and flourished is a tribute to their diplomatic skills, and it is perhaps a pity that they were frustrated in their hopes of becoming Her Majesty's representatives in Paris and the Vatican.

# 7

# CHIPS AND X.-B.

Henry (later Sir Henry) 'Chips' Channon (1897–1958) and Alan Lennox-Boyd (later 1st Viscount Boyd of Merton) (1904–83) were well-known Conservative MPs who served in parliament from the 1930s to the 1950s. Both married daughters of one of Britain's richest peers, Rupert Guinness, 2nd Earl of Iveagh, head of the brewing dynasty, and eventually became directors of the Guinness company. They were also both actively homosexual. Their wives were aware of this fact and do not seem to have minded: if anything, they found it advantageous to have husbands who, while charming and attentive, left them to get on with their own infidelities. (The Channon marriage eventually broke down, but this was more on account of the wife's boredom with London social life than through any revulsion at her husband's proclivities.) The two men were close friends (as we are repeatedly told by Lennox-Boyd's otherwise discreet biographer); for thirty years they helped each other in various ways (not least in the management of their respective 'queer' lives). They were, however, very different personalities, who left a mark on their times for quite different reasons. Lennox-Boyd was a serious politician with deeply held principles who was elected to parliament at twenty-six and became a minister at thirty-three, ending his career as a much-praised Colonial Secretary in the last decade during which Britain ran a colonial empire. Channon, a man of few principles and limited political gifts, but a shrewd and witty observer of the social and political scene, is remembered as one of the twentieth century's outstanding diarists.

Channon was born in Chicago, the grandson of an English immigrant who had made a fortune out of a fleet of ships on the Great Lakes, to the extent that Chips (it is not clear how the sobriquet originated) was never faced with the necessity of earning a living. As a boy before the First World War he visited Paris and was bowled over by its beauty and sophistication; he returned there to work for the Red Cross in 1917, becoming an Honorary Attaché at the United States Embassy and befriending eminent homosexuals such as Marcel Proust and Jean Cocteau – clearly he had winning ways. On the recommendation of Evan Morgan, heir to Viscount Tredegar and a notorious homosexual rake, he went on to spend eighteen riotous months at Christ Church, Oxford (the smartest of the Oxford colleges), where he was again socially successful: he resolved to make his home in England (though he did not become a naturalised British subject until just before his marriage in 1933). Though many were repelled by his naked social ambition, there can be no doubt of his success in penetrating not only London society but also a clandestine fraternity of sexually ambiguous English aristocrats and European princelings: his royal 'conquests' included Prince Paul of Serbia (future Prince Regent of Yugoslavia), whom he once described as 'the person I have loved most', the Kaiser's nephew and King of Italy's son-in-law Prince Philipp of Hesse, and Prince George, Duke of Kent, fourth son of King George V. (Prince Paul and Prince George married sisters, daughters of Channon's 'adored' Princess Nicholas of Greece.) He was also admired by many smart women, including Diana Cooper and the future Queen Mother. The secret of his success was not just racy charm but a talent for making himself useful to the people he wanted to know. In his early thirties he published three books, two unremarkable novels (in which he expressed disenchantment with his native America), and a biography of the homosexual King Ludwig of Bavaria.

Channon's social career entered a new trajectory with his marriage in 1933, aged thirty-six, to the glamorous Lady Honor Guinness, aged twenty-four. (Channon, who knew Evelyn Waugh, was surely part of the inspiration for the character of Rex Mottram in *Brideshead Revisited*, the vulgar but shrewd American-born political aspirant who marries Lord Marchmain's daughter Julia and becomes closely involved with her family.)* With her millions added to his own ample means, they moved into a sumptuous house in Belgrave Square and an estate at Kelvedon in Essex, where (in the words of his *DNB* entry) 'the hospitality was as lavish as the interiors were ornate' – the blue dining room of the Belgravia house was inspired by the Amalienburg pavilion at the Nymphenburg Palace in Munich. Any qualms the Iveaghs may have had about their son-in-law must have been quickly overcome, for at the 1935 general election they used their influence to secure for him the Conservative candidature in the safe seat of Southend-on-Sea, which had been held by Lord Iveagh himself until he inherited his peerage in 1927,

* In his published diary for 25 April 1945, Channon notes that he is reading the novel without mentioning that one of the characters is obviously based on himself: possibly such a mention was removed by his highly protective literary executor, Peter Coats.

and since then by his wife. A month before Channon was elected to parliament, Honor gave birth to a son, named Paul after the Regent of Yugoslavia, their only child and his father's pride and joy. Paul would eventually succeed his father as MP for Southend, which was thus held by three generations of the same family for eighty-five years.

Channon kept diaries for most of his life: the originals have not been made public, but a selection covering the years 1934–53, edited by Robert Rhodes James, was published in 1967.* Fashions change: when the published diaries first appeared, they were lambasted by the critics for their snobbery, vulgarity and outrageous opinions; to a later generation, it is these very qualities which render them priceless. As a shrewd, gossipy, epicene, still rather starry-eyed American, luxury-loving and enamoured of peers and princes, moving in ruling circles and witnessing great events, his view of politics and society, albeit partial, is riveting. In the five years up to the outbreak of war, the diaries cover three big themes. First, the reign and abdication of Edward VIII: Channon, who adored the King for his glamour, became something of a friend of both Edward and Mrs Simpson, and was able to follow their drama from close quarters thanks to his intimate friendship with the King's brother the Duke of Kent, who lived next door to the Channons in Belgrave Square. Secondly, the Nazis, with whom he hobnobbed when Ribbentrop invited him to the Berlin Olympics: Chips found them rather exciting, and hoped they would favour his German princeling friends (they did in fact make Philipp of Hesse governor of the statelet formerly ruled by his family).

---

* In his will, Channon expressed a wish (not binding on his executors) that his diaries should become available for public scrutiny sixty years after his death; it is currently (2014) rumoured that a more revealing edition of them may be published by his grandson in the near future.

Thirdly, the 'appeasement' policy of Neville Chamberlain: Channon ardently supported this, and viewed it from a ringside seat after he had been appointed Parliamentary Private Secretary to R. A. Butler, Undersecretary for Foreign Affairs, in February 1938, an appointment probably owing something to the fact that Butler's boss, the Foreign Secretary Lord Halifax, was Honor Channon's uncle. (Though as Home Secretary in the 1950s Butler did nothing to implement the Wolfenden recommendations, he writes in his memoirs that he delighted in the company of Chips, whom he also found an invaluable aide owing to his ear for gossip.)

Seeing that they came out in 1967, at the start of which year all homosexual behaviour remained illegal, it is hardly surprising that the published diaries avoid all overt reference to Channon's queer life – in his preface to a 1993 reprint, Rhodes James admitted that much had been removed on the subject. However, much can also be discerned by reading between the lines. Taken in combination, there is something inescapably homosexual about his love of lords, his passion for lavish décor, his fascination with the Nazis, his malicious wit. His great friends include Harold Nicolson, Bob Boothby, Osbert Sitwell and Somerset Maugham. During the 1930s he exhibits strong romantic feelings for Prince Paul and Prince George, and during the 1940s for two other attractive (if less socially exalted) men, the playwright Terence Rattigan and the horticulturist Peter Coats. Channon in fact fell madly in love with Rattigan (as described by the latter's biographers) at their first meeting in 1944, showered him with expensive gifts, and had an intermittent affair with him lasting several years: Rattigan dedicated his play *The Winslow Boy* to Channon's son Paul. As for Coats, he lived in a close and barely concealed relationship with Channon at Belgrave Square after Chips and Honor had amicably divorced in 1945 (she wanted to marry a Czech airman and live with him in Ireland – it is noteworthy that, so as not to harm his political career, she allowed Chips to divorce her on the grounds of her adultery, rather than the normal 'gentlemanly' arrangement which was the other way round). While seeking romance, Channon was also addicted to a rougher kind of sex. When Tom Driberg was elected to parliament in 1942 Channon obligingly gave him a tour of the gentlemen's lavatories at the Palace of Westminster, which Driberg described in his memoirs as 'an act of pure, disinterested, sisterly friendship, for we had no attraction for each other'. After the war, Chips and Coats sometimes hosted discreet dinner parties which were attended by guardsmen in uniform: at one of these, a guardsman expired of a heart attack during a sexual performance, and Chips had to use all his resourcefulness (no doubt coupled with a liberal distribution of cash) to get the corpse smuggled out of the house and deposited in the park. Sexual debauchery, fuelled by alcohol and drugs, undermined Chips's own health and led to his early death in 1958 at the age of sixty-one. A year earlier he had received a knighthood as a long-serving MP: while the peerage he craved eluded him, his son Paul became Lord Kelvedon on his retirement as MP for Southend-on-Sea in 1997.

Alan Lennox-Boyd belonged to the tradition of homosexual imperialists: his attachment to the British Empire stemmed from the fact that many of his ancestors had played a role in it as soldiers, merchants and administrators. His father was almost fifty at the time of his birth and soon disappeared from the scene to live with a mistress, leaving his four young sons to be brought up by their formidable mother. Handsome, narcissistic, doted on by their mother, and incestuously adoring of her and each other, they all developed homosexual leanings. (Alan's brothers, none of whom married, all died on active service, one working as a British spy in Nazi Germany before the war, the other two during it.) As an undergraduate at Christ Church, Oxford, where he met his future brother-in-law Chips,* Lennox-Boyd cut a dash which carried him to the presidency of both the Union and the Conservative Association. Through the Christ Church don Professor Lindemann he met Winston Churchill, who was immediately taken with him and helped launch him into politics. In 1931, still only twenty-seven, he captured the marginal seat of Mid-Bedfordshire – a considerable achievement as he had been effectively fighting as an independent, having been disowned by the Conservative leadership as the sitting Liberal MP was a member of the National Government (in which Conservatives and Liberals had agreed not to oppose each other at the general election). He managed to hold the seat for the next thirty years, largely thanks to charm and flair: even during his years as a government minister, he often spent afternoons touring Bedfordshire villages in his chauffeur-driven Bentley, stopping to chat to constituents about their concerns and offering them lifts.

In parliament Lennox-Boyd at first continued to be a rebel, supporting Churchill in his opposition to Indian self-government; but he was restored to official favour by his approval of Neville Chamberlain's policy of appeasing the dictators. The year 1938, during which he turned thirty-four, marked a turning point in his life. In February he entered the government as Parliamentary Secretary to the Ministry of Labour (an appointment carrying an element of irony, as it had been held by the Liberal he had been asked not to challenge in 1931); and in December he married Lady Patricia ('Patsy') Guinness, the younger sister (by nine years) of Lady Honor Channon. It was at Chips's house in Belgrave Square

---

* Channon had come down from the university before Lennox-Boyd went up to it, but frequently returned to Oxford.

that Lennox-Boyd both met his future wife (who liked what she saw of her sister's unusual marriage) and heard of his government appointment (which coincided with Chips's own invitation to become PPS to Butler, who happened to be the previous holder of Lennox-Boyd's new office). Though Patsy married Lennox-Boyd despite warnings from friends, whose suspicions seemed confirmed when they were joined on their honeymoon by one of Alan's bachelor brothers, the marriage turned out well: she was happy to have a homosexual husband, and proved the perfect political wife. Some had the impression that the union involved an element of role-reversal, as she was a rather masculine, cigar-smoking woman, while he engaged in such 'feminine' pursuits as flower-arranging, and was more interested than she was in food and clothes.

In May 1940 Lennox-Boyd, who was both patriotic and brave, left the government to serve for three years in motor torpedo boats, returning to office in 1943 as Parliamentary Secretary to the Ministry of Aircraft Production. He probably owed this appointment to the influence of John Llewellin (1893–1957), Conservative MP for Uxbridge, a misogynistic Old Etonian bachelor who was Minister for that department, and who appears to have been close to Lennox-Boyd, under whom he would later serve as Governor-General of the Central African Federation.* After the war Lennox-Boyd became the Conservatives' colonial specialist; on his party's return to power in the 1950s, he served (after a spell as Minister of Transport) as Colonial Secretary for six years. He conducted a spirited rearguard action on behalf of what remained of the empire, yielding to nationalist demands in

---

* On 5 April 1943 Stuart Preston told James Lees-Milne (as recorded in the latter's diary) that 'a cabinet minister was mad about' Lennox-Boyd. This surely refers to Llewellin: it is hard to see who else it might be, except perhaps Hugh Dalton (see Chapter 13).

some territories while consolidating others and extolling the benefits of British rule: it was not his fault that, owing to the national failure of nerve after Suez, and hostility to Britain's colonial role from both the Americans and Soviets, his impe-rial rescue mission ultimately proved unavailing. He was also assiduous in cultivating Britain's allies in the Arab world, becoming a close friend of the anglophile (and homosexual) Prince Abdulilah, Regent and later Crown Prince of Iraq: the Iraqi revolution of 1958, which led to the horrific murder of both the Prince and his nephew the King, was a blow for him both personally and politically. (The revolutionaries discov-ered intimate letters from Lennox-Boyd among the Prince's papers, which they released to the world's press.) On the whole he was regarded as a popular and successful minister, and there was some talk of his succeeding Selwyn Lloyd (another closet queen) as Foreign Secretary. At this point, a number of Tory MPs who were aware of his private life warned the Prime Minister Harold Macmillan against any such move. In the event, Lennox-Boyd, still in his mid-fifties, left politics with a viscountcy soon after the 1959 general elec-tion to become chairman of Guinness, leading a prosperous life until his death in a road accident at the age of seventy-eight.

Although Lennox-Boyd's homosexuality was evidently known to some of his fellow MPs, no one in his constituency (except for its grandest resident, the 13th Duke of Bedford at Woburn, yet another closet queen) seems to have had any inkling of it. (His successor as MP for Mid-Beds, Stephen Hastings, knew about it from working for MI6, and was amazed that none of his constituents had suspected it.) And although his wife both knew about it and was untroubled by it, their three sons (so the author is informed by one of them) were barely aware of it – they were rather surprised when

Philip Murphy's biography of their father, published in 1999, made a few brief references to it. (Before they went to Eton, their father had taken them aside and explained to them what to do in the event of trouble from 'queers'.) As with his brother-in-law and confidant Chips, Lennox-Boyd's homosexual relationships seem to have included both the intensely romantic and the purely carnal. Some interesting revelations are contained in the diaries of James Lees-Milne, a sometime friend of the family. Hearing of Lennox-Boyd's death, Lees-Milne recalled: 'With him [during the 1930s] I slept more than once, as indeed with his brother George, but they were not romantic occasions.' In 1943, Chips told Lees-Milne that Lennox-Boyd was madly in love with Lees-Milne's American friend Stuart Preston, and begged Lees-Milne to urge the reluctant Preston to yield to the advances of 'X.-B.' (the thinly disguised designation which Lees-Milne gives Lennox-Boyd in a volume of his diaries which appeared while the latter was still alive). In 1948, Lennox-Boyd told Lees-Milne that, although Patsy was 'a wonderful wife', he found it 'tiresome' having to lead 'a life of dissimulation' as he was 'in love with a young man'. Soon afterwards, Lees-Milne met the youth in question, Major Alexander Beattie of the Coldstream Guards, a Canadian in his late twenties and a former bodyguard of Winston Churchill, who struck Lees-Milne as 'a good-looking and amiable ass'. Beattie, known as 'Sweetie' at the Colonial Office (where he was disliked by the officials because he distracted the Secretary of State at important moments such as the Suez crisis), was the great love of Lennox-Boyd's life; during the late 1940s, he accompanied Lennox-Boyd on overseas journeys during which they were entertained together by British representatives – though once he resumed office in 1951, Lennox-Boyd accepted advice that in future it would be more appropriate for him to be accompanied on his travels by his wife. (In 1953, Beattie emulated his lover by marrying an earl's daughter – Lady Rozelle Pierrepont, only surviving child of the 6th and last Earl Manvers of Thoresby Hall; they divorced in 1961.) A later protégé of Lennox-Boyd was Roy Miles (1935–2012), a flamboyant young man from the North of England who began life as a hairdresser and eventually established himself as a successful London art dealer.

Blessed with seductive charm, quick intelligence, *savoir faire* and considerable wealth, Channon and Lennox-Boyd led enchanted closet-queen lives. If they ever got into trouble, they evidently managed to extricate themselves from it without scandal. In their wild youth they seem to have enjoyed much thrilling sexual adventure; they subsequently experienced both reasonably successful marriages and fulfilling homosexual relationships. They were probably lovers for a time, and remained the closest of friends, seeing each other almost every day when they were in London. They collaborated on many projects: during the war they tried to help the lonely and penniless Lord Alfred 'Bosie' Douglas; in 1958 they organised a memorial service for their murdered friend Prince Abdulilah – almost the last thing Chips did before his death, which left Lennox-Boyd disconsolate.

# 8

# HAROLD AND HINCH

Blessed with cherubic looks, subtle intelligence and a charming personality, Harold Nicolson (1886–1968) distinguished himself in three different spheres – as a diplomat, writer and politician. The son of an ambassador who became head of the Foreign Office, he began by following his father's profession: he took part in the conferences which drafted the post-1918 peace treaties, going on to serve at the British embassies in Tehran and Berlin. He might have reached the top ranks of the service had he not resigned from it in 1929, aged forty-three. He had become bored with the work and wanted to devote himself to literature, having already had some success as a writer; he also wanted to see more of his wife, Vita Sackville-West (1892–1962), herself a noted novelist and poet, whom he had married in 1913, and who refused to accompany him to foreign posts. Over the next three decades he wrote approximately a book a year, including history, biography (he was the official biographer of King George V), novels and *belles-lettres*, works distinguished by their perceptive insights and elegant style. In 1935, Nicolson was approached by the chairman of the National Labour Party, the 9th Earl De La Warr, his wife's cousin, to stand in their interest at the forthcoming general election: he had barely heard of the party (consisting of the minority within the Labour Party which had broken away from the mainstream in 1931 to follow Ramsay MacDonald into the National Government), but approved of its programme (which combined support for the Conservative-dominated coalition with mildly left-wing policies), and was duly elected as National Labour MP for West Leicester by a majority of 87 votes. Up to then his only experience of politics, at the previous general election, had been as a candidate of the short-lived 'New Party' led by the fiery demagogue Sir Oswald Mosley (for whom Nicolson felt a certain fascination), which had failed to win a single seat.

Nicolson loved the clublike atmosphere of the House of Commons, and was popular with MPs of all parties. In domestic policy he was a social liberal; in foreign policy he strongly believed that Britain should stand up to Hitler. His parliamentary contributions (the most famous of which was a speech lambasting the Munich agreement) were always eloquent, well argued and heard with respect. When Churchill (whose calls for rearmament Nicolson had consistently supported) became Prime Minister in 1940, Nicolson was given junior office in the wartime coalition as Parliamentary Secretary to the Ministry of Information (where the new minister, Duff Cooper, was a friend); but he was considered somewhat ineffectual, and only lasted a year in the job. For the rest of the war he played a valuable role, as a francophile and a fluent French speaker, in helping smooth the difficult relations between the British government and the Free French. At the 1945 election he lost his seat, and an attempt to win another as a member of the regular Labour Party ended in failure. In later life he did, however, become a minor celebrity,

not only as a book-writer but also as a broadcaster and journalist – millions listened to his 'fireside chats' on the BBC,
while the intelligentsia avidly devoured his weekly book
review in the *Observer* and weekly essay in the *Spectator*.

Nicolson would probably be remembered as a mere footnote
to the diplomatic, political and literary history of his time were
it not for two publications which took place in the 1960s and
70s. All his life he had been an assiduous diarist, and a selection
of his journals covering the years 1931–62, published in three
volumes appearing in 1966–8, brought him instant fame. Witty,
poignant and incisive, they capture the drama of the great events
he watched from the wings, provide fascinating insights into the
leading public figures of the day, give a flavour of the club-based
London social life of the period, and enable us to follow the feelings and thoughts of an observer who encapsulated some of the
best qualities of the England of his time. Since their appearance,
few works dealing with the period have failed to draw on them;
and they are a major historical source on the doings of the long
parliament of 1935–45 in which Nicolson served. They are discreet: Nicolson rarely reports malicious gossip, and says little
about the private lives of himself or anyone else. However, the
diaries reveal the identity of his close friends, and many of these
were homosexual or bisexual. Certainly most of the fellow MPs
to whom he felt closest came into this category: as well as figures
discussed in previous chapters, such as Bob Boothby, Chips
Channon and Philip Sassoon, they included four young parliamentarians to be considered in the next chapter, all of whom lost
their lives during the Second World War.

Nicolson was still alive, though reduced by a series of strokes,
when his diaries were published: they were edited by his son
Nigel (1917–2004), himself a distinguished writer and former
parliamentarian (he had been a Conservative MP for
Bournemouth during the 1950s, eventually being 'deselected' by

his local party for what they considered his excessively liberal views). In 1973, five years after Harold's death, Nigel scandalised the nation by publishing another work in which he revealed that both his parents, while apparently happily married, had been essentially homosexual. It is difficult nowadays, reading *Portrait of a Marriage*, a book which appears to be a model of restraint and good taste, to understand the furore which it aroused forty years ago. To write at all about the unconventional sex lives of the recently dead was then considered unaccept-able;* for a son to write such things about both his parents seemed unforgivable (and indeed, many of those who knew Nigel were so shocked that they never spoke to him again). In fact, the book mostly concerned a single traumatic (if some-what farcical) episode in the life of his mother. In 1919–20, while Harold was attending the Paris Peace Conference, Vita fell madly in love with a younger woman, Violet Trefusis (*née* Keppel); they ran off together, hotly pursued by their husbands who with some difficulty persuaded them to return. Vita had written an account of this affair, to be published after her death: as her literary executor, Nigel felt he could not publish it with-out putting it in the context of his parents' unusual marriage. However, while revealing their homosexual tastes, he was oth-erwise discreet: the main point of the book is to show that, apart from the one episode, they managed to combine the indulgence of those tastes with a happy and fulfilling partnership.

The book is a little disingenuous, for one of the reasons the marriage worked so well is that they did not see much of each other. Throughout the 1920s, Harold was serving abroad, while Vita remained in England. From the 1930s to the 1950s, they generally met only at weekends, which they spent together at

* Michael Holroyd had broken the taboo with his life of Lytton Strachey, published in 1969 – though his subject had been dead not for five years but thirty-seven.

Sissinghurst Castle in Kent, an ancient property which they acquired in 1930 and where they collaborated on creating a paradisal garden: during the week, Vita lived at Sissinghurst and Harold at his London flat, where they wrote their respective books and engaged in their respective homosexual love affairs. When they were apart they wrote to each other every day (some ten thousand of these letters are now housed at the Lilly Library in Indiana), discussing everything except their extramarital sex lives, concerning which they respected each other's privacy. In fact, though they both felt emotionally drawn to their own sex, their love lives were quite different. Vita was passionate by nature (a trait she believed she had inherited from her grandmother, a Spanish dancer); she had a series of all-consuming love affairs, each lasting two or three years. Harold, who had a strong libido and sought a daily erotic adventure well into middle age, took a pragmatic view of sex. He gathered around him a circle of attractive, well-bred young men of literary bent, who in return for his hospitality and mentorship were happy to oblige him in his somewhat unromantic urges. (Nigel compared his sexual experiences to 'a quick visit to a picture gallery between trains'.) Many of his lovers went on to become established literary names, such as Robert Byron, Christopher Hobhouse, James Lees-Milne, James Pope-Hennessy, Alan Pryce-Jones and Richard Rumbold. (Another was to acquire a different kind of notoriety – the Soviet agent Guy Burgess.) Only twice in his life does he seem to have been seriously in love with a man for any length of time: in the 1920s with Raymond Mortimer, later a famous literary critic (who was upset by Nigel's *Portrait*, though he was not mentioned therein); and in the 1930s with a fellow MP, Robert Bernays.

Nicolson, who to outward appearances was a manly and 'normal' Englishman, took extraordinary precautions to ensure that no one outside his private world suspected his homosexuality, even to the extent of appearing somewhat homophobic.

One example will suffice. He was a great Byron enthusiast, and in the privacy of his intimate circle enjoyed discussing Byron's homosexuality. However, in 1924, for the centenary of the poet's death, he wrote *Byron: The Final Journey*, an account of Byron's sojourn in Greece during the last year of his life; and during his research in the archives of John Murray (who had been Byron's publishers and were now Nicolson's) he discovered a letter which left little doubt that, during his last months, Byron had shared a bed with his Greek page Lukas Chalandritsanos, who was also (so the letter indicated) the unnamed addressee of his erotic poem 'Love and Death'. Far from wishing to make use of the letter, Nicolson wrote to Sir John Murray, head of the firm, that its discovery had come as 'a shock', and he feared its publication would 'prove deleterious'. Sir John concurred; he thought publication 'would create a most disagreeable impression', and did not believe 'that either of us is bound to disclose this letter'. He added that he was 'glad that the discovery has come through you who regard such questions as I do'. During the 1920s Nicolson also produced studies of three other sexually ambiguous men of letters, Verlaine, Tennyson and Swinburne, which refrained from mentioning their homosexual side. In both his diaries and his personal correspondence, Nicolson always guarded himself against writing anything that might betray his (or anyone else's) proclivities if it fell into the wrong hands: his love letters are consequently curious to read. A man like Harold Macmillan, to whom Nicolson was close politically and of whom he saw much during his decade in the House of Commons, was apparently unaware of his homosexuality.

Harold and Vita had two sons, Benedict ('Ben') and Nigel, born during the first years of their marriage. Both felt unloved by their mother and saw little of their father (though he was undoubtedly fond of them, as they were of him). Both were bisexual, and led rather troubled lives. During the 1930s, Nigel fell in love with a fellow Balliol undergraduate, James Pope-Hennessy, whom he introduced to his father: on discovering that James had become Harold's lover, he received an emotional shock from which he never quite recovered. The brothers both married and had children, but neither marriage lasted long. Nigel, as we have seen, became a distinguished man of letters (as well as co-founding the publishing firm of Weidenfeld & Nicolson): he was an impressive figure, capable of much kindness and generosity, yet came across as a cold personality. Ben, an art historian who became editor of the *Burlington Magazine*, was a raffish, bohemian type who smoked and drank to excess and dropped dead at the age of sixty-three. Perhaps the stable from which they emerged was not quite as happy as Nigel's *Portrait* would have us believe.

The phenomenon of male homosexuals marrying lesbians was not uncommon in the establishment world of the first half of the twentieth century. Such unions provided both parties with socially necessary camouflage; and where affection, common interests and mutual respect existed, they could be surprisingly successful (though there was always a risk that one party would leave the other in order to devote himself or herself to the homosexual life). Two of Harold Nicolson's friends also contracted such marriages. Lord Gerald ('Gerry') Wellesley, a diplomatic colleague of Harold before the First World War (who later became a distinguished architect, and unexpectedly succeeded as 7th Duke of Wellington on the death in action of his nephew in 1943), married Dorothy ('Dot') Ashton, who, having borne him two children, abandoned him to devote herself to affairs with Vita and other women. And James Lees-Milne, one of Harold's coven of handsome young men in the 1930s, later famous as a diarist and architectural historian, married Alvilde Chaplin, a notoriously bossy woman (she was a general's daughter) who had a passionate affair with Vita in the 1950s. Other examples of the genre are the diplomat Sir Charles Mendl, who married the American decorator Elsie de Wolfe; Christopher Hussey, architectural conservationist and editor of *Country Life*, who married Betty Kerr-Smiley (niece of Ernest Simpson of Abdication fame); and the courtier Sir Michael Duff, who married his cousin, Lady Caroline Paget.

In politics too such marriages were far from rare. It has been noted that statesmen such as Edwin Montagu and Samuel Hoare married women who were considered 'masculine' (Venetia Montagu, though she conducted many affairs with men, seems to have been bisexual). There are several examples closer to our own time (some of them too close to permit inclusion here). An interesting case is that of the eccentric Viscount Hinchingbrooke (1906–95), known as 'Hinch', heir to the 9th Earl of Sandwich, who sat as Conservative MP for South Dorset from 1941 to 1962. Although he never held government office, Hinch was constantly in the public eye owing to his flamboyant disagreements with his own party. His views were wayward and unpredictable. During the war, he was one of a group of 'reformist' young Tory MPs who urged the Conservatives to adopt policies of the Labour Party, including the welfare state and nationalisation; after the war he turned into a right-wing blimp, opposing the retreat from empire. (He was one of the eight 'Suez rebels' who suspended their party membership in protest against Eden's decision to withdraw from the Canal Zone.) Despite having an American mother he became strongly anti-American (he considered NATO an American plot to take over the world), while admiring the Soviet Union, which he often visited. He was fiercely opposed to the efforts of Macmillan and subsequent premiers to take Britain into 'Europe'. In 1962 he inherited his father's earldom and seat in the House of Lords; at the subsequent by-election in South Dorset, he supported an independent anti-EEC candidate against the official Conservative, as a result of which the seat was won by Labour. In 1963 he supported legislation enabling peers to disclaim their peerages and stand for the House of Commons, and in 1964 he disclaimed his own, becoming plain Victor Montagu, and hoping to be swept back into Parliament. His efforts to secure re-election as an independent proved unavailing, and his old party wanted no more to do with him, though he remained an idiosyncratic figure on the margins of politics, one of the leaders of the doomed campaign to keep Britain out of the 'Common Market'. Like Harold Nicolson, his friend in the wartime House of Commons, Hinch was a homosexual married to a lesbian. His first wife, the artist Rosemary Peto, whom he married in 1934, described by James Lees-Milne as 'like a very jolly able-bodied seaman', bore him no fewer than seven children, though the great love of her life was Renée Fedden, wife of the National Trust official (and former lover of Anthony Blunt) Robin Fedden, with whom she lived after divorcing Hinch in 1958. His second marriage of 1962 to Lady Anne Holland-Martin (*née* Cavendish), sister-in-law of the Prime Minister Harold Macmillan, disintegrated after a few months. Hinch – a narcissist who was handsome in youth and distinguished-looking in middle life – retained a fondness for young men into old age: visitors to Hinchingbrooke Hall, his ancestral property in Huntingdonshire, and Mapperton, his Jacobean house in Dorset, were warned to avoid solitary walks. That his homosexuality strayed into the realms of paedophilia was revealed in 2014 with the publication of a searing memoir by his son Robert, describing his father's sexual attentions to him between the ages of seven and twelve.

# 9

# CASUALTIES
# OF WAR

Harold Nicolson's friends included four young MPs who shared his homosexual tastes, all of whom died on active service during the Second World War – Victor Cazalet, Rob Bernays, Jack Macnamara and Ronnie Cartland. (After their deaths, he wrote that Bernays, Macnamara and Cartland had been his best friends in the House of Commons: as their names were read out during the commemorative service at St Margaret's, Westminster on VE day, he was in tears.) As MPs, they were not obliged to serve in the armed forces, but they all considered it their patriotic duty to do so. They were also – like Nicolson himself – all profoundly unhappy about the 'appeasement' policy of the Chamberlain government: Cartland and Macnamara joined Nicolson in abstaining in the parliamentary vote on the Munich Agreement in October 1938, attracting the ire of the whips, while Bernays came close to resigning as a junior minister over it; following the betrayal of the Czechs, Cazalet dedicated himself to the cause of Hitler's next victims, the

Poles.* Another young soldier-MP in Nicolson's circle, Sir
Paul Latham, lacked the caution and discretion essential to
the survival of homosexuals in public life: he too found both
his military and his parliamentary career abruptly terminated during the war, for the rather different reason that he
was caught misbehaving with men under his command.

Victor Cazalet (1896–1943) was a neighbour of Harold and
Vita in Kent. (In the 1930s he built a new country house for
himself just a few miles from Sissinghurst, Great Swifts,
designed by Paul Hyslop, the architect boyfriend of Nicolson's
ex-lover Raymond Mortimer.) The scion of a wealthy mer-
cantile family of Huguenot descent, well-connected (he was a
godson of Queen Victoria, who had stayed at the family's villa
near Nice), accomplished both as an all-round sportsman and
an amateur pianist, debonair and handsome (if rather short –
hence his nickname 'Teenie'), awarded the MC for heroic
exploits on the Western Front, he captured Chippenham for
the Conservatives in 1924, aged twenty-seven, and held the
seat until his death almost twenty years later. He was a rather
saintly man, having become an ardent Christian Scientist at
Eton (a passion he combined rather oddly with being
President of 'Pop')†; he tended to give everyone the benefit of
the doubt, rarely spoke ill of anyone, and was happy for others
to take credit for his achievements. Though he was far from
stupid – he narrowly missed getting a 'First' at Oxford, and his

---

* A book has recently been published about these fervent young parliamentary
anti-appeasers, *Troublesome Young Men* by Lynne Olson (Bloomsbury, 2007) –
though the author fails to notice that most of them possessed another common
attribute.

† The Eton Society or 'Pop' is the self-electing body of boys who act as school prefects: they normally consist of the school's social and sporting elite, and enjoy
certain privileges such as the right to wear decorative waistcoats. (One unstated
privilege in times past was the enjoyment, if they wished to have it, of the sexual
services of the prettiest boy in the school, known as 'pop bitch'.)

diaries show literary talent – his virtuous outlook won him the reputation of being naive in his judgements, and while popular with leading figures in all the political parties, he never acquired any office beyond that of PPS. He did however do much to advance various causes in which he believed – including Zionism, the cause of General Franco in the Spanish Civil War, and the Polish cause before and during the Second World War. On becoming premier in 1940, Churchill, who had admired Cazalet as a young man (though they had fallen out politically in the 1930s), offered him no job in his administration, but made him the liaison officer between the Polish leader General Władysław Sikorski and the British government. For three years, Cazalet won general admiration for his handling of this role (which included smoothing over disagreements among the Poles as well as helping conduct their often difficult relations with their allies), until he perished with Sikorski on 4 July 1943 when the aircraft in which they had just taken off from Gibraltar crashed into the Mediterranean (a mysterious accident which, coming as it did just a few weeks after the Germans had announced the discovery of the mass grave at Katyn of Polish officers murdered by the Russians, has given rise to various conspiracy theories).

Though Cazalet had many female admirers, he never married. The closest relationships in his life seem to have been with his Scottish mother, whom he adulated and called his 'angel', and his sister Thelma, a feminist who was herself elected a Conservative MP in 1931. In her memoirs, Thelma (who reciprocated her brother's adoration) deals indignantly with 'insinuations' concerning his sexuality. 'The reason Victor never married', she claims, stressing his sporting achievements, 'is that he dreaded becoming too engrossed with one person, and too fond of his own children to bring them up properly.' It is indeed possible that this other-worldly and rather puritanical man, who abstained from alcohol and tobacco and devoted much of his spare time to boys' clubs, never had sexual relations with anyone (as also seems to have been the case with that other mother-worshipping Christian Scientist, Lord Lothian); but most of the important friendships in his life were with homosexual or bisexual men. At Eton, his soul-mates (who remained friends for life) included two aesthetes who shared his passion for music, the future harpsichord-maker Tom Goff and Vita's cousin Eddy Sackville-West. At Oxford, he knew Anthony Eden during his 'queer' phase, and hobnobbed with Chips Channon and Prince Paul of Serbia. His great friends between the wars included Bob Boothby, the novelist Hugh Walpole, and the German tennis champion Gottfried von Cramm (sent to prison on account of his proclivities). Harold Nicolson (who often accompanied Cazalet on the journey between Kent and Westminster) was an old friend, though he was often exasperated by Cazalet's enthusiasms, many of which he did not share, and took a jaundiced view of Cazalet's passion for entertaining the great. ('Victor's mania for knowing important people is becoming an obsession', he wrote in 1937. 'Were he not so mean about supplying food and drink, he would rapidly become one of London's leading hostesses.') Cazalet's closest friend in the 1930s House of Commons was said to be Hamilton Kerr (1903–74), the young, American-born Conservative MP for Oldham, another lifelong bachelor who combined sporting and artistic interests. After the war Kerr became MP for Cambridge, in which position he was succeeded in 1966 by Robert Rhodes James, who a decade later would publish a biography of Cazalet which managed as usual to convey nothing about the subject's private life.

The son of a North London vicar, Robert ('Rob') Bernays (1902–45) made his mark (despite a stammer) as President of the Oxford Union in 1925, and subsequently earned his living as a journalist with the Liberal *Daily News*. Having been sacked by the paper in 1930, he spent some months as private secretary to Lord Beauchamp, and accompanied that Liberal grandee on the jaunt to Australia which preceded his downfall. (Bernays later assured Nicolson that he had been appalled by Beauchamp's flaunting of his proclivities, and had left his employment on account of it. But he kept in touch with Beauchamp, with whom he spent two nights in Paris in 1936, and also wrote speeches for Beauchamp's MP son.) Bernays captured the seat of Bristol North from Labour at the 1931 general election, and held it in 1935 – victories only made possible by the fact that he faced no Conservative opponent, belonging as he did to the Liberal faction allied to the Conservatives in the National Government. He rose to be a junior minister in the departments of Health and Transport during the premiership of Neville Chamberlain (1937–40); he also kept a diary, published fifty years after his death and now regarded, along with Nicolson's, as an important historical source on the parliamentary politics of the period. Nicolson, sixteen years his senior, first met him on entering parliament in 1935, and they soon became close friends: as non-Conservative supporters of the National Government, they held similar political views; but they also seem to have fallen in love, a passion which may have been consummated during ten idyllic weeks they spent together on a parliamentary delegation to East Africa in the winter of 1937. In letters to Vita, Nicolson referred to 'my beloved Rob'; in letters to his sister, Bernays wrote that 'he is very fond of me as I am of him' and that he hoped one day to marry a woman with whom he had 'the kind of mental affinity which I have with H'. However, when Bernays did marry in 1942, aged forty, it was to someone very different to the gentle Harold – Nancy Britton, daughter of a Bristol Liberal political family, a strident character who went on to become a colonel

in the ATS (the British Army's women's branch). Like Harold
and Vita, they had two sons – who never knew their father, as
he died in January 1945 while visiting British troops in Italy
and Greece when his plane disappeared over the Adriatic.
Nicolson had learnt of the death of 'Teenie' with equanimity;
but on hearing about 'Rob', he felt 'crushed'.

Apart from Nicolson, Bernays's closest parliamentary friend
was Walter Elliot (1888–1958), an exuberant Scottish doctor
who sat in the House of Commons for almost forty years,
serving in the cabinet from 1932 to 1940 in the successive
posts of Agriculture, Scottish and Health Secretary. Both
Bernays and Elliot were fond of Katharine 'Kay' Tennant, a
jovial, masculine woman (popularly known as 'the happy
hippo'), whose favourite hobbies were playing golf and driving tractors. Bernays was dismayed when Elliot suddenly
married her in 1934; he wrote to his sister that, while 'of course
it was not a "grand passion", I am not capable of that', he
thought that he and Kay might have formed 'a union of mind
and heart and interests and friends and all the things which
make for happiness'. (It sounds as if he aspired to a marriage
much like that of Harold and Vita.) Notwithstanding this disappointment, the Bernays–Elliot friendship flourished after
May 1938 when Elliot was appointed Secretary of State for
Health, with Bernays as his Undersecretary. Both men disapproved of Munich and were expected to resign from the
government over it, but finally decided not to do so – dis-
maying their friends and ensuring that their ministerial
careers ended when Churchill became Prime Minister.
Through Bernays, Nicolson too became a friend of Elliot, and
the three of them often dined together: if not homosexual,
Elliot (whose marriage to Kay produced no children, and
whose other parliamentary friends included 'Hinch' and
Brendan Bracken) seems to have been sympathetic to the

cause, warning Nicolson in 1940 to be wary of the homophobic Viscount Davidson, who held a senior post at the Ministry
of Information and was 'out to destroy' him.

John ('Jack') Macnamara (1905–44) was born in Assam in
north-eastern India, the son of an Irish doctor employed by a
tea company. He hardly knew his parents, who sent him to
England at the age of three, to be looked after by a succession
of Saki-esque aunts. This experience seems to have made him
profoundly misogynistic – in 1938, he wrote that, much as he
disliked Hitler, he admired him for having put German
women in their place. After education at Cheam and
Haileybury, schools specialising in the sons of empire, the
blond and handsome Macnamara was recruited by the secret
service, helping to counter 'subversion' during the turbulent
period which featured the General Strike of May 1926. (That
same year he was briefly arrested by the French authorities in
Tunisia as a British spy, though it is possible that he was drawn
to that country for reasons other than espionage.) From 1927
to 1933 he served as a regular officer with the British Army in
India (possibly a cover for continued intelligence work): he
made himself unpopular with the 'memsahibs' by refusing to
dance with their daughters, but seems to have been admired
by several native princes, who had him to stay in their palaces.
Back in England, Macnamara became involved in Conservative politics. He unsuccessfully contested a by-election in
East London, being opposed by local Jews who suspected him
of fascist leanings. (They may not have been entirely mistaken:
though later a fervent opponent of 'appeasement', he was for
a time a member of the Anglo-German Fellowship, a Nazi
front organisation; and his autobiography *The Whistle Blows*
[1938] is peppered with mildly anti-semitic remarks.)
However, at the 1935 general election, having just turned
thirty, he won the contest at Chelmsford, having been adopted

there on the recommendation of its former Conservative MP
Colonel Charles Howard-Bury, a famous soldier and explorer
who was a homosexual and an admirer of Macnamara.

Macnamara seems to have been an earnest and idealistic
MP, if rather easily swayed in his views. During his first year
in parliament he associated closely with the raffishly homosexual Guy Burgess (1911–63), just down from Cambridge,
who acted as Macnamara's assistant until he got a job as a BBC
talks producer. Though Burgess, in order to preserve his
'cover' as a Soviet agent (a role of which Macnamara almost
certainly knew nothing), had resigned from the Communist
Party to which he had belonged at university, and even followed Macnamara into the Anglo-German Fellowship, he
seems to have influenced Macnamara in a left-wing direction – for example, getting him to sympathise with the
Republican cause in the Spanish Civil War. Macnamara and
Burgess visited Nazi Germany together in 1936, Burgess later
boasting to his friend Goronwy Rees that they had enjoyed
themselves with boys of the Hitler Youth; they also visited
Paris to meet Burgess's friend Edouard Pfeiffer, the homosexual *chef de cabinet* of the French politician (then War Minister,
later premier) Daladier, who organised erotic entertainments
for them. Burgess was a lover of Harold Nicolson, and by the
spring of 1936 Nicolson and Macnamara were also seeing
much of each other, staying up until the early hours at
Nicolson's flat at King's Bench Walk: Nicolson wrote that
Macnamara struck him as the best of the MPs newly elected
in 1935, though still requiring 'much experience of public
affairs and public behaviour' (an education to which Nicolson
doubtless felt he might contribute). Whatever his earlier views
on Hitler, by the time of Munich Macnamara had concluded
that Nazi Germany would have to be fought: most of his parliamentary interventions stressed the urgency with which

Britain's armed forces needed to prepare for the coming struggle. On the outbreak of hostilities in 1939, he returned to full-time soldiering, while remaining an MP. For two and a half years he commanded a territorial battalion, the 1st London Irish Rifles, based in Sussex. (Nicolson several times visited him there to 'address the troops'; Macnamara in turn called on Nicolson whenever he was in London, usually with some young friend in tow.) Macnamara was a favourite of Winston Churchill, who entertained him at 10 Downing Street and chose him first to command the new Royal Air Force Regiment (designed to secure and defend airfields) when it was created in 1942, then to be Deputy Chief of Combined Operations: in the latter role, Macnamara masterminded such operations as the airlifting of supplies to Tito's partisans in Yugoslavia, and the kidnapping by Patrick Leigh Fermor of the German commander in Crete. He was killed in December 1944 by German mortar fire while revisiting his old battalion, then manning a front along the Senio River in Northern Italy.

Macnamara was a close friend of William Teeling (1903–75), another homosexual Irishman filled with British patriotism who fought for the Empire and was involved in Conservative politics (they met in the early 1930s campaigning in the East End, where they were candidates in neighbouring constituencies). During the 1930s Teeling worked as a journalist, walking across England and America and living rough to report on the effects of the Slump; he also visited Nazi Germany where, like Macnamara, he was interested in the Hitler Youth. He served in the RAF during the war, and became MP for a Brighton seat at a by-election in 1944, just a few months before Macnamara's death. Teeling wrote an obituary appreciation of his friend in *The Times*, lamenting that the House had lost one of its most valiant members. Teeling married in 1942, principally, it would seem, to make himself acceptable to candidates' selection committees: he showed no great regret when his wife suddenly died in 1953. Teeling continued to represent the voters of Brighton until 1969, becoming a well-known right-wing Conservative MP who lamented decolonisation and championed the right of the Irish peers to sit in the House of Lords, and being knighted for services to his party in 1962.

Ronald ('Ronnie') Cartland (1907–40) was the younger brother of the novelist Barbara Cartland, who after his death published a biography of him in which she portrayed him as a spotless paragon. Certainly he seems to have been a young man of unusual courage, high principles and independence of mind. His grandfather was a once prosperous Birmingham industrialist who committed suicide after suffering ruin; his father then worked for the Conservative Party, hoping to become an MP, but was killed in action in 1918. After Charterhouse, where he was regarded as a model schoolboy, Cartland followed in his father's footsteps by working for the Conservatives, and managed to get adopted in 1933 as their candidate in the Birmingham constituency of King's Norton, largely thanks to the patronage of Neville Chamberlain, whose family had 'ruled' Birmingham since the 1870s. Having won his seat at the 1935 election, however, Cartland did not hesitate to attack Chamberlain, first for not doing enough, as Chancellor of the Exchequer, to help the poor, and then, as Prime Minister (from May 1937), for his appeasement of Hitler. His most famous moment occurred on 2 August 1939 when he spoke out against Chamberlain's motion to adjourn the House for two months (which had been framed as a confidence motion), accusing the Prime Minister of having 'ideas of dictatorship', and declaring prophetically: 'We are in a situation that within a month we may be going to fight – and we may be going to die.' This was regarded as treason by Tory whips and loyalists, but made him a hero to those MPs who wanted to stand up to Hitler. When war broke out a month later, Cartland duly went off to fight in France, dying a hero's death in May 1940 with a unit which sacrificed itself in order to hold back the Germans from Dunkirk during the Allied evacuations. He had been greatly admired by Churchill, who wrote a preface to Barbara's biography in which he eulogised him in much the same terms as he had Rupert Brooke in 1915.

Cartland's closest relationships (like Cazalet's) were with his mother, a colonel's daughter, to whom he wrote constantly, addressing her as 'my own darling', and his sister Barbara, whom he met daily when they were both in London, regarding her as his greatest confidante and inspiration. Otherwise he seems to have had little interest in women, though he was extremely attractive to them; when one of his admirers, Ruth Leonard, offered to act as his unpaid secretary, he accepted her offer, but never addressed her by her Christian name, and replied to her letters by offering advice on religion. He was close to Harold Nicolson, with whom he agreed politically, and whom he seems to have regarded as a father-figure (though he is hardly mentioned in Barbara's biography). Many of his other friends were homosexual, including (inside the House of Commons) Alan Lennox-Boyd, Paul Latham, Jack Macnamara and Philip Sassoon, and (outside it) Peter Coats (who described Cartland as a 'particular friend'), Noël Coward and Rom Landau (a Polish-born mystic, sculptor and Arabist). Though (again like Cazalet) he was profoundly Christian, and somewhat fastidious and abstemious in his habits, he does not seem to have been entirely celibate.

The son of an industrialist who became managing director of Courtaulds, Paul Latham (1905–55) inherited his father's fortune and baronetcy in 1931, in which year, aged twenty-six, he was also elected Conservative MP for Scarborough and Whitby. He used his wealth to transform the fifteenth-century Herstmonceux Castle, Sussex, into a luxurious modern residence, and gave fabulous parties there, regular attenders at which included his fellow MPs Rob Bernays, Bob Boothby, Brendan Bracken, Malcolm Bullock, Ronnie Cartland, Chips Channon and Harold Nicolson. Latham was strikingly handsome, tall and slim, with cold blue eyes and curly fair hair (though a childhood accident had left him with an artificial left leg). He could be charming, but was essentially a sadist who delighted in causing pain and discomfiture to others; he was also a promiscuous and predatory homosexual. For more than a decade he conducted a sado-masochistic affair with Eddy Sackville-West (later 5th Baron Sackville), Vita's cousin and a talented writer and musician, who was finally driven (in 1937) to a nervous breakdown by the relationship. In 1933 he married Lady Patricia Moore, daughter of the 10th Earl of Drogheda, whom he enjoyed humiliating in public: she bore him one son. He seems to have grown bored with politics, as shortly before the war he informed his constituents that he would not be recontesting the seat at the next general election. However, before that intention could be put into effect, Latham entered the history books as the only serving MP of modern times to go to prison because of homosexuality.*

---

* The MP and art collector William John Bankes would probably have gone to prison in 1841, after being caught (for a second time) with a guardsman in Green Park, but fled abroad. Edward de Cobain, a Belfast MP and sometime Grand Master of the Orange Order, was sentenced to a year's hard labour for 'gross indecency' in 1893 – though he had been expelled from the House of Commons a year earlier after he had left the country to evade arrest. An ex-MP and minister, Sir Ian Horobin, considered in the next chapter, was sent to prison for four years in 1962 for indecent assault. Among peers, Lord Beauchamp also went abroad in 1931 to avoid disgrace and imprisonment; while Lord Montagu of Beaulieu went to prison for twelve months after a trial in 1954 based on dubious evidence.

In 1939 he volunteered for military service, and became an officer in the 70th Searchlight Regiment, Royal Artillery. In June 1941, by which time he had attained the rank of acting major, his batman complained to the police that Latham had taken him to London and sexually assaulted him there; a search of his house then resulted in the discovery of letters which provided evidence of homosexual conduct with other men in his unit, as well as with several civilians. The following month, invoking a procedure last used in 1815, King George VI officially informed the House of Commons that a member who served in the Army was to face a court martial. 'I fear this means he has been getting into a mess with the soldiers', wrote Nicolson in his diary. 'I am sorry and sickened. Poor Paul, he has not had a happy life, and he will feel about his son.' Latham tried to kill himself by driving his motorcycle into a tree, but only succeeded in causing himself serious injury; at his court martial (where he was represented by the most famous barrister of the day, the former Labour Attorney-General Sir Patrick Hastings, KC), he was charged with attempted suicide in addition to thirteen homosexual offences, of which he was convicted of ten. (Among the facts produced in evidence were that he had given a cheque for £70 to a Cambridge undergraduate who had spent the night at his flat: Latham denied any wrongdoing, explaining that, out of charity, he had wanted to help the young man with his debts.) He was sentenced to two years' imprisonment (of which he served eighteen months), resigned as an MP, was divorced by his wife while in prison, and found himself in reduced financial circumstances following his release (obliging him to sell Herstmonceux Castle after the war to the Royal Observatory).

Latham's pre-war friend James Lees-Milne twice visited him in Sussex following his release from prison, writing of the encounters in his diary. The first visit took place in May 1943.

He was very thin but healthier and handsomer than I remember him. He still has a frightening look of craziness in the crimped gold hair, anthropoidal head, albino eyebrows and cold blue eyes. He talked incessantly of himself. Paul has become incredibly sentimental, yet his conversation is more depraved than anyone's I have ever heard. He is obsessed by sex and already haunts the most dangerous places, as he told me. He also enjoys repeating disobliging things said about one. He is a sadistic man. He had the grace to acknowledge Eddy [Sackville-West]'s great kindness in helping him, yet he is irritated by Eddy's devotion. I am terribly sorry for him but would pity him more if he were less wayward and less egocentric.

Three years later, in April 1946, Lees-Milne found him much improved:

Just the same in appearance, like a bounding retriever puppy, hatless, his hair still yellow, clustering and curly. Complexion slightly sunburned. He was giggly and rather endearing. We dined with his old mother. She is a dear. Paul is angelic to her. He says she has always been and always will be his best friend. He is greatly improved. Far less hysterical and more reconciled. Less sex mad. Seems to take a far saner view of life. I sat on Paul's bed until 3 a.m. out of affection and a desire to console. Paul says that no one has ever insulted him since he came out of prison, but I noticed that the people in the Eastbourne hotel stared at him.

Latham subsequently turned to religion, and attempted to atone for a reprobate life by ministering to the poor and the sick while himself dying of cancer in his late forties.

# 10

# BELISHA AND BOYLE

Although Leslie Hore-Belisha (1893–1957) and Sir Edward Boyle (1923–82) belonged to different generations – one was born exactly thirty years after the other – their political careers bore some striking similarities. They were brilliant undergraduates at Oxford, where they were both memorable Presidents of the Union, regarded by their contemporaries as future prime ministers. After working for a few years as journalists, both became MPs while still young: Belisha was thirty when he won his Plymouth seat in 1923, Boyle just twenty-seven when elected a Birmingham MP in 1950, becoming 'the Baby of the House'. Both quickly won a reputation for skilful oratory which held the attention of the chamber. They did not have to wait long for government office: after distinguishing themselves in the same job, that of Financial Secretary to the Treasury, they were both promoted to become the youngest member of the cabinet. For a time, they were household names – Belisha as a popular War Secretary when war broke out in 1939, Boyle as a reforming Education Secretary at a crossroads in British education in the 1960s – and looked as if they might reach the top. But their ambition failed; their careers fizzled out; and by the time of their quite early deaths (Belisha aged sixty-three, Boyle aged fifty-eight), they had been forgotten by the public.

In other respects they were very different. Boyle was born with a silver spoon in his mouth, whereas Belisha had to struggle to establish himself. Belisha was a Liberal who eventually became a Conservative, Boyle a Conservative who effectively ended as a Liberal.* Boyle was a man of almost obsessive probity, whereas many regarded Belisha as something of a trickster. And although they were both egocentric characters who enjoyed the sound of their own voices, Belisha frequently irritated people with his brashness, while Boyle was generally liked for his good manners. However, they possessed one distinguishing common characteristic – they were both unusually close to their mothers, who represented the great inspiration of their lives. It was their tragedy that they both lost the parent upon whom they had so depended while relatively young – Boyle was thirty-eight when his mother died, Hore-Belisha, forty-three. That had some bearing on the subsequent deflation of their careers. Boyle never married. Belisha, aged fifty, married a woman young enough to be his daughter; but the marriage, which produced no children, was not a success, and they had ceased to live together by the time of his death.

Isaac Leslie Belisha hailed from a family of Sephardic Jewish Manchester businessmen – his grandfather David Belisha had been one of the promoters of the Manchester Ship Canal in the 1880s. An only child, he lost his father before he was a year

---

* Although Boyle never formally left the Conservative Party, and used the Carlton Club as his London base until his death, he confided to friends that, having left the House of Commons, he voted Liberal at the 1970 general election. After being raised to the peerage that year, he sat in the House of Lords as a crossbencher.

old, and (to quote his biographer) 'the young widow and her infant son were to remain closely dependent on each other throughout his childhood and ... until the end of her life'. He was educated at the Jewish House at Clifton, where he excelled at debating and public speaking. When he was eighteen his mother married again: her new husband was an eminent civil servant, C. F. A. (later Sir Adair) Hore, and Leslie changed his name, dropping the 'Isaac' and prefixing his stepfather's surname to his own. (It was later said in jest that he was 'one of the Elishas of Mount Horeb':* this was not originally an antisemitic jibe, but thought up by the historian Philip Guedalla, another witty Sephardic Jew in Liberal politics.) In 1913 Hore-Belisha went up to St John's College, Oxford, his stepfather's *alma mater*, and became a leading light of the Oxford Union, where he was celebrated for his irony and repartee. He enlisted during the First World War and rose to be a major in the Royal Army Service Corps, serving in France and the Balkans and being mentioned in despatches. After the war he returned to Oxford to finish his degree, and was elected President of the Union. He had become something of an aesthete. 'In his rooms he had an abundance of purple cushions. His guests stood in the pale light of lamps mounted upon brackets of carved Venetian bronze ... He opened magnums of champagne and handed round Turkish coffee made in pots that he had brought home from Salonika.' (It was the Oxford of *Brideshead Revisited*: Evelyn Waugh came up to the university the term after Hore-Belisha went down.)

After leaving Oxford, H.-B. (as he was known to friends and colleagues) was called to the Bar but mainly earned his living as a journalist: he became a popular writer for the *Daily*

---

* Where, according to the Book of Deuteronomy, God gave Moses the Ten Commandments.

*Express* and *Evening Standard*, and befriended their proprietor Lord Beaverbrook, who was to be an important ally in his career. In 1922 he was adopted as Liberal candidate for the seat of Plymouth Devonport, which he captured from the Conservatives the following year: he held it for twenty-two years, an impressive achievement at a time when his party was in disarray. He soon made his mark in the House, though as a Liberal it seemed unlikely that he would enjoy public office. However, in 1931 H.-B. became chief organiser of the group of Liberal MPs led by Sir John Simon (later known as the National Liberals) which supported the National Government, and was appointed a junior minister at the Board of Trade. The following year he was promoted to be Financial Secretary to the Treasury, where he found favour with his boss, the Chancellor of the Exchequer Neville Chamberlain. In 1934, aged forty, he was given a department of his own as Minister of Transport, and immediately launched a campaign to reduce road accidents, which had reached alarming figures. He introduced speed limits, driving tests, the Highway Code and pedestrian crossings. He had a flair for publicity, and soon became a national celebrity: he regularly appeared on the newsreels with advice for motorists and pedestrians, while his 'Belisha beacons' were endlessly talked about, becoming the subject of jokes on the radio and the stage. The campaign worked: despite an increase in traffic, there were almost a thousand fewer deaths on the roads in 1935 than in 1934, and more than twelve thousand fewer injuries. In June 1936, having become one of the government's brightest stars, he joined the cabinet. H.-B. was a romantic admirer of King Edward VIII, by whose abdication in December 1936 he was dismayed. That same month he suffered a more personal and devastating blow with the death of his mother.

Around this time H.-B. struck up an unlikely friendship with

'Chips' Channon, who often mentions him in his diary. On first meeting H.-B. in 1935, Channon had been contemptuous – 'an oily man, an opportunist, with a Semitic flair for publicity'; '"the Jew boy", bungling and self-important' – but within a short time he was writing affectionately of 'Leslie', who became one of his favourite fellow MPs. Perhaps they were drawn to each other by the fact that they were both outsiders. In 1936 they were united by their romantic desire to 'save' King Edward. In 1938 Channon visited the house near Buckingham Palace to which H.-B. had recently moved, having spent much time and money on its refurbishment and decoration. Channon found it 'snug and luxurious, like the *boîte* of a well-kept tart ... and a touch Jewish'. (The military men summoned there also found it a touch feminine – the first thing one saw on entering was 'a bronze bambino in a niche raising its hand in greeting'.) Channon was particularly struck by H.-B.'s bedroom, which had been turned into 'a sort of *chapelle ardente* to his mother's memory. There are photographs of her taken at all times, and personal relics, as well as a striking portrait, painted of her from memory. She adored him and he worshipped her; she was the passion of his life; he only wants to succeed, he confided in me, to justify her faith in him.'

In May 1937 Chamberlain became Prime Minister and appointed H.-B. Secretary of State for War. With the prospect of another European war looming, it was urgently necessary to reform and modernise the Army, and Chamberlain felt that Hore-Belisha had the brains and drive for the job. His first achievements were impressive. He launched a successful campaign to boost recruitment, reminiscent of his earlier campaign to promote road safety: he introduced a raft of measures to improve the lot of the private soldier, and publicised these as before by regular appearances on the newsreels. He abolished some archaic practices and simplified others. He amalgamated the Cavalry with the Royal Tank Corps. He developed Britain's air defences. He inaugurated a system under which junior officers were promoted sooner and senior ones retired earlier; and he himself retired some twenty top generals (including the hidebound Chief of the General Staff, Deverell), replacing them not with the officers who considered themselves next in line, but with energetic younger men who shared his reformist views. Chamberlain seemed delighted, writing to his sister that 'my new S. of S. is doing what I put him there for and had already stirred the old dry bones up until they fairly rattle'. After Munich, which he regarded as a shameful expedient, H.-B. set about persuading a reluctant cabinet that, in the event of war, Britain needed to send a large army to France, not merely a small force as formerly envisaged, and that this would involve the reintroduction of conscription; after Hitler's seizure of what remained of Czechoslovakia in March 1939 he got his way. There was not much time or money to effect the necessary transformation; but it is to H.-B.'s credit that, by September 1939, Britain was in reasonable military shape to face hostilities.

Inevitably, these rapid changes won H.-B. many enemies. He was hated by officers who saw their privileges and traditions undermined, or who were passed over for promotion. He caused resentment among his officials by preferring the (generally excellent) advice of the war correspondent of *The Times*, Captain Basil Liddell Hart, to their own. Even among those officers whom he promoted to top positions, and who agreed with many of his reforms, he tended to be disliked. These men, who mostly belonged to guards regiments, did not take kindly to being ordered about by a former major in the RASC; they also considered that, as a politician, he interfered in operational matters which it was for the Army alone to decide. Moreover, being very English, insular and reserved, they looked askance at his flamboyance, his 'chutzpah', his love of publicity, his habitual unpunctuality, his perceived effeminacy, his 'foreign' air. Undoubtedly, some of them despised him for being Jewish. Such feelings about the Secretary of State were shared by Lord Gort (CIGS until the outbreak of war, then Commander of the British Expeditionary Force in France), Henry Pownall (Director of Military Operations at the War Office, then Gort's Chief of Staff) and Edmund Ironside (Gort's successor as CIGS, who referred to H.-B. in his diaries as 'the Jew'). They found sympathy for their views among Conservative MPs, and at court. (As a National Liberal, H.-B. had few allies in the Conservative Party; and he was out of favour at court owing to his friendship with the Duke of Windsor, having been the first cabinet minister to visit the ex-King in exile.) H.-B. made things worse for himself by his tactlessness and insensitivity; indeed, he seems to have been largely unaware of the feeling against him. Soon after the outbreak of war, a plot was hatched to get rid of him, in which the key figure seems to have been Pownall. An opportunity came in November 1939 when H.-B. visited the front in France. Knowing of his love of luxury and fine cuisine, Gort and Pownall saw to it that he endured physical discomfort and disgusting food. H.-B. accepted these privations with good humour, but on his return he expressed severe criticism of the slowness with which the BEF were fortifying their sector of the front. H.-B. had a valid point, but some of his criticisms displayed ignorance, and his strictures were represented as an unjustified attack on the competence and honour of Gort and his staff; visits to the front by the King and the Prime Minister followed, during which dislike of the minister, and the difficulty of getting on with him, were widely expressed.

Chamberlain personally liked H.-B. and believed that he had 'done more for the Army than anyone since Haldane', but dreaded finding himself in the position of Lloyd George during the First World War, at loggerheads with the generals in cir- cumstances where the King sided with the latter. On 4 January 1940 he summoned H.-B. and, with some embarrassment, explained that because of 'prejudice' against him he had decided to move him from the War Office to the Board of Trade. This came to H.-B. as a totally unexpected shock, and he chose to resign rather than accept the proposed move. When Chamber- lain expressed surprise, as H.-B. had always struck him as 'an ambitious man', H.-B. replied (as he wrote in his diary): 'My mind was centred on the War Office. My heart was there also. I had a job of work to do ... and I had hoped to see it through. My idea of ambition was fulfilling oneself and not just holding an office in the government. After my mother died I lost ambition in the ordinary sense and I had hesitated at the time whether to continue in politics or occupy myself more spiritually.' And so H.-B. left the government, and shortly afterwards resigned also as chairman of the National Liberals. He began to spend much time at Roman Catholic religious retreats (it is not clear whether he actually converted), but remained a backbench MP.

On hearing of H.-B.'s departure, Pownall wrote in his diary: 'A fine day's work for the Army and for the proper conduct of the war.' A Low cartoon showed a crowd of blimpish officers in a mess toasting a slashed portrait of H.-B. with the words: 'Gad, gentlemen, here's to our greatest victory of the war.' In fact, the man they had brought down had accurately predicted how they might lose the war. H.-B. had often voiced his concern that the Germans might break through either in the lightly fortified British sector of the front, or (as proved to be the case) in the weak northern part of the French sector; he also expressed doubts about the plan to rush into Belgium in the event of that country being invaded by the enemy. He reiterated these anxi- eties in a letter written to Chamberlain on leaving office –

though for security reasons he was unable to make any reference to such matters in his resignation statement to the House
of Commons, as a result of which his departure caused puzzlement. (The popular press assumed he had been got rid of by the
'brass hats' owing to his championship of the common soldier.)
Whether H.-B. would have been able to make a difference had
he remained in office must remain a matter of conjecture.
Certainly his successor, Oliver Stanley, a charming lightweight
(and son of Lord Derby who had held the post during the First
World War), was not the man either to make the changes
needed to avoid disaster or to impress them on the French.

One man who regarded H.-B.'s downfall as a tragedy that
almost cost Britain the war was Liddell Hart. He blamed
Churchill, H.-B.'s colleague at the Admiralty since September
1939. Churchill was the only member of the cabinet whom
Chamberlain had consulted before deciding to remove H.-B.
from the War Office; and Beaverbrook and Brendan Bracken,
who were friends of H.-B., begged Churchill to intercede for
him, but in vain. Churchill seems to have borne a grudge
against H.-B. arising from the fact that, in 1938, H.-B. had
humiliated Churchill's son-in-law, Duncan Sandys MP, before
a House of Commons select committee after Sandys had disclosed some classified information about Britain's air defences;
he may also have been jealous of H.-B.'s public popularity, which
rivalled his own. (Long after he left office, H.-B., 'the soldier's
friend', was recognised and cheered wherever he went.) In his
war memoirs, Churchill regretted not having been able to
include H.-B. in his wartime coalition, but he could surely have
found a place for him had he wished. From the backbenches,
H.-B. delivered occasional criticism on military matters, which
always made Churchill extremely angry. An astonishing fact is
that, in the middle of the war, Hore-Belisha visited Ireland in the
hope of finding evidence for the ludicrous story that Bracken

was Churchill's illegitimate son, which he apparently planned to use to discredit both men. (Although Bracken had been his friend before the war, H.-B. turned against him after Bracken had been appointed Minister of Information in 1941, one job H.-B. would dearly have loved for himself.) Only in his Caretaker Government of May–July 1945 did Churchill bring back H.-B. as Minister of National Insurance: during his ten weeks in office, H.-B. secured the passage of legislation providing for family allowances and compensation for industrial injuries. Having lost his seat at the 1945 election, H.-B. joined the Conservatives; but a vague feeling of hostility against him lingered among them, he was unable to find a safe seat, and having failed to be re-elected for a marginal one in 1950 he abandoned parliamentary politics. Britain's most famous transport minister ended up chairing the transport committee of Westminster City Council. As a belated acknowledgement of his services to the nation he was raised to the peerage in 1954 (which, Harold Macmillan noted in his diary, was not popular with Conservative backbenchers). He died of a heart attack three years later: a greedy eater, he had long been fat and unfit (Gort nicknamed him 'Beli', a reference to his girth).

During his years in office, H.-B. had three devoted assistants. On joining the government in 1931 he appointed as his parliamentary private secretary Viscount Elmley MP, son of the recently disgraced Lord Beauchamp (and former President of the Hypocrites, the Oxford dining club whose meetings usually ended in homosexual orgies), who served him in this capacity for seven years until succeeding to his father's peerage in 1938. At the War Office, Belisha appointed Major Charles Haydon to be his Military Assistant, a post which had not existed since the days of Haldane, whose duties began early in the morning when he attended upon H.-B. at home while he bathed and dressed. Haydon (who went on to

Henry 'Chips' Channon (*above*) and Alan Lennox-Boyd (*left*) enjoyed long and successful political careers while leading racy homosexual lives behind the scenes; intimate friends, they married sisters, Guinness heiresses.

Harold Nicolson (*left*), diplomatist, politician and man of letters, and Viscount Hinchingbrooke (*below*), pictured here after marrying his second wife Anne in 1962, were friends in the wartime House of Commons. They were also both homosexuals married to lesbians: Nicolson had two sons by his marriage to Vita Sackville-West, 'Hinch' no fewer than seven children by his first wife Rosemary.

Three bachelor Conservative MPs, friends of Harold Nicolson, who lost their lives in the Second World War: Victor Cazalet (*right*), pictured here with his sister Thelma, also a Tory MP; ck Macnamara (*below left*); and Ronnie Cartland (*below right*).

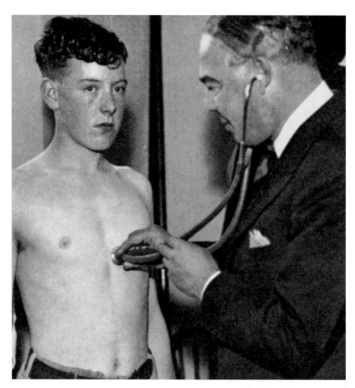

Leslie Hore-Belisha, Secretary of State for inspects a recruit, 193

Sir Edward Boyle with his admirer Margaret Roberts (later Thatcher) at a dinner of the Oxford University Conservative Association, 1947.

Enoch Powell (*right*) and
Edward Heath (*below*) were
both mother's boys from
lower-middle-class provincial
backgrounds who repressed
their homosexual feelings
in the interests of ambition;
having entered parliament in
1950, and served together in
cabinet in the early 1960s, they
became bitter rivals.

The Oxford economics don G. D. H. Cole (*above*) influenced ma[ny] undergraduates who w[ent] on to make their mark [as] Labour politicians, so[me] of whom, such as the future Foreign Secreta[ry] Tony Crosland (*left*), shared his homosexua[l] tastes.

Jeremy Thorpe (*right*), posing with his violin in 1974, and Norman St John-Stevas (*below*), xing an eight in a frivolous boat race in 1950: they were among he most stylish and charismatic liticians of their generation, but never liked each other.

'Princes of Darkness' –
Michael Portillo (*left*) and
Peter Mandelson (*below*).

become a distinguished general) always spoke affectionately of H.-B., who in turn seems to have been very fond of him: when they visited Rome in April 1938, H.-B. was almost late for an audience with Mussolini as he insisted on stopping at a jeweller's to buy Haydon an expensive cigarette case. Miss Hilde Sloane was H.-B.'s highly protective secretary. When he died, she inherited his papers, and typed out a selection from his handwritten diaries which she made available to the writer R. J. Minney, who produced a short biography concentrating on H.-B.'s years at the War Office. This selection is now preserved at Churchill College, Cambridge; the original diaries and the rest of H.-B.'s papers she seems to have destroyed.

H.-B.'s marriage in June 1944 caused surprise to his friends as they regarded him as 'a confirmed bachelor because of his undimmed devotion to his mother'. His wife, Cynthia Elliot (1916–91), was twenty-three years his junior, 'tall, dark, attractive and vivacious'. They had met before the war, during which she had been captured by the Germans while serving in France with a women's mobile canteen unit; she spent three years working as a nurse in prisoner-of-war camps before being repatriated in a prisoner exchange in 1943. She must have had private means, as Sir Robert Bruce-Lockhart, a friend of Hore-Belisha from the days when they were both on Beaverbrook's payroll, wrote that H.-B., who after leaving office had been reduced by financial necessity to writing a weekly article for the *News of the World*, ceased to be 'hard up' upon his marriage. (Bruce-Lockhart added cryptically that there was another mystery in H.-B.'s life, apart from the mystery of his resignation.) H.-B. presumably looked to his wife to provide him with the coddling and adoring attentions he had received from his mother; and she presumably became exasperated with the role, eventually leaving him, and remarrying within months of his death.

*

Unlike Hore-Belisha, Sir Edward Boyle, 3rd Baronet, was born
to wealth and privilege, though the fortunes of his family had
been quite recently established. His grandfather, the 1st
Baronet, Conservative MP for Taunton at the time of his death
in 1909, was a clever and energetic surveyor who had become
rich in the building boom of the 1880s and 90s. His son,
Edward's father, the 2nd Baronet, was by contrast languid and
unassertive; spared the necessity of earning a living, he
devoted himself to scholarly and charitable pursuits. In his forties, he married Beatrice Greig, a talented musician (she
played the cello) with a strong personality. They lived in some
style at Ockham, a beautiful Jacobean manor house in East
Sussex, and in a double house in Queen's Gate, Kensington.
Edward, born in 1923, was the eldest of three children; the
strongest influences on his upbringing were his mother and
his equally formidable paternal grandmother. He was an
unusual boy: awkward and unathletic, with a Bunteresque
shape and personality, he had learnt to read and write by the
time he was four, and soon amassed a considerable knowledge
both of literature and classical music. At his prep school, he
astonished other boys by regaling them with detailed information on subjects of which they were totally ignorant, a habit
which remained with him for the rest of his life. However, as
he talked with infectious enthusiasm, and was obviously moti-
vated not so much by a desire to show off as to share with
others the things that fascinated him, he was generally popular both there and at Eton, where he ran the political society.
After leaving school he did war work as an intelligence officer
at Bletchley Park, where his ability to handle large quantities
of information stood him in good stead.

Boyle was at Bletchley when his father died in 1945, and he
succeeded to the baronetcy at the age of twenty-one.
Henceforth his mother was the one person with whom he

enjoyed a close relationship. 'She had a proper admiration for her son's abilities', wrote Boyle's friend John Boyd-Carpenter, 'but she also maintained firm control over his domestic life.' They lived together, at Ockham and in a London flat; until she became seriously ill in the late 1950s she devoted herself to his comfort and well-being, encouraged him in his career and acted as hostess at his house parties and dinner parties. Their attachment to each other, and her coddling ministrations, ensured that he never quite grew up, and few who knew them were surprised that he remained a bachelor.

At Oxford, Boyle was admired for his knowledge and learning (though he caused surprise by only getting a third in history). Despite their differing views, he befriended the future Labour politician Tony Benn: they were considered the top undergraduate debaters of their day, served successively as President of the Union, represented Oxford in a famous debating tour of the United States, and soon after leaving the university were elected to parliament within two weeks of each other. Boyle also became chairman of the University Conservative Association, where he bowled over Margaret Roberts (later Thatcher) with his charm, sophistication and apparent omniscience: she always retained a soft spot for him (as Prime Minister, learning that he was fatally ill, she arranged for him to be made a Companion of Honour), though with the passing years their outlook diverged, Boyle being by both upbringing and temperament a 'One Nation' Conservative. Boyle was still an undergraduate when he was adopted as prospective Conservative candidate for the Birmingham seat of Perry Barr; at the general election of February 1950 he failed to dent its large Labour majority, but in November that year he successfully contested the neighbouring seat of Handsworth at a by-election after the death of its Conservative MP, holding it for the next twenty years. In the interval between his university and ministerial careers he served as assistant editor of the *National Review*, owned and edited by his Eton friend John Grigg.

In the House of Commons, Boyle soon won a reputation as a skilful (though courteous) debater, a good conversationalist and an affable colleague. After his party returned to power in October 1951 he served for two and a half years as a PPS before being appointed the youngest member of the government in July 1954 as Parliamentary Secretary to the Ministry of Supply. (Churchill told a friend that he had been reluctant to make the appointment as Boyle was younger than he himself had been on becoming a minister, but felt he had no choice but to give him a job owing to his talent and popularity.) When Eden succeeded Churchill as premier in April 1955 he was promoted to be Economic Secretary to the Treasury: the two Chancellors under whom he served, R. A. Butler and Harold Macmillan, were pleased with his work and enjoyed his company, sharing as they did his love of conversation and interest in political ideas. Then, in the autumn of 1956, came the Suez crisis, and the aborted Anglo-French invasion of Egypt. The deeply conscientious Boyle felt that Eden's policy was both foolish and dishonest, and that he could not remain a member of his administration: in the most famous action of his career, he resigned from the government. (One may compare H.-B., who in 1938 was disturbed by Munich, but chose not to resign, unlike Duff Cooper, his colleague at the Admiralty.) However, only ten weeks later his former boss Macmillan was Prime Minister, and invited Boyle to return to the front benches as junior minister at the Department of Education: Boyle found the decision to rejoin the government more difficult than that to leave it, but accepted, he told friends, because of his interest in the young. During the next two and a half years he visited most of the 146 local education authorities in England and Wales, and was responsible for drafting and presenting to the House the government's White Paper *Secondary Education for All*. After the Conservative victory in the 1959 election, he was promoted to be Financial Secretary to the Treasury, where he served with distinction under Derick Heathcoat Amory and Selwyn Lloyd.

In 1961, Boyle's mother died. During her last years she had suffered from both physical and mental illness, causing him much distraction and distress, and her passing seems to have affected him with relief as well as grief. But did it leave him rudderless? Like Hore-Belisha, he seems, at this point, to have 'lost ambition in the ordinary sense'. In July 1962, Macmillan, in his 'long knives' reshuffle, appointed Boyle to the cabinet as Education Secretary at the age of thirty-eight. The great debate taking place was of the respective merits of comprehensive and grammar schools: Boyle could not make up his mind, and left the important decisions to be made by his Labour successors. He also recommended that his ministry be amalgamated with the Department of Science, as a result of which Quintin Hogg became Secretary of State of the new Department of Education and Science and Boyle himself was demoted to the rank of Minister of State (though remaining in the cabinet). When the Conservatives lost the 1964 election, and Edward Heath became party leader, Boyle was offered other portfolios, but chose to remain Shadow Education Secretary. He and Heath had much in common – both were bachelors who had been close to their mothers; both were centrist, meritocratic politicians; both were former Presidents of the Oxford Union, and deeply interested in classical music – yet somehow they failed to get on. Boyle was disturbed by what he saw as a shift to the right in the Conservative Party, and by Enoch Powell's 'Rivers of Blood' speech of 1968; he was also worried by developments in his Birmingham constituency, where there was an influx of naturally Labour-voting Commonwealth immigrants, and the local Conservatives tended to support Powell's views. When, in 1969, he was offered the Vice-Chancellorship of Leeds University, he accepted with alacrity, surrendering the shadow education portfolio to Margaret Thatcher. The following year he gave up his seat, was raised to the peerage and took up his university post, which he held until his death from cancer in 1982. He was a popular and effective Vice-Chancellor, and able to indulge his love of music by becoming involved in the Leeds Piano Competition – though his right-wing critics noted with a touch of *Schadenfreude* that, during his first years in office, he had to cope with a nightmare of radical student unrest.

Though he had many female friends, Boyle never showed any discernible romantic interest in anyone of either sex. When once asked whether he had ever been in love, he replied that, as a boy, he had been infatuated with the violinist Jelly d'Arányi (who was some thirty years his senior, and a lesbian). He was an ardent supporter of the campaign to decriminalise homosexuality, but this should be seen in the context of his support for other liberal causes such as racial tolerance and the abolition of the death penalty. As Education Secretary, his junior minister was Christopher Chataway, the famous Olympic runner who had gone into Conservative politics: they made an odd pair – Chataway, in his early thirties, a handsome young adonis; Boyle, still only in his late thirties but looking far older, fat, stooped and shuffling – but Chataway was never conscious of any homosexual interest. The historian Michael Howard, a friend of Boyle from prep school onwards, recalls that, whenever the conversation touched upon sex, 'he fell impatiently silent until he could get it back on to a topic on which he was expert and no one else in the group was'. He was rumoured to have a fondness for choirboys – he went into ecstasies over their singing, and was indignant when music written for their treble voices was sung by female sopranos – but his feelings for them were almost certainly innocent. John Grigg wrote of his Eton schooldays: 'His rotund shape and bubbling good nature misled many . . . into assuming that he was at ease with life. In fact . . . he was a mass of nerves. His finger-nails were bitten to the quick, and he seldom sat still.' Twenty years later, Chataway also witnessed the nail-biting, but assumed that, if there were any buried sexual tensions, they were heterosexual. Like H.-B., Boyle seems to have compensated for the lack of a sex life with over-indulgence in food and drink, to the detriment of his physical health and shape.

Did these two men, who were so different yet had so much in common, ever meet? There appears to be no correspondence with Hore-Belisha among Boyle's voluminous papers in Leeds University Library; but there was one moment when they surely encountered each other. At Oxford in 1945, Boyle befriended William Rees-Mogg, future editor of *The Times* and then an aspiring politician: they were fellow young hopefuls in both the Union and the Conservative Association. As a schoolboy during the war Rees-Mogg had written a fan letter to Hore-Belisha, and subsequently got to know him: rather oddly, he believed that H.-B. was destined to rise high in the counsels of the postwar Conservative Party and possibly become Prime Minister. He invited H.-B. to Oxford, and even founded a Hore-Belisha Society there: one may assume that he introduced Boyle to his hero. And so the man of the future rubbed shoulders with the has-been, two mother-worshipping ships that passed in the night.

# 11

# WOLFENDEN BLUES

A lan Lennox-Boyd was by no means the only closet queen to serve in the Conservative administrations of 1951–64 – a period marked by unprecedented persecution of homosexuals by the police and prosecuting authorities, and by the government's refusal to give legal effect to the recommendation of the Wolfenden Report of 1957 that private, consensual homosexual acts between men over the age of twenty should cease to be criminal. Another was Harry (eventually 1st and last Viscount) Crookshank (1893–1961), a confirmed bachelor who held the key cabinet post of Leader of the House of Commons from 1952 to 1955, a period when the government had to manoeuvre carefully with a small majority. Crookshank was born in Cairo, where his father ran the Egyptian prison service. His father died while he was in his teens and he remained close to his rich American mother and his unmarried sister, with whom he lived for the rest of their lives. After education at Eton, and gallant war service in the Grenadier Guards (where the subalterns in his battalion included three fellow Etonians also destined for notable careers in Conservative politics – 'Bobbety' Cranborne, Oliver Lyttelton and Harold Macmillan), he briefly served as a diplomat before entering parliament as MP for Gainsborough, Lincolnshire, which he represented for more than thirty years. A natural rebel, Crookshank was frequently at odds with his party leaders, but was an impressive parliamentary performer and held junior office as Minister of Mines in the 1930s and as Postmaster-General during the Second World War. During the Conservatives' years of opposition from 1945 to 1951 he was one of their stars in harrying the Labour government, and although there was little love lost between him and Winston Churchill, of whose wartime premiership he had been a stern critic, Churchill on returning to power in 1951 felt obliged to appoint him to his cabinet, first as Minister for Health, then as Commons Leader. Crookshank hoped for promotion under Anthony Eden, whom he admired, and was devastated when Eden, a few months after becoming Prime Minister, sacked him from the government at the end of 1955, sending him to the House of Lords.

Possibly Crookshank's sexual reputation played a part in the sudden termination of his career, for since the late 1940s he had been close to a man half his age, Desmond Kilvington, a heavy-drinking merchant seaman from Brighton, who accompanied him on his election campaigns, moved into his house in Pont Street after his mother died in 1954, and was introduced to all and sundry as his 'cousin'. Following his retirement as MP for Gainsborough Crookshank persuaded the Conservatives of the neighbouring seat of Grimsby to adopt Kilvington as prospective candidate, but as their true relationship became apparent Kilvington was dropped by the Grimsby Conservatives before the 1959 election: it was, to quote the author of Crookshank's entry in the *DNB*, 'a time when Conservative anxieties about homosexuality in the party

were particularly acute'. (In the event, Grimsby elected another
sexually ambiguous MP – Labour's Tony Crosland.) Ailing
and bitter, Crookshank did not long survive this brush with
scandal. His fellow Grenadier Macmillan (now Prime
Minister) read the address at his funeral.

The cabinet reshuffle which dismissed Crookshank
appointed as Foreign Secretary another clandestine homosexual, Selwyn Lloyd (1904–78). The son of a Liverpool
dentist, brought up in a Methodist household, Lloyd was educated at Fettes, a tough Scottish public school, and later
practised as a barrister on his native Merseyside. After distinguished war service he was elected Conservative MP for
the Wirral in 1945. Though lacking charisma, he won a reputation for hard work, shrewdness and reliability, and when
his party returned to power in the 1950s he rapidly ascended
the ministerial ladder, becoming Foreign Secretary under
Eden, in which capacity he attended the notorious Sèvres
meeting of October 1956 at which the British, French and
Israeli governments secretly coordinated plans for seizing
back the Suez Canal after its nationalisation by Nasser. Blessed
with considerable deftness and a cool head, Lloyd managed to
survive the subsequent political and military fiasco which
ended Eden's career, and remained Foreign Secretary until
1960, when Harold Macmillan made him Chancellor of the
Exchequer. In July 1962 he was a victim of the so-called 'night
of the long knives' when Macmillan sacked one-third of his
cabinet; but only fifteen months later he returned to office as
Lord President of the Council and Leader of the House of
Commons, having played a prominent role in the manoeuvres
which led to Sir Alec Douglas-Home succeeding Macmillan
as premier in October 1963. In 1971 – unusually for an MP
who had held such high public offices – he was elected
Speaker of the House of Commons (in which position he was

succeeded in 1976 by another closet queen, Labour's George Thomas).

Although Lloyd seemed the model of dull respectability, he managed discreetly to indulge his tastes throughout his life. At Fettes, as a pretty younger boy indiscriminately offering favours to older boys, he acquired the nickname 'Jezebel' (after his initials J.S.B.L.). These activities led to a scandal, but while three senior boys were expelled, Lloyd persuaded the authorities that he was an innocent victim. During the war he established a close friendship with Lieutenant-General Miles Dempsey, who commanded the British Second Army on D-Day and whom Lloyd served as Deputy Chief of Staff. In 1951, having been appointed to his party's front bench on the eve of its return to power, Lloyd, aged forty-six, married his secretary, aged twenty-three; but though they had a daughter, the marriage broke up after a couple of years (Lloyd retaining custody of the child). As Chancellor from 1960 to 1962 Lloyd lived at Chequers, where he entertained young servicemen. He was infatuated with his handsome (and heterosexual) godson and personal assistant Jonathan Aitken (himself destined for a chequered career in politics), who had some trouble parrying his advances. He was also attracted to Peter Walker (1932–2010), a handsome youth who left school at sixteen and proceeded to make himself into a millionaire before becoming Conservative MP for Worcester in a by-election in 1961, aged twenty-nine: as Lord President he appointed Walker his PPS, the prelude to a front-bench career which would last a quarter of a century. (Walker followed Lloyd's example by marrying his secretary in 1969, on the eve of the Conservatives' return to power: Lloyd became godfather to the first of their five children and remained a family friend.) In his memoirs *Stroll On*, Tony Booth – the actor who played Alf Garnett's son-in-law in the TV sitcom *Till Death Us Do Part*, and became Tony Blair's father-in-law – describes how, one summer evening in the early 1960s, walking in the Mall by St James's Park, he received (and rejected) a sexual pass from an inebriated middle-aged man whom he at once recognised as Selwyn Lloyd; after asking for a light, the man invited him for a drink to 'a very nice place I've got above Admiralty Arch' (which was Lloyd's official residence as Lord President in 1963–4).*

That Lloyd should have taken such risks seems surprising in view of the fact that, only a few years earlier, one of his own junior ministers at the Foreign Office had found his career abruptly terminated as a result of nocturnal frolics in St James's Park. This was Ian Harvey (1914–87), who subsequently wrote a memoir, *To Fall Like Lucifer* (1971), in which he frankly discussed his homosexuality and the scandal which ended his career. Harvey was a mother's boy whose father was killed in the First World War and who greatly resented his stepfather. He became aware of his proclivities as a small boy when he found himself admiring the 'baddies' in pantomimes, while despising the boy heroes who were played by girls. At his prep school he was initiated into sex by a young Welsh master, whom his mother thanked for taking such a close interest in her son. Like Lloyd, Harvey went on to Fettes, where an older boy, the son of friends of his parents, was asked to 'look after' him. Harvey began a passionate affair with this (unidentified) boy which endured for more than a decade until the paramour was killed in action in 1940. This, Harvey writes, was the only homosexual relationship he ever had with a member of his

---

* In his memoir *Cold Cream: My Early Life and Other Mistakes* (2008), Ferdinand Mount, who worked for Lloyd in 1962–3, casts doubt on this story on the grounds that such behaviour would have been out of character (p. 248). However, Mount goes on to say that 'it is not clear whether [Lloyd] was ever gay in the active sense', whereas I am reliably informed that he was.

own class. After a successful career at Oxford, where he became President of both the Conservative Association and the Union (being succeeded in both positions by Edward Heath), and was drawn to Anglo-Catholicism, Harvey worked in advertising. As a wartime artillery officer he led a celibate life, though he formed a close platonic friendship with a fellow officer who later became, like Harvey himself, a colonel in the Territorial Army and who eventually committed suicide after being arrested for gross indecency.

After the war Harvey resumed his advertising career, and captured the seat of Harrow East for the Conservatives in 1950. He married (being under pressure to do so from his constituency association) the sister of the Labour politician Christopher Mayhew, by whom he had two daughters. By this time, Harvey, who often attended official or business dinners in central London, had got into the habit of enjoying rapid, alcohol-fuelled adventures with guardsman prostitutes in Kensington Gardens or St James's Park before returning to the family home in Richmond. He was aware of the risks he was running (especially after the Labour MP William Field, whose mother had once been housekeeper to Harvey's grandfather, was forced to resign his seat after a conviction for 'importuning' in a public lavatory), and swore to himself that each such encounter would be the last, but continued to indulge the habit even after he had been appointed a Foreign Office minister by Macmillan in January 1957. On the night of 18 November 1958, after attending a reception at the Polish Embassy and then a late vote at the House of Commons, Harvey, somewhat the worse for drink, was employing the services of a uniformed guardsman in St James's Park when both were arrested by a park warden accompanied by a police officer. Harvey made his predicament worse by trying to escape, and then giving a false name. The following morning he submitted his resignation to his boss Selwyn Lloyd (which must have been an interesting encounter between the two Fettesian closet queens). Thanks to a good barrister, Harvey and the guardsman were merely convicted of breaching park regulations and each fined £5 (Harvey insisting on paying the soldier's fine), but his Oxford contemporary Ted Heath, now Government Chief Whip, made it clear that, in view of the press exposure the episode had received, he must immediately give up his parliamentary seat (though the party arranged for him to resume his advertising career with the firm which handled its publicity). By an unhappy coincidence, his disgrace occurred only a few days before the House of Commons was due to debate the Wolfenden Report, fourteen months after its publication (though the government had resolved in any case to do nothing to implement its recommendations). Harvey subsequently fought a battle against alcoholism and depression, and his marriage broke down; but he eventually found a role for himself as chairman of the Conservative Group for Homosexual Equality.

The political careers of two other promising ministers in the Macmillan government – both of whom had served as President of the Cambridge Union – were terminated by homosexual disclosures, though both managed to avoid public disgrace. Charles Fletcher-Cooke (1914–2001) was a flamboyant wit who became one of the youngest KCs after the war and was elected Conservative MP for Darwen, Lancashire in 1951. In 1959 he married a glamorous divorcée, Diana, Lady Avebury: at the wedding reception, friends noted that the cake was made of cardboard and thought this a fitting metaphor for the marriage itself. Soon afterwards, he was appointed a junior minister at the Home Office. In February 1963 (by which time Fletcher-Cooke had separated from his wife), an eighteen-year-old borstal boy named Anthony

Turner was arrested for speeding in East London, driving Fletcher-Cooke's Austin Princess without a licence. It transpired that he had been living with Fletcher-Cooke, who explained that he had met the boy through Robin, Viscount Maugham (which, as Lady Bracknell would say, was no guarantee of respectability of character), and was 'looking after' him owing to his professional interest in the rehabilitation of delinquents. Fletcher-Cooke was obliged to resign as a minister; but he managed to hold on to his parliamentary seat, which he continued to represent until 1983, eventually being knighted for services to his party. Denzil Freeth (1924–2010), a High Anglican stockbroker, was elected MP for Basingstoke in 1955. A handsome man and a brilliant speaker, he was appointed junior science minister in 1961 (under the notoriously homophobic Lord Hailsham) and was thought to be making a success of this job when an investigation at the time of the Profumo Affair in 1963 revealed that he had been present at homosexual parties also attended by the Admiralty spy John Vassall. This information was not made public at the time (the government wanted no more scandals), but Freeth was quietly removed from office when Macmillan retired a few weeks later, and obliged to give up his seat at the 1964 general election. His career had narrowly survived an earlier incident in 1962 when he had been arrested wandering the streets naked near his flat in Pimlico – conduct which, he explained, had been due to worry over the health of his mother. (Had their careers not been cut short by scandal, it is quite possible that Harvey, Fletcher-Cooke and Freeth, all talented politicians as well as accomplished parliamentarians, would have gone on to attain cabinet rank.)

Two ministers in the Macmillan government took an interest in teenage boys. Derick ('Derry') Heathcoat Amory (1899–1981) was Lloyd's predecessor as Chancellor of the

Exchequer. Like Lloyd he came from a Nonconformist background, though his family had for several generations been rich
textile manufacturers in Devon, where they lived as gentry and
played a prominent role in local affairs. A product of Eton and
Christ Church and a confirmed bachelor, Amory served on
Devon County Council before being elected to parliament in
1945 for the local seat of Tiverton, and was a leader of scout
troops both in Tiverton and at the House of Commons. He was
a popular minister: as Secretary of State for Agriculture he abolished food rationing; and as Chancellor he presided over the
reflation which won Macmillan the 'You've Never Had It So
Good' election of 1959. He caused surprise by resigning from
the government soon after that election, ostensibly on grounds
of age (he was six years younger than the Prime Minister), and
immediately retiring from the House of Commons. A short
time earlier, Bob Edwards, a journalist on the *Daily Express* (and
soon to become its editor), had got hold of 'extraordinary details
of parties with teddy boys at Margate' attended by Heathcoat
Amory: the paper's owner, Lord Beaverbrook, refused to allow
the story to be used, but it probably cooked the minister's political goose. Ian Horobin (1899–1976), a war hero who had
shown exemplary courage as a prisoner of the Japanese, sat as
Conservative MP for Oldham East from 1951 to 1959, serving
as Parliamentary Secretary to the Minister of Power during his
last year in the House of Commons. In 1962 Macmillan recommended him for a life peerage, and his elevation had been
gazetted when Horobin suddenly withdrew his acceptance of it
owing to the fact that, in the interim, he had been charged with
indecent assault. For almost forty years, he had served as
Warden of Mansfield House University Settlement, a club for
boys and young men in the East End, where he lived in a small
flat: his work there was recognised with a knighthood in 1955,
but his homosexual tastes were common knowledge among the

boys, who were well rewarded if they agreed to satisfy his fairly innocent desires, and with some of whom he formed affectionate relationships. However, in 1961 his activities were denounced to the authorities by a clergyman, and after a trial at which he was defended by a former parliamentary colleague, the future Attorney-General Peter Rawlinson, QC,* he was sent to prison for four years. Horobin, who spent his last years in Tangier, remained unrepentant about his way of life, telling his friend the poet John Betjeman: 'I broke the law with my eyes open all my life until I went to prison. I broke it in prison. I broke it immediately I came out of prison, and I have not the slightest intention of ever paying any attention to it.'

Some mystery still surrounds Thomas ('Tam') Galbraith (1917–82). Son of the Conservative politician Lord Strathclyde, a notorious bruiser, Galbraith was himself a gentle and courteous man who, after wartime service in the navy, was elected to parliament in 1948 and served for most of the 1950s, with Ted Heath, as a government whip. He married in his fortieth year and had several children (including the present Lord Strathclyde, sometime Leader of the House of Lords in the Cameron government), though the marriage was not a happy one. From 1957 to 1959 he was a junior minister at the Admiralty, and in 1962 he came under suspicion when personal letters from him were discovered among the papers of the homosexual Admiralty clerk John Vassall who had been unmasked as a Soviet spy. It was thought odd that a minister should have communicated by post with an official of his own department; and the press hinted at possible romantic involvement, even suggesting that Galbraith might have tried to shield Vassall from exposure. Galbraith, who by this time was Undersecretary of State for Scotland, was

---

* He had also defended Montagu, Pitt-Rivers and Wildeblood at their trial at Winchester in 1954.

obliged to resign from the government while his conduct was investigated by two official inquiries. The correspondence (though it revealed that the two men had visited each other's private residences) turned out to be of an innocent and even trivial character, and Vassall later denied in his memoirs that there had been any sexual relationship, though it is possible that some unstated mutual attraction existed. The inquiries exonerated Galbraith of improper behaviour, and in 1963–4 he served again as a junior minister; but following his brush with scandal he became a heavy drinker and suffered the breakdown of his marriage and an untimely death.

Enoch Powell (1912–98) was one of the most brilliant politicians of his generation, considered by some to be more than a trifle mad. He was the only child of primary school teachers in the Black Country; like Edward Heath (who was to be his hated rival) he was a mother's boy, though his messianic fervour probably derived from his father's Welsh ancestry. He also resembled Heath in showing early promise as a musician – though Powell gave up his beloved clarinet in early youth because (as he later put it) he feared it might release passions he could not control. At Trinity College, Cambridge, where he was an outstanding classical scholar, he fell under the influence of the great classicist and poet A. E. Housman: he admired Housman's collections *A Shropshire Lad* (which was covertly homosexual) and *Last Poems* (which was overtly so), and wrote poetry in a similar style throughout his life. Powell (again like Heath) was a solitary and self-absorbed character with few social graces who shunned intimacy with his fellow human beings; but in old age he confessed to Canon Eric James, a former Trinity College Chaplain, that he had been in love with a fellow male undergraduate at Cambridge (probably Edward Curtis of Clare College), and that this infatuation had inspired love verses published in his *First Poems*. ('I love the fire/ In youthful limbs that wakes desire ... ') In 1937

Powell was appointed Professor of Greek at the University of Sydney, from where he wrote to his parents, with astonishing frankness, that he was repelled by his female students, while feeling 'an instant and instinctive affection' for Australian males between the ages of seventeen and twenty-three. This, he added, might be 'deplored, but it cannot be altered', and it therefore had to be 'endured – and (alas!) camouflaged'.

After distinguished war service (during which he rose from the ranks to become the youngest brigadier in the British Army, and established a close friendship with a comrade in arms, the couturier Hardy Amies), Powell turned to politics. His fastidious, pedantic mind led him to take some eccentric positions: having voted Labour in 1945, he then joined the Conservatives in the hope that they might prevent the British withdrawal from India, but once they had failed to do so he became the most insular of 'Little Englanders'. He was elected Conservative MP for Wolverhampton South-West in 1950 and served in the governments of Eden and Macmillan, eventually reaching the cabinet as Health Secretary in 1960, and twice renouncing office on grounds of principle. Powell was a brilliant logician, a rousing orator and a man of passionate sincerity; but he was tactless and truculent, unwilling to moderate his opinions to take account of fashionable orthodoxies or avoid giving offence. In April 1968, while Shadow Defence Secretary, he made the 'Rivers of Blood' speech warning of the perils of coloured immigration, which overnight made him both a hero to millions and a political pariah. He famously remarked that 'all political careers end in failure', and he himself failed not only to stem immigration but to achieve two other aims close to his heart – to keep Britain out of 'Europe', and to secure the integration of Northern Ireland into the United Kingdom. But he had the satisfaction of contributing to the defeat of Heath, who had taken Britain into the EEC, when he urged his large following in the country to vote Labour at the February 1974 general election. (In the leadership ballot of Conservative MPs a decade earlier, Heath had won 150 votes to Powell's 15.) Like other Tory politicians who were ambitious for office but not known for their interest in women, such as Selwyn Lloyd and Ian Harvey, Powell married around the time of his party's return to power in 1951, in his fortieth year; his wife Pamela (by whom he had two daughters) was a party worker who had campaigned for him in the recent general election. However, although this solitary and obstinate man cannot have made an ideal husband, his marriage, unlike those of Lloyd and Harvey, endured, and indeed seems to have been happy: the recently published poems which he wrote to his wife on their wedding anniversaries clearly show his love for her. Though often thought of as a black-hearted reactionary, Powell was one of the few Conservative MPs (another was Margaret Thatcher) who consistently supported giving legal effect to the Wolfenden recommendations in the decade leading up to their enactment in 1967. (As an Ulster Unionist MP in the 1980s he resisted the extension of the Wolfenden provisions to Northern Ireland, but made it clear that this was on constitutional rather than moral grounds.)

Finally it may be observed that, of three men who served as Prime Minister for all but the last year of this period – Winston Churchill (1951–5), Anthony Eden (1955–7) and Harold Macmillan (1957–63) – none was a stranger to homo-sexuality. As we have seen, Churchill was a confirmed misogynist, attracted by young men. Eden was curiously the opposite of Churchill – he was notoriously unclubbable, and preferred the company of women to men. A handsome man, he was extremely vain and narcissistic, took enormous care over his appearance, and was (like Balfour) thought to possess feminine characteristics. His wartime colleague P. J. Grigg, Secretary of State for War, regarded him as 'a poor feeble little pansy'; another colleague, 'Rab' Butler (who had chosen Chips Channon to be his PPS in 1938) described him as 'half mad baronet, half beautiful woman'. He was certainly actively homosexual as an Oxford 'aesthete' after the First World War, when his lovers included the dilettante Eddy Sackville-West (later 5th Baron Sackville), the bibliophile Eddie Gathorne-Hardy, and the artist Eardley Knollys. (Needless to say, there is no hint of this in his official biography by Robert Rhodes James [1978].) After his marriage in 1923 to Beatrice Beckett, both his romantic and social lives seem to have centred on women; but his second wife, Winston Churchill's niece Clarissa, whom he married in 1952, and who was considered rather masculine just as he was thought somewhat feminine, had many homosexual friends. (Writing to Bernard Berenson after the Suez fiasco, Hugh Trevor-Roper opined that the 'vain and foolish' Eden had been 'wholly managed' by his wife and that the homosexual photographer Cecil Beaton had been her 'Rasputin'.) As for Macmillan, it was long rumoured that, aged fifteen, he had been expelled from Eton for homosexuality – though his latest biographer D. R. Thorpe contends that it is more likely that he was removed from the school by his mother when she discovered that he was being 'used' by older boys. (He is also rumoured to have been seduced by the future theologian and detective novelist Ronald Knox, who tutored him in school holidays.) Certainly Harold's elder brother Daniel had a 'reputation' at the school, where his lovers included the future economist John Maynard Keynes. (In old age, Macmillan caused surprise when, succeeding his brother as chairman of the family publishing firm, he commissioned Skidelsky's life of Keynes which dealt frankly with the latter's homosexuality, including the dalliance with Daniel.) In adult life Macmillan, though he married Lady Dorothy Cavendish (Bob Boothby's eventual paramour) and had four children by her, was uninterested in sex, and found it puzzling that it drove men to take such risks with their careers. In the diaries of his premiership, published in 2012, he expressed sorrow and regret over the events which ended the ministerial lives of Harvey, Fletcher-Cooke and Freeth – though when, in 1963, he faced a scandal (which would prove fatally damaging to his premiership) arising from the sexual activities of the War Minister John Profumo, he wrote with relief that it was 'women this time, thank God, not boys'.

It seems unlikely that Sir Alec Douglas-Home (formerly 14th Earl of Home), who was Prime Minister between the autumns of 1963 and 1964, had homosexual leanings. However, in July 1965 Douglas-Home was succeeded as Conservative leader by the unmarried Edward Heath, who had played a significant role in the politics of the previous ten years, having served as Government Chief Whip (1955–9), Minister of Labour (1959–60), Lord Privy Seal (1960–3), President of the Board of Trade (1963–4) and Shadow Chancellor of the Exchequer (1964–5), and who must now be considered.

# 12

# TEDDY BOY

Edward 'Ted' Heath (1916–2005), leader of the Conservative Party from 1965 to 1975 and Prime Minister from 1970 to 1974, is a curious case. He was born in Broadstairs, Kent of working-class origins, which he never tried to conceal. He was not close to his father, a carpenter who eventually ran a modestly successful building firm, a jocularly vulgar man who flirted with women. But he worshipped his mother, who had a certain refinement, having once worked as a lady's maid in a country house: she lived for her 'Teddy', and pushed him to achieve great things. As a bright teenager, he was also patronised by several middle-aged gentlemen whose houses his father repaired, including Alec Martin, future chairman of Christie's, who taught him to be interested in pictures. Thanks to a determination (inculcated by his mother) to work hard and succeed, Heath was the star of his grammar school and went on to Balliol College, Oxford, where he became President of both the Union and the Conservative Association: he seems to have been popular with everyone while intimate with no one. Unlike his Oxford contemporary and future rival Harold Wilson, he was not brilliant, but an intelligent and dedicated plodder. During the war he served in the artillery, exhibiting impressive organisational skills and ending as a lieutenant-colonel. After a series of clerical jobs he was elected MP for Bexley in 1950 and spent the rest of that decade as a Conservative whip, a role to which his personality – upright, loyal, thorough, affable but aloof – was well suited. That as Government Chief Whip he managed to keep the parliamentary party together after the Suez fiasco was a considerable achievement. As a middle-ranking cabinet minister in the early 1960s he abolished two unpopular features of British life, National Service and Retail Price Maintenance. Apart from music (he was an organ scholar at Balliol, and considered a career as an orchestral conductor), he had few interests outside politics; he lived frugally in a tiny flat, spending weekends with his family in Broadstairs, saving part of his modest salary. That he possessed unusual energy, leadership qualities and ability to absorb new subjects was demonstrated when, having taken up yacht racing in his late forties in response to medical advice to exercise more, he managed to win two top international races, the Sydney–Hobart and the Admiral's Cup, within six years.

It nevertheless seems odd that the Conservatives should have chosen Heath as leader following their defeat in the 1964 election (though the only other candidates on offer, the lizard-like Reginald Maudling and the mad genius Enoch Powell, would probably have been even less suitable). He was a bachelor and a 'loner'; he lacked charisma and the common touch; apart from his piercing blue eyes, he was of unattractive appearance; his manner was gauche and his accomplishments limited (despite his enthusiasm for 'Europe' he was proficient in no foreign language). It was felt that he was the best person to present the Conservatives as a modern, centrist, meritocratic party; it was also hoped that his straightforwardness would provide a refreshing contrast to the tricky showmanship of Labour's Harold Wilson (who summed up the difference between them nicely when he remarked that 'I'm a shit and he's a cunt'). Heath lost badly to Wilson in 1966 but, to the general surprise, defeated him in 1970. His premiership was dogged by social and economic problems. The cause dearest to his heart was Britain's accession to the European Economic Community, a step regarded with indifference by the public and hostility by many in his own party: showing his usual efficiency and determination, he achieved it within three years. Though he had unusual integrity for a politician, both colleagues and voters tended to find him arrogant, awkward and aloof. ('He had learned from his mother that he was the centre of the universe', writes his official biographer Philip Ziegler, 'and the fact that he was now Prime Minister was merely the outward and visible evidence that this was indeed the case.') He was finally destroyed by union militancy after a strike by the coalminers, coming on top of an Arab oil embargo, had brought the country to a halt. After losing two elections to Wilson in 1974, Heath lost the party leadership the following year to Margaret Thatcher, who had been the only woman in his cabinet: throughout her years as Leader of the Opposition and Prime Minister he regarded her with an intense loathing which he never troubled to conceal, his rancorous behaviour ('the incredible sulk') becoming something of a national joke. When she fell from power in 1990 he refused to follow her into the House of Lords, but in 1992 became a Knight of the Garter and Father of the House of Commons (an honorific position awarded to the longest continuously serving MP).

(It is interesting that, while several sexually ambiguous men served as cabinet ministers in Conservative governments of the 1950s and 1960s, including Heath himself, it is difficult to identify any others in his own administration – with the possible

exception of Peter Walker, the former PPS and protégé of
Selwyn Lloyd who, following his marriage in 1969, aged thirty-
seven, seems to have been a devoted family man while serving
in cabinet throughout the premierships of both Heath and
Thatcher. Even among the Heath government's junior ranks,
only two figures stand out – William van Straubenzee
[1924–99] and Norman St John-Stevas [1929–2012], both bachelors who served under Margaret Thatcher at the Department
of Education. Stevas will be discussed in Chapter 16. Van
Straubenzee, who like Heath had a distinguished wartime career
in the Royal Artillery, was a prominent lay Anglican who lived
in a flat in Lambeth Palace and counted many homosexual cler-
ics among his friends. After his first election defeat in 1974,
Heath appointed him Shadow Education Secretary, but sacked
him after a few months for reasons which are unclear. Though
Walker, Stevas and van Straubenzee were all social liberals and
close to Heath politically, none of them could claim anything in
the nature of personal friendship with him.)

At first sight, Heath looks typical closet-queen material, the
mother's boy who never grows up and feels unable to love
other women. Indeed, though he made an effort to be polite
to the wives of colleagues, he exhibited a lifelong indifference
towards women which almost amounted to repugnance. Like
his hero Winston Churchill, he was notorious for ignoring the
ladies at the dinner table (even when he was host), and talking across them. Around the time he went to Oxford, a
doctor's daughter in Broadstairs, Kay Raven, fell in love with
him; his mother hoped they would marry; he saw her on visits
home and maintained a friendly if undemonstrative correspondence with her. When, after waiting fifteen years for him
to propose to her, she finally married someone else, he affected
to be devastated: he kept a photograph of her by his bedside
for the rest of his life. When he became Conservative leader,

it was hoped that he would consider marriage to one of his musical friends, such as the pianist Moura Lympany; but as soon as any name was suggested, such friendship as he had shown towards the woman in question suddenly cooled. His attitude towards Margaret Thatcher speaks for itself: it obviously wounded him to the depths that he should be supplanted by a female. 'When I look at him and he looks at me', Thatcher once remarked, 'it doesn't feel like a man looking at a woman, more like a woman looking at another woman.' When he retired from the House of Commons after more than fifty years of service, his constituency hesitated between two candidates to replace him, a 'eurosceptic' man and a woman: despite his passion for 'Europe', Heath threw his influence behind the former, who was duly selected.

However, if Heath avoided all intimacy with women, he never showed much desire for intimacy with men either. Even at Oxford, he steered clear of the close platonic relationships which were common among the male undergraduates: Ziegler quotes a letter sent by one 'Freddy', hurt that 'Teddie' had spurned his advances. Another biographer, Andrew Roth, claims that in 1939–40, while awaiting his army call-up, Heath underwent 'a disturbing experience'; but he provides no further details, and certainly during his years as a regimental officer Heath was never 'one of the lads', but an aloof figure. During his political career he was respected by colleagues, but seems to have had only two fairly close friends: Madron Seligman, a Jewish industrialist and Balliol contemporary who later became a Member of the European Parliament; and Toby Low (later Lord Aldington), a banker and junior minister in 1950s governments who became deputy chairman of the Conservative Party. Both were married with children and appear to have been thoroughly heterosexual; at least part of their attraction was that they were rich men, able to offer

lavish hospitality and financial support to the originally impe-
cunious Heath along with advice on how to build up his own
fortune. Otherwise there is no record of his forming a close
and lasting association with anyone, let alone a known homosexual or attractive younger man. (It has been suggested that
Heath was not really capable of friendship in the ordinary
sense because of his self-centredness: he talked much about
himself but rarely showed interest in the lives of others. Such
was his egocentricity that, when asked what he regarded as his
main achievement, he replied: 'Don't you think becoming
Prime Minister is sufficient?')

Apart from exhibiting no sexual weaknesses in his relations
with his fellow human beings, Heath was intolerant of such
weaknesses in others. As Chief Whip, he showed little patience
with those (such as his Oxford contemporary Ian Harvey)*
who got into trouble, and used his knowledge of the sexual
peccadilloes of MPs to keep them in line (admittedly a traditional practice of the job). As Prime Minister, he not only
sacked one minister (Lord Lambton) who had been exposed in
the press as a raffish frequenter of prostitutes, but also another
(the war hero Earl Jellicoe) who admitted to the occasional use
of call girls but had been untouched by scandal. (He did, however, following the inconclusive general election of February
1974, offer a seat in his cabinet to the Liberal leader Jeremy
Thorpe, despite knowing something of Thorpe's louche homosexual life.) Whenever homosexual law reform was debated in
the House of Commons (as happened on some half-dozen
occasions between the publication of the Wolfenden Report in
1957 and the enactment of its main recommendations in
1967), he took care to be absent – except for the debate on Lord

---

* Harvey dedicated his memoir *To Fall Like Lucifer* – published in 1971, just after
Heath came to power – 'to those in peril on the sea', apparently an elliptical reference
to Heath's homosexuality.

Arran's first bill in May 1965, when Heath, about to stand for the party leadership, voted against the reform proposals (which were narrowly defeated). Only in old age did he put his head above the parapet by supporting the lowering of the age of homosexual consent to eighteen and then sixteen.

Inevitably, Heath's unmarried state (he remains Britain's only bachelor prime minister apart from Balfour and Pitt the Younger) led to speculation about his private life. It was widely assumed among 'the chattering classes' that he was 'queer'; there was much innuendo to this effect in the satirical magazine *Private Eye*; homophobic abuse was chanted by militant trade unionists demonstrating in Downing Street against his Industrial Relations Bill. It was noted that the only hobbies he was known to pursue, as a musician and a yachtsman, tended to bring him into contact with desirable young men. It has even been claimed that there was a KGB plot to compromise him by inviting him to meet a handsome *agent provocateur* in the form of a Czech cathedral organist. Much bizarre rumour circulated: that he liked dressing up as a woman; that he was having an affair with his good-looking police detective. After his death, Brian Coleman, a gay Conservative member of the London Assembly, alleged that Heath had regularly 'cottaged' along motorways, an allegation for which no source was produced and which was received with widespread scepticism. In fact, to date, no convincing evidence has surfaced to suggest that Heath ever had a physical or even a platonic relationship with anyone. The most that can be said is that, in old age, when he became a belated supporter of homosexual law reform, he developed friendships with some attractive younger gay Conservative MPs (such as Alan Duncan and Matthew Parris) which were mildly flirtatious and skittish.

An interesting account of Heath is given in the memoirs of

the Old Harrovian nightclub owner Jeremy Norman, whose
boyfriend Derek Frost decorated Arundells, the house in the
cathedral close at Salisbury where Heath went to live in 1985.
Having never previously concerned himself with interior decoration, Heath threw himself eagerly into the task – 'the
long-buried gay designer gene expressed itself in his enthusiasm'. He showed himself in no hurry for the job to be
completed, and for years afterwards would telephone Frost
and Norman, who lived half an hour's drive away, asking them
to visit him as he wished to complain about some shortcom-
ing or suggest some improvement. 'It was as if he did not want
to let go of either the experience or the relationship which it
engendered ... We sensed that, in his own highly inhibited
way, he was reaching out to us as a gay couple.' Though Heath
evidently enjoyed their company, and they exchanged hospitality, he never dropped his guard with them (he called them
'Jeremy' and 'Derek' but never invited them to call him 'Ted'
rather than 'Sir Edward'). When they asked him why he had
failed to support homosexual law reform, he explained that he
had always been in favour of it but that 'the rank and file of the
party would never have stood for it'. At parties given by
Norman and Frost, Heath was at ease with other gay couples
but never addressed a word to Norman's old mother (which
was just as well as she was an ardent Thatcherite). On their last
visit to Arundells, about nine months before Heath's death, 'a
curious and unexplained character greeted us at the front
door, a young, educated, oriental man who seemed to be a
close friend and confidant ... he stayed on with us during our
chat'. (There is an unsubstantiated rumour that Heath, who
after his premiership developed good contacts in both Beijing
and Hong Kong, was discreetly 'supplied' with Chinese youths
in his later years; but even if this were true, it seems unlikely
that the comforts sought from them would have amounted to

much after such a long period of chastity.)

Norman concludes that Heath was 'a deeply closeted gay man' who 'decided early on in life to sublimate his sexuality to his political ambitions'. Similarly, Michael McManus, who was Heath's private secretary in the 1990s and helped him with his memoirs, writes in his *Tory Pride and Prejudice* (2011) that he was 'left in no doubt whatsoever that Heath was a gay man who had sacrificed his personal life to his political career, exercising iron self-control and living a celibate existence as he climbed the "greasy pole" of preferment'. This assessment (shared by others who knew Heath down the years) is surely correct. Thanks to the influence of his mother, the keynote of his personality was a belief that he was a man of destiny allied to tremendous will-power and a basic integrity. At the outset of his career he seems to have concluded that, if he was to realise his ambitions (particularly coming from the background that he did), any homosexual feelings would have to be rigorously suppressed; and he stuck to this policy for the rest of his life. Not a natural dissembler, he would have found it difficult to lead the double life of an active closet queen. Quite possibly he managed to persuade himself that he was above the sexual fray, even that he might have made a satisfactory husband to Kay Raven. But his true nature revealed itself through his rampant misogyny, and the significant if limited attachments of his later years. Meanwhile, in place of sex, he had the consolations of music (it was said that his piano was his only real friend), and of food and drink: a greedy gastronome, from his mid-fifties onwards he was monstrously fat. (In China, where he was often entertained by the communist leaders, it was said that he had 'the appetite of an emperor and the face of a eunuch'.)

# 13

# THE DEAR LOVE
# OF COMRADES

Did the Labour Party, with its professed belief in 'equality' and the brotherhood of man, provide a safer environment for homosexuals than the Conservative Party? Certainly there was a strain in early British socialism which preached sexual toleration and the rejection of bourgeois morals. Its outstanding figure was Edward Carpenter (1844–1929), a handsome clergyman who regularly visited Paris to consort with male prostitutes, and who resigned from holy orders in his early thirties to devote himself to radical causes. Inspired by the American poet Walt Whitman, the English 'Christian socialists' Morris and Ruskin, and Hindu mysticism, he wrote a stream of tracts advocating a wealth-sharing society, reverence for nature, and sexual freedom. He led a close-to-nature existence at Millthorpe, an estate near Sheffield where he practised market gardening with his working-class lover George Merrill, which became a place of pilgrimage for socialists and homosexuals: he believed that both categories reflected what Whitman called 'the dear love of comrades'. It is surprising that he did not get into trouble, especially after the publication of such works as *Homogenic Love* (1894) and *The Intermediate Sex* (1912); but he had a personality which commanded respect, and was careful to keep his relationship with Merrill monogamous and private.

In 1884, Carpenter was one of the founders of the Fabian Society, which had as its object 'the restructuring of society ... in such a manner as to secure the general welfare and happiness'. The Society (which exists to this day, and has generally consisted of middle-class intellectuals) played a significant role in the development of the Labour Party: it remained sympathetic to Carpenter's ideas about sexual freedom, and attracted not only those interested in heterosexual free love (such as H. G. Wells) but also the sexually ambiguous, including members of the Bloomsbury Group (and, surprisingly, Lord Rosebery in the years after his premiership). One of its leading lights was the Oxford economist G. D. H. Cole (1889–1959), founder of a movement known as 'guild socialism' which advocated the control of industry by the workers. He was a romantic homosexual, who penned the lines:

A look from thee, and thy body warm,
And the music mingling clear,
And out again to the heedless swarm
Where I may not call thee dear.

During the First World War (in which he was a conscientious objector) Cole married Margaret Postgate, a bluestocking who shared his views. They formed a successful academic partnership, and had three children; but in the biography of her husband which she wrote after his death, she admitted that he was a misogynist who never had time for any woman other than herself and only with difficulty accepted the principle of equality or even votes for women. When he was invited to contribute an entry to *Who's Who*, she had to stop him giving as his recreation '*to diaphtheirein tous neous*' (ancient Greek for 'the corruption of young men'). The Coles also wrote detective novels together, some of which (notably *Death of a Millionaire* [1925]) feature homosexual characters portrayed in a (for the time) surprisingly positive light. Though Cole was outside the mainstream of the Labour Party, he influenced several generations of Oxford undergraduates, some of whom (including the future Prime Minister Harold Wilson) went on to achieve prominence in the party; he formed close (doubtless mostly platonic) friendships with his favourite male pupils, and taught them that their socialist beliefs need not inhibit them from enjoying the good things in life. (Cole's brother-in-law and friend Raymond Postgate combined the roles of communist, detective novelist, and President of the Food and Wine Society.)

However, while the Fabians were relaxed about alternative sexual preferences, the British labour movement as a whole was deeply rooted in the fierce evangelical Christianity which also spearheaded the crackdown on homosexuality during the Victorian era. Radical reformers such as W. T. Stead and Henry Labouchere who sought to clear the streets of child prostitutes saw homosexuality as an equivalent scourge: hence the Criminal Law Amendment Act of 1885, which raised the age of (heterosexual) consent from thirteen to sixteen, incorporated the 'Labouchere Amendment' which criminalised virtually all homosexual behaviour between males as 'acts of gross indecency'. Such episodes as the Cleveland Street scandal and the trials of Oscar Wilde confirmed radical politicians – and such working-class people as read the newspapers – in the view that homosexuality was a decadent, aristocratic vice which led depraved 'gentlemen' to corrupt innocent proletarian youths.* Thus, as the Labour Party rose to be a force in the land, the chapel-going, working-class trade unionists who made up its backbone tended to be one of the most homophobic elements in the political firmament, obliging those members who were 'queer' (many of whom came from loftier backgrounds) to lead closeted lives.

Hugh Dalton (1887–1962), who occupied a series of senior cabinet positions from 1940 to 1951, might be described as a hereditary closet queen. His father John Dalton (1839–1931) was the clergyman to whom Queen Victoria entrusted the education of her grandsons, the future Duke of Clarence and King George V; he also happened to be a close friend of Edward Carpenter, to whom, amazingly, the job of tutor to the royal princes seems originally to have been offered. In his mid-forties John married the sister of a midshipman to whom he had taken a fancy on HMS *Bacchante*, the training ship on which the princes, accompanied by their tutor, sailed round the world in the 1870s. For almost half a century he was a Canon of Windsor, known at court as a sinister intriguer: when he died, Hugh found his papers to be full of correspondence with young men in which 'a strong homosexual strain is clear'. Hugh's godfather was the ill-fated and bisexual Clarence, though he rebelled against his court background and came to regard royalty with contempt, a feeling which was thoroughly reciprocated (in a rare exercise of his prerogative, George VI prevented him becoming Foreign Secretary in 1945). Though brought up to revere Victorian ideals of healthy young manhood, Dalton himself was a sickly, unattractive and somewhat charmless boy; at Eton, it was his envy of the handsome, muscular and dashing contemporaries destined to form

---

* During the debate on the 1967 bill, the Labour MP James Wellbeloved expressed the view that all 'queers' were 'toffs' and that there was no such thing as a working-class homosexual.

the future ruling class which drove him towards radical politics, as well as confirming his homosexual tastes. At Cambridge, where his mentors included two famous (though celibate) homosexual dons, Arthur Benson (who had been his father's best man) and Goldworthy Lowes Dickinson, he joined the University Fabian Society and fell madly in love with another of its members, Rupert Brooke. His undergraduate flirtations seem to have strayed beyond the purely platonic: he and Brooke went on hikes during which they slept naked under the stars; and at a Fabian summer school in Wales in 1908, Dalton (known to other young Fabians as 'Daddy') made advances to James Strachey, 'waving an *immense* steaming penis in his face and chuckling softly' (as Brooke wrote to James's brother Lytton). Dalton, along with John Maynard Keynes, was invited by Lowes Dickinson to discuss homosexuality with Dr Magnus Hirschfeld when the pioneering German 'sexologist' visited Cambridge in 1910. Stirred by male camaraderie, Dalton fought gallantly in Italy during the First World War. Afterwards he became one of the leading men in the Labour Party, combining his political career with teaching at the London School of Economics. His idealism was tempered by patriotism and pragmatism: he was always sceptical about Soviet communism, and was one of the first senior Labour figures to accept that Britain needed to rearm to face Hitler. During the Second World War he served as Minister for Economic Warfare (which included running the sabotage organisation SOE) and President of the Board of Trade. In the postwar Labour government he became Chancellor of the Exchequer, and was at one moment thought of as a possible alternative to Attlee as Prime Minister. In November 1947 he was forced to resign owing to a budget leak, but he returned to the cabinet within a year, ending his ministerial career as Minister of Local Government and Planning.

Dalton's formidable wife Ruth, whom he married just before the outbreak of war in 1914, shared his political beliefs and was an ally in his career; but although they had one daughter (who died in childhood), his romantic interest remained fixed on his own sex. His homosexuality expressed itself through his close fatherly interest in the careers of various young male socialists. (It is unlikely that he went to bed with any of them, though he was much given to hugging and embracing.) Three of his protégés became leading figures in party and government: Hugh Gaitskell (1906–63), Richard Crossman (1907–74) and Tony Crosland (1918–77). Gaitskell was Chancellor of the Exchequer under Attlee in 1950–1, and succeeded Attlee as party leader from 1955 until his early death. Crossman, one of the party's foremost intellectuals, held various cabinet posts under Harold Wilson, and achieved posthumous fame through his indiscreet diaries which revealed the workings of government. The brilliant and abrasive Crosland also served under Wilson, and was Foreign Secretary under Callaghan at the time of his sudden death. All three (who in youth were noted for their good looks) had been greatly assisted in their rise by Dalton, who during the war employed Crossman in SOE and Gaitskell as his private secretary at the Board of Trade, and who helped Crosland find a winnable seat at the 1950 election. And all three had been to Oxford, where they were influenced by G. D. H. Cole and enjoyed homosexual experiences.* Gaitskell was a flamboyant aesthete, whose youthful *amours* included John Betjeman and (in 1930s Vienna) the American writer John Gunter. Crossman was a friend of W. H. Auden, and in an early diary describes an Easter holiday with another young poet 'who

---

* Gaitskell and Crossman, though never close friends, were contemporaries at both Winchester and New College.

kept me in a little whitewashed room for a fortnight as his mouth was against mine and we were completely together'. The dashing Crosland was an eager seducer of his male contemporaries, and had what he later described as 'an exceedingly close and intense friendship' with his fellow socialist undergraduate and future cabinet colleague Roy Jenkins – to be considered in the next chapter.

Of the three, Crossman went on to become resolutely heterosexual, while both Gaitskell and Crosland carried a strong whiff of bisexuality into their later lives. Ann Fleming (Gaitskell's lover) wrote to Evelyn Waugh of a dinner party in 1958 at which Gaitskell and friends from Oxford days 'held hands and recited verse because in early life they had loved each other in the same set' – until the arrival of her husband Ian 'silenced the eminent "homos"' who 'did not seem too pleased'. Crosland exercised his charms on both Dalton and Gaitskell in order to advance his career: the heterosexual Woodrow Wyatt, who knew them all, wrote that 'there was a scintilla of platonic homosexuality in [Gaitskell's] affection for Tony' and that 'Hugh Dalton ... was in love with Tony and as his literary executor Tony had the odd task of dealing with the emotional letters Dalton wrote him'. As Dalton wrote in 1951: 'Thinking of Tony, with all his youth and beauty and gaiety and charm ... I weep. I am more fond of that young man than I can put into words.' Dalton's lovesickness for Crosland (as described in the memoirs of the socialist banker Nicholas Davenport) became an embarrassing joke in the Labour Party: Crosland, while taking advantage of Dalton's patronage, responded coolly, which only seemed to fill Dalton with masochistic delight. It nevertheless seems likely that Crosland himself (whose first marriage was a disaster and whose second produced no children) continued to have homosexual feelings which he repressed in the interests of ambition.

In parliamentary votes, Gaitskell, Crossman and most others of their background supported the Wolfenden recommendations: although Gaitskell did not live to see their enactment in 1967, his widow Dora, as a life peer in the House of Lords, was particularly active in the cause of homosexual law reform. On the other hand, a man such as George Brown, Labour's bibulous Deputy Leader and Foreign Secretary, a politician of working-class origin who had not been to university, was violently opposed to the decriminalisation of homosexuality – 'this is how Rome fell!', he thundered to Barbara Castle. When in November 1962, at the time of the Vassall affair, Brown launched a tirade in the House of Commons hinting at queer goings-on in high places, frontbench colleagues such as Crossman squirmed with embarrassment. While it is significant that Wolfenden became law under a Labour and not a Conservative government – as a higher proportion of Labour MPs were willing to support it, and the Labour Home Secretaries Soskice and Jenkins took a more enlightened view than their Conservative predecessors – most Labour voters would probably have agreed with Brown.[*]

As Carpenter's example shows, homosexuality and left-wing politics were often combined in the outlook of those who rejected Victorian values and sought to overcome class barriers. Whereas Dalton in Edwardian times managed to scandalise his father's royal employers merely by becoming a Fabian socialist, by the 1930s the Labour Party's championship of traditional family life meant that such 'rebels' had to move further to the left to express their sense of rejection: hence the Marxist affiliations of such homosexuals as the 'Cambridge

---

[*] However, there were rumours that Brown was himself homosexual, which were believed by the knowledgeable civil servant Sir Freddie Warren (Private Secretary to the Chief Whip, 1958–79). Despite his opposition to the 1967 bill, he absented himself from both the debates and the votes.

spies' Burgess and Blunt, the poet Auden, the composer Tippett, and Tom Driberg. One young rebel of the 1920s who found that active membership of the Labour Party, coupled with a homosexual lifestyle, was quite enough to shock his parents' generation was Oliver Baldwin (1899–1958), eldest son of Stanley Baldwin, who was Conservative Prime Minister three times between 1923 and 1937 and the leading British statesman of the period. After gallant service in the First World War, Baldwin spent several adventurous years knocking around Algeria, Egypt and Armenia, working for the secret service and enjoying the delights (including homosexuality) which those lands had to offer. Returning to England on the eve of his father's first premiership, he joined the Labour Party – a step which certainly involved an element of defiance against his rich (though enlightened) family, as the mild conservatism of his father could have accommodated his social conscience, and he loathed communism as a result of his experiences in Armenia, where he had been imprisoned by the Bolsheviks and witnessed the appalling atrocities they had inflicted on the local populace. He continued to live off a comfortable private income, and winter luxuriously in Algeria. As Labour MP for Dudley from 1929 to 1931 he admired the handsome patrician radical Sir Oswald Mosley, whom he was almost tempted to follow when Mosley resigned from the Labour government to found his 'New Party'. Baldwin maintained good personal relations with his father despite their political differences; but his mother, to whom he had been close in childhood, was deeply hurt – she ceased to visit the Commons gallery as she could not bear to see her husband and son sitting on opposite sides of the House. Meanwhile Baldwin had settled down to an enduring homosexual 'marriage' with an aristocratic charmer named Johnnie Boyle: they lived on a farm in Oxfordshire owned by Johnnie's brother-in-law Lord Macclesfield, where they employed good-looking male staff, and held weekend parties attended by like-minded friends such as Harold Nicolson and Beverley Nichols. His family seem to have been surprisingly accepting of this domestic set-up – except for his father's first cousin Rudyard Kipling, to whom he had formerly been close, but who was so shocked to learn of Baldwin's 'beastliness' that he broke off all further contact. When his father received an earldom on his retirement from the premiership in 1937, Oliver happily assumed his courtesy title; and when he was again elected to parliament in the Labour landslide of 1945 it was as Viscount Corvedale MP. Though he had a distinguished reputation as a journalist, the fact that he was known to be cohabiting with another man precluded him from office in either the 1929 or the 1945 Labour governments, and during the Second World War confined him to low-grade intelligence work in the Middle East. However, when his father died in 1947, and Oliver succeeded to the earldom, he was appointed to the vacant governorship of the Leeward Islands, a colony consisting of six sugar islands in the Caribbean with a population of 120,000. He sailed out to his post accompanied by a homosexual private secretary and a handsome cook-valet from the Oxfordshire farm, followed soon afterwards by his lover Johnnie. The 2nd Earl began his governorship with good intentions; but his championship of the downtrodden blacks against the white sugar planters, coupled with 'the strange and unnatural happenings at Government House' (substantiated, in Colonial Office eyes, by complaints from naval captains whose crews had been whisked off by the governor for nude bathing sessions), soon led to demands for his recall. Retired after two years in office, Baldwin retreated with Johnnie to their pleasant life in the country, where he took to the bottle and died aged fifty-nine. (Although almost all who knew

Oliver and Johnnie were aware of their relationship, they still had to exercise prudence, writing letters in code language and vetting those they admitted to their household: it is unlikely that the nude-bathing sailors in Antigua were treated to much more than admiring looks.)

Another upper-class homosexual who was driven towards left-wing politics by a desire to shock his respectable family was Gavin Henderson, 2nd Baron Faringdon (1902–77), whose grandfather the 1st Baron had made a fortune in rail-way finance in late Victorian times and set himself up as a country gentleman at Buscot Park, Oxfordshire. After Eton, Henderson was prominent among the 'Brideshead generation' at Oxford* and the 'bright young people' in London; he threw wild parties, used his wealth to finance a lavish lifestyle for himself and his friends, and was unrestrained in his pursuit of working-class youths. His worried family arranged for him to marry Honor Philipps, daughter of the shipping magnate Lord Kyslant. On the day the marriage was announced in November 1926, Henderson fled to Australia, where he remained for four months; when finally persuaded to return, he went on an alcoholic rampage, smashing up a nightclub and throwing a stag party at Henley at which his friends set the Thames alight with twenty gallons of petrol; at his wed-ding, he caused consternation by including Florence Mills's troupe of black girls among the guests, before abandoning his wife to spend the night with a sailor. The marriage lasted only a few weeks, and was formally annulled in 1931. (Honor went on to find another homosexual husband.) On inheriting his grandfather's title, estate and fortune in 1934, the new Lord

* Evelyn Waugh satirised him in *Vile Bodies* (1930) as the rakish Lord Parakeet, 'birdlike and gay, making rude little jokes in a shrill, emasculate voice' – originally called 'Kevin Saunderson' until the publishers insisted he change the name to something less resembling the inspiration.

Faringdon became a welcome recruit to the Labour Party's meagre caucus in the House of Lords. He filled Buscot with radical politicians, and republican refugees from the Spanish Civil War: staying there, Beverley Nichols marvelled at the spectacle of 'Gavin, still very much the lord of the manor, still very much a connoisseur of good claret ... playing host to people whose main object in life ... is to strangle lords of the manor in the last ditch'. In 1939 he registered as a conscientious objector, and enlisted as a fireman (he seems to have had a penchant for firemen, later serving as parliamentary spokesman for the National Association of Fire Officers). In 1942, Hugh Dalton described him as 'a pansy pacifist of whose tendencies it might be slander to speak' (Dalton disapproved of the pacifism, but may have felt a pang of envy at the sexual self-indulgence). Owing to his reputation, there was no question of Faringdon holding office in postwar Labour governments; but he nevertheless became a substantial figure in the Labour Party, being elected to its National Executive and to the London County Council, becoming chairman of the Fabian Society, and hosting party gatherings at Buscot. Like his friend Tom Driberg, Faringdon was an inveterate supporter of radical causes – which did not stop him 'living like a lord', with his two palatial country houses (he inherited another from his mother) and his green Rolls-Royce. Opinions about him varied: some thought him funny, generous and kind; while James Lees-Milne, who knew him as a party-goer in the early 1930s and later in connection with his donation of Buscot to the National Trust, found him sinister with his 'lithe, panther movements', 'cat-like eyes' and 'dangerous, evil and malevolent' personality.

Among the MPs elected to parliament in the 'Labour landslide' of 1945 were two confirmed bachelors, Thomas Skeffington-Lodge (1905–94) and William Field (1909–2002).

The flamboyant and haughty Skeffington-Lodge was MP for
Bedford from 1945 to 1950. Like Faringdon and Driberg (both
close friends), he was a 'champagne socialist' on the left of the
party: he came from an old landowning family in Yorkshire,
connected with the Cabot Lodges of Boston, Massachusetts.
Having been narrowly defeated at Bedford in 1950 by Winston
Churchill's son-in-law Christopher Soames, he hoped to enter
the House of Lords; having failed to revive a defunct peerage
to which he believed himself entitled, he tried to get a new one
from the Labour Party, but was given short shrift by Attlee,
who both knew of his homosexual reputation and had been
annoyed by his left-wing pronouncements. He stood as a
Labour candidate in elections for the next twenty years (in
1955 he opposed Alan Lennox-Boyd in Mid-Bedfordshire)
but never succeeded in getting re-elected, though like
Faringdon he became a prominent Fabian. As a resident of
Brighton, he was a well-known and somewhat outrageous
figure in the gay life of that city; in 1970 he spitefully issued a
libel writ against his neighbour, the novelist Francis King,
whose latest work, *A Domestic Animal*, had mildly satirised his
political and social pretensions in the character of Dame
Winifred Harcourt: the action, though settled, ruined King
(who later avenged himself by writing another novel, *The
Action*, based on the episode). Skeffington-Lodge owned a
hotel near the Vauxhall works in Luton, where he was
rumoured to offer free accommodation to lorry drivers in
return for their favours: when he stood for parliament for the
last time, at the Brighton Pavilion by-election of 1969 (caused
by the retirement of the homosexual Conservative MP Sir
William Teeling, mentioned in Chapter 9), his successful Tory
opponent Julian Amery hinted at this rumour by describing
him as 'the bed-and-breakfast candidate'. Field, a solicitor's son
who had seen wartime service in the Intelligence Corps,

became leader of Hammersmith Council in 1945 and the following year entered the House of Commons at a by-election in Paddington North, former seat of Brendan Bracken. A popular parliamentarian, he was appointed PPS to John Strachey, a junior minister at the War Office, and seen as a future frontbencher. But in 1953 he was arrested, charged, convicted and fined for 'importuning' in a London public lavatory. Field defended himself vigorously and appealed against his conviction, being represented at the appeal by his friend John Maude, QC, a former Conservative MP. When the conviction was upheld, Field promptly resigned his seat and disappeared from view, burying himself in deepest Dorset, where he devoted himself to a study of Egyptology.

Middle-class socialist homosexuals such as Cole and Dalton, while behaving with discretion, were fairly relaxed about their preferences, which they made little attempt to conceal from their friends; while a flamboyant upper-class queen such as Faringdon (who was known to preface his parliamentary speeches 'My dears' rather than 'My lords') positively advertised those preferences. It was quite otherwise with a man of working-class background such as George Thomas (1909–97), who lived in terror of the exposure of his guilty secret. The son of an alcoholic Welsh coalminer who abandoned the family during the First World War, he was brought up by his formidable mother with whom (as with so many closet queens) he had a relationship of reciprocal worship and with whom he lived up to her death in 1972. Thomas, who was blessed with handsome looks and a beautiful voice, became a schoolteacher and an official of the National Union of Teachers; he was also an ardent Methodist and rose high in the counsels of that denomination. Elected to parliament for a Cardiff constituency, he served in Harold Wilson's 1960s Labour government, finally reaching the cabinet as Secretary of State for Wales. (As a junior Home Office minister in 1965 he cautiously tried to help the Liberal MP Jeremy Thorpe out of problems he was experiencing as a result of his homosexual life; when, thirty years later, the present writer, then working on a biography of Thorpe, tried to ask him about this, Thomas reacted with anger and alarm.) From 1976 to 1983 Thomas served as Speaker of the House of Commons (succeeding another closet queen, Selwyn Lloyd), in which role he became a national celebrity; to the disgust of former Labour colleagues, he was seduced by the grandeur of his position, and became a great sucker-up to royalty and admirer of Margaret Thatcher (who expressed her appreciation by having the heirless Thomas created a hereditary peer on his retirement, as Viscount Tonypandy). Though twice engaged to be married, Thomas was compulsively homosexual; his sexual encounters, usually taking place anonymously in locations such as cinemas, were numerous, furtive and guilt-ridden – though his proclivities were no great secret at Westminster, where he showed a more than fatherly interest in various young MPs and parliamentary employees. (In 2014 it was suggested that he had also had inappropriate contact with boys in care homes in his constituency.) His homosexuality was exposed after his death by his friend and confidant Leo Abse, another Welsh Labour MP (who was himself bisexual, and instrumental in bringing about the reform of the law). Abse wrote that, while Thomas was a tough politician who showed complete fearlessness in dealing, for example, with his Welsh Nationalist opponents, he would 'dangerously over-react and panic if there was the slightest sign of a crack in the thin ice upon which he skated all his life ... The slightest tremor of scandal ... reduced him to a jelly.' Abse helped Thomas out of blackmail situations in both Cardiff and London, and was consulted by Thomas when the latter, soon after retiring from

the speakership, discovered to his horror that he had contracted a venereal disease from a rent boy (Abse advised him
to plead 'problems with the waterworks'). Abse explained that
he had decided to 'reveal' Thomas's homosexuality 'because I
believe that the gifts he gave to the nation fundamentally arose
because of, not despite, his sexual orientation', that he brought
'a feminine sensibility and empathy' to political life.

Homosexuality may provide the key to the mysterious dis-
appearance of an Edwardian socialist politician of proletarian
background, Victor Grayson. Born in 1880, Grayson was
brought up in a working-class family in Liverpool – though
the fact that they lived unusually well for their station, coupled
with an irregularity in his birth certificate, suggests that he
may have been the illegitimate son of a wealthy person. After
leaving school he worked as a mechanic, and later trained to
be a Unitarian minister, but abandoned his studies to devote
himself to socialist politics. In 1907 he stood as the
Independent Labour Party candidate at a by-election in the
Yorkshire industrial constituency of Colne Valley and was
elected, aged twenty-six, with a majority of 153. During his
two and a half years in the House of Commons he built up a
reputation as a fiery platform speaker (he has been described
as 'the greatest mob orator of his generation') and a radical
journalist (he became political editor of the socialist weekly
*The Clarion*). After losing his seat in 1910 he quarrelled with
the mainstream Labour Party and in 1912 was one of the
founders of the British Socialist Party (which in 1920 would
transform itself into the British Communist Party). However,
in 1914 he shocked socialist colleagues by his uncompromising support of the war against Germany. Owing to ill-health
(probably brought on by heavy drinking) he did not immediately enlist, but embarked on a speaking tour of Australia
and New Zealand to promote recruitment: he finally joined a

New Zealand regiment in 1916 and was 'invalided out' the following year after fighting on the Western Front. Grayson was attractive to women, and in 1912 married Ruth Nightingale, a young actress of boyish appearance: they had one daughter, but the marriage was not happy, and she died in the influenza epidemic of 1918. Friends and colleagues were aware, however, of his homosexual preferences, which were confirmed by the discovery in the 1980s of love letters written to Harry Dawson, a fellow Merseyside socialist with whom he had an affair lasting some years. (Were they, one wonders, acquainted with Edward Carpenter?) After the war Grayson, who had previously led a hand-to-mouth existence, suddenly became prosperous, living in a smart flat in St James's and spending money freely. This transformation in his fortunes appears to have owed something to his acquaintance with Maundy Gregory, a homosexual conman who became Lloyd George's principal agent in the sale of honours – though it is not clear whether Grayson was involved with Gregory in his shady activities, or was blackmailing him. One day in September 1920 he was visited by two men with whom he left in a car, taking luggage. He was never officially heard of again. A book published in 1970 suggests that he was murdered by Gregory, but another published in 1985 (by another former Labour MP for Colne Valley) argues persuasively that he disappeared voluntarily, and was still alive in London in 1948. (As Noel Annan writes, life held such terrors for 'compromised' homosexuals that they often sought to remove themselves from the world in one way or another. 'Lewis Harcourt took an overdose, Victor Grayson disappeared, and Lord Beauchamp fled into exile . . . ')

# 14

# TONY AND ROY

Anthony ('Tony') Crosland (1918–77) and Roy Jenkins (1920–2003) became close friends as Oxford undergraduates in the autumn of 1939, soon after the outbreak of war. They were both clever, personable young men filled with socialist idealism, who hoped to make their mark in left-wing university politics as a prelude to successful political careers on the national stage. In terms of background, personality and outlook, however, they were very different. The public-school-educated Crosland was an upper-middle-class product, the son of a senior civil servant. He knew almost nothing about the working class whose interests he purported to champion – and when, less than a year later, he encountered members of it during his military service, he found that he did not like them much. The grammar-school-educated Jenkins was the only child of a South Wales miner who, through his own efforts, had acquired a good education, risen through the trade union movement, and been elected Labour MP for Pontypool in 1935. Though the family's roots were proletarian, they had become local bigwigs, lived well, and had great ambitions for

their son.* Whereas Jenkins's parents were tolerant and unfa-
natical when it came to both politics and religion, Crosland's
had belonged to a fundamentalist puritan sect, the Exclusive
Brethren: this may partly explain the fact that, while Jenkins
was always moderate in his views and measured in their
expression, Crosland tended to take up uncompromising positions and defend them fiercely. Thus, at the time they met,
Crosland was a supporter of Stalin's Russia, while Jenkins, like
his father, was wedded to the principles of democratic socialism. Intellectually, Crosland was by far the more brilliant –
though Jenkins possessed a good mind, along with a streak of
Welsh guile. Jenkins was by nature phlegmatic, Crosland
volatile and temperamental. Whereas Jenkins was shy and
courteous, Crosland was arrogant and abrasive. Both were
fond of alcohol; but while Jenkins cultivated an appreciation
of fine wines, Crosland was given to drunken debauches.
Jenkins took a romantic view of the past, and loved the historic fabric and traditions of Oxford; Crosland did not allow
his thoughts to be affected by such sentimental considerations.

Crosland was the older by more than two years, so that he
was starting his second year at Trinity College when Jenkins
arrived in 1938 at Balliol next door. (They were well-suited to
their respective colleges, the traditional ethos of Balliol being
industrious and high-minded, that of Trinity, patrician and
devil-may-care.) The handsome and self-assured Crosland
was already a glamorous figure on the undergraduate scene,
who dressed stylishly and raced around in a red sports car.

---

* Notwithstanding (and probably in reaction against) their respective social backgrounds, both Crosland and Jenkins came to affect aristocratic speech
mannerisms, a habit which Jenkins may have copied from Crosland. These affec-
tations were later mocked by their colleague Richard Crossman, who as the son
of a high court judge, a third-generation Wykehamist and a descendant of the
Plantagenets through the Danvers family considered himself to be of a higher
social class to them both.

Jenkins, the grammar-school boy from the provinces, was dazzled by him: though he often saw him at meetings of the University Labour Club, for a year he worshipped him from afar. Then, one evening in the autumn of 1939, Crosland called on Jenkins to discuss some Labour Club business, and stayed on. 'Thereafter', writes Jenkins in his memoirs, 'we saw each other nearly every day until he left for the army in the summer of 1940.' As an undergraduate, Crosland was actively homosexual; and at the outset their relationship certainly included a sensual element. As Jenkins's biographer John Campbell puts it: 'Roy was not by nature gay ... but it is clear that he fell for a time so wholly under Crosland's spell that he might have tried anything.' Crosland later wrote to Jenkins's mother that, during the first seven months of 1940, the two of them had enjoyed 'an exceedingly close & intense friendship of a kind that neither of us are ever likely to experience again. We used to spend practically the whole day together ... in complete mutual absorption and (as I then thought) complete mutual loyalty. The proof of our friendship is that during the whole period neither of us had any relations with members of the other sex – we were each too wrapped up in our interwoven lives.' Their surviving correspondence for those months not only testifies to the loving nature of the relationship, but highlights their difference in personality. Crosland's letters to his 'pansy Beau Geste' (as he refers to Jenkins in one of them) are racy and teasing, as well as patronising – he was clearly the dominant partner; Jenkins writes guardedly and conventionally, already showing the bland elegance of style for which he would become known.

During university vacations, Crosland went to stay with Jenkins at his family home in Pontypool. He was touched by the warmth of the welcome he received from Jenkins's parents; indeed, as he had lost his own father and was not close to his mother, he began to see them as substitute parents for himself. His letter to Mrs Jenkins quoted above (written in 1942 by way of explaining that his friendship with Roy was not what it had been) shows that she became his confidante. He also had long talks about socialism with Arthur Jenkins, MP, who eventually persuaded him to drop his support for Soviet Russia and embrace the democratic socialist cause. As a result, both Crosland and Jenkins left the communist-dominated university Labour Club in April 1940 to found a new Democratic Socialist Club. This proved a great success: most other Labour Club members followed them into the new society, which the Labour Party also recognised as its affiliate. Crosland and Jenkins served successively as its Chairman; its President (as well as its first speaker) was G. D. H. Cole, who taught them both economics.* (Crosland was greatly influenced by Cole's teachings and writings; Jenkins was more sceptical, judging by the remark in his memoirs that Cole managed to write the same book over and over again, achieving huge sales each time.)

In his memoirs, Jenkins states that his friendship with Crosland was 'the most exciting' of his life. It seems to have been his only amorous friendship with another man. In August 1940, when Crosland left to begin his military training, Jenkins attended the annual Fabian Summer School at Dartington Hall in Devon. There he met Jennifer Morris, an undergraduate from Girton College, Cambridge and daughter of the Town Clerk of Westminster. They fell in love and began a serious affair. When he learnt of the relationship (not from Jenkins but another source), Crosland (as he later confessed to Jenkins's mother) was 'jealous and bitter'. Jenkins

* As part of their course in Philosophy, Politics and Economics: Jenkins had gone up to Oxford to take this course; Crosland, who originally read Classics, switched to it in his third year.

tried to reassure him that he still looked on him as his dearest friend, and for the next two years they continued to meet fairly frequently (sometimes, rather uncomfortably, with Jennifer); but (to quote again from Crosland's confessional letter to Mrs Jenkins), 'from being David and Jonathan'* they were now just 'two normal people on conventionally friendly terms'. In 1943 they were separated, Crosland going to fight as a paratrooper in North Africa, Jenkins to work as a code-breaker at Bletchley Park. In January 1945, Roy married Jennifer. After the war, Crosland returned to Oxford to finish his degree, and was elected President of the Oxford Union (it was one of the great disappointments of Jenkins's life that he had narrowly failed to achieve this honour in 1940-1). The battle-hardened Crosland was now bisexual, but his interest in women seems to have been purely carnal – he still reserved his romantic feelings for men. His first marriage in 1952, to the vinegar heiress Hilary Sarson, was a disaster, his wife leaving him after suffering a few months' cruelty and neglect. Although his second marriage in 1964 to the American journalist Susan Barnes seems to have been happy and successful, friends suspected that he continued to have homosexual feelings which he repressed, fearing they would get in the way of his political advancement, and that this partly accounted for what Jenkins, in the entry on Crosland which he eventually wrote for the *Dictionary of National Biography*, called his 'uncontrolled demon of discontent'. (It is interesting that Crosland did not participate in any of the votes on the Sexual Offences Bill which slowly made its way through parliament in 1966-7 and finally gave effect to the Wolfenden recommendations.) There can be no doubt of Jenkins's keen and exclusive interest in women: while happily married to Jennifer,

---

* Whose love 'was wonderful, passing the love of women' (2 Samuel 1:26).

by whom he had three children (Crosland had none), he also had affairs with Leslie Bonham Carter, wife of a prominent Liberal, and Caroline Gilmour, wife of a prominent Conservative. (Jennifer does not seem to have minded particularly, nor did the husbands of the two mistresses who remained Jenkins's good friends.)

As ambitious young socialists seeking to get into parliament and then into office, Crosland and Jenkins were rivals – though in the early days their rivalry was perfectly amicable. Jenkins won the first round when a by-election in April 1948 took him to Westminster as 'the Baby of the House'; Crosland had to wait until the general election of February 1950 before being returned for South Gloucestershire, a seat found for him by his admirer Hugh Dalton. Both hoped for junior office in the Attlee government; their hopes were raised in April 1951 when their friend John Freeman resigned as junior war minister, but the vacancy was filled by another young hopeful, Woodrow Wyatt. Together with Freeman, Wyatt and Tom Driberg, Jenkins and Crosland formed a secret canasta school in the Westminster precincts: the other four were much amused by Driberg's rackety homosexuality (he assured them that he was an expert at bribing the police, should the latter try to interfere with their illegal gambling), and acted as ushers at the bizarre event that was Driberg's wedding in the summer of 1951. After Labour lost the October 1951 general election, Crosland and Jenkins placed themselves on the centre-right of the party. They became protégés of the leading centrist figures Dalton and Gaitskell, who preferred Crosland to Jenkins, not only because he was more obviously brilliant, but also because of homosexual interest: as described in the last chapter, Dalton was pathetically in love with Crosland; while according to Wyatt 'there was a scintilla of platonic homosexuality in [Gaitskell's] affection for Tony ... Hugh not only loved his

mind but also his looks and eternal undergraduate youthfulness'. Crosland lost his seat in 1955 (to return as MP for
Grimsby in 1959), but during his years out of parliament
enhanced his reputation as one of the party's foremost
thinkers with his book *The Future of Socialism* (1956), which
advocated a more equal society while opposing state owner-
ship of industry: this was eventually adopted as party policy,
while demonising Crosland in the eyes of the left. It was a
blow to both Jenkins and Crosland when Gaitskell, who had
become party leader in 1955, died in 1963 after a short illness.
They did not care for either of the main candidates for the succession, Harold Wilson and George Brown – a choice between
a crook and a drunk, as Crosland put it. However, when
Wilson won the leadership, and went on narrowly to win the
general election in October 1964, they both hoped for a place
in his government.

To Crosland's intense jealousy, Jenkins was given a depart-
ment of his own (albeit outside the cabinet), as Minister of
Aviation. Crosland was offered the position of number two to
George Brown at the new Department of Economic Affairs,
which he almost turned down, as Brown, supported by
Wilson, was opposed to the devaluation of sterling which
Crosland (correctly) regarded as necessary. However, only
three months later, in a reshuffle caused by Patrick Gordon
Walker's resignation as Foreign Secretary, Crosland was promoted to the cabinet as Education Secretary. His delight was
somewhat soured when he learned that the post had first been
offered to Jenkins, who refused it because he hoped to land a
greater prize, the home secretaryship, on the retirement of the
ailing incumbent, Sir Frank Soskice. Soskice duly retired at the
end of 1965, to be replaced by Jenkins; though he served at the
Home Office for less than two years, Jenkins built up a great
reputation there, both for his efficient handling of public order

issues and his role in bringing about a raft of reforming liberal measures, including the partial legalisation of homosexuality and abortion. Jenkins and Crosland retained their posts after Labour's landslide victory at the 1966 general election; in a reshuffle of September 1967, Crosland was moved to a position of equal seniority as President of the Board of Trade. Then, in November 1967, after the government was forced into the devaluation which Crosland and others had long advocated, James Callaghan resigned as Chancellor of the Exchequer. Being acknowledged as Labour's leading economic mind, Crosland was confident of being chosen to succeed him – indeed, Callaghan himself assured him that he would be. However, Wilson finally chose Jenkins, partly because he regarded Jenkins as the steadier character (and better parliamentary performer) to take charge at a time of crisis, partly because he felt a certain antipathy towards Crosland. This was a devastating blow to Crosland, made all the more bitter since, as head of the second economic ministry, he was now subordinate to Jenkins. An element of enmity now entered into their relations, demonstrated by the fact that, during Jenkins's two and a half years as Chancellor, Crosland constantly tried to obstruct him in niggardly ways. That their friendship was not yet dead was shown in the autumn of 1969 when Jenkins stood up for Crosland in the face of Wilson's (probably not very serious) threat to sack Crosland over his opposition to the government's proposed industrial relations legislation (which was dropped anyway owing to protests from other quarters): indeed, Jenkins's insistence that Crosland was indispensable may have been a factor in Wilson's decision to promote Crosland that November to head a new 'super-ministry' of Local Government and Regional Planning (later the Department of the Environment).

When Labour unexpectedly lost the 1970 general election,

the relations between Jenkins and Crosland at first became easier, now they were no longer rivals for office. Crosland supported Jenkins in the ballot of Labour MPs for the post of deputy party leader,* which Jenkins easily won. Jenkins then suggested that they work closely together as allies – but as this effectively meant working for Jenkins (who, unlike Crosland, had a sizeable personal following among Labour MPs) to become party leader and prime minister, with Crosland as number two, Crosland backed away with hurt pride. And an issue soon arose to bring their relations to a new low. In 1967, Jenkins and Crosland had both supported Wilson's decision to apply for British membership of the European Economic Community (EEC); the application had been vetoed by De Gaulle, but in 1969 De Gaulle stood down as French President, and had Wilson won the 1970 election, his first move would have been to renew it. In the event, it was enthusiastically (and this time successfully) renewed by Heath, the new Conservative premier; but as there was a strong contingent of anti-EEC Tory MPs led by Enoch Powell, Heath needed opposition support to get the measure through: he allowed his MPs a free vote in the hope that Labour would do the same. However, with opportunistic hypocrisy, Wilson and Callaghan decided to pander to the (admittedly widespread) anti-EEC feeling in the Labour Party and oppose the policy which they had espoused when in government, on the grounds that the terms obtained by Heath were inadequate. Nevertheless, Jenkins and his fellow pro-EEC Labour MPs resolved to defy their party whip and support the government in the crucial vote in October 1971, which sixty-nine of them did, assuring Heath a comfortable majority. Crosland, however, abstained, which Jenkins regarded as an act of treachery. Jenkins soon had his revenge. In 1972 he resigned

---

* Formerly held by George Brown, who had lost his seat at the general election.

from both the shadow cabinet and the deputy leadership over
the European issue. When Crosland stood in the ensuing contest for deputy leader, the 'Jenkinsites' denied him their votes,
ensuring the victory of the lacklustre Ted Short.

In fact, Crosland had never been a committed 'European'
like Jenkins – he just felt, as an economist, that Britain would
be better off in than out. And his abstention did him little
good: he failed to receive the shadow chancellorship vacated
by Jenkins, which went to Denis Healey. Nevertheless, it was
a sad departure for a man who, up to then, had always prided
himself on his integrity, never afraid to speak out for what he
believed was right, whatever the consequences for his career
and popularity. Indeed, around this time friends were dismayed to observe that he compromised his principles in other
ways, as well as making up to people he had formerly despised.
When Labour unexpectedly returned to power in 1974,
Jenkins and Crosland unenthusiastically resumed their former
roles as Home Secretary and Environment Secretary: the
chancellorship for which Crosland longed remained with
Healey, while the foreign secretaryship after which Jenkins
hankered went to Callaghan. When Wilson resigned in March
1976, both Crosland and Jenkins stood in the ensuing leadership election (then consisting of a series of ballots of Labour
MPs), along with Callaghan, Healey, Tony Benn and Michael
Foot. Crosland came bottom of the first ballot, with seventeen
votes, and was eliminated; Jenkins received a disappointing
fifty-three votes and, realising that he could never beat
Callaghan, withdrew. (He would have stood a far better chance
had he challenged the then unpopular Wilson in 1968 or 1972,
as his friends had urged him to do.) In the final ballot,
Callaghan defeated Foot to become party leader and Prime
Minister. Jenkins confidently expected to be appointed to the
vacant foreign secretaryship: when it went to Crosland, who

knew little about foreign affairs, Jenkins experienced feelings of jealousy and bitterness similar to those suffered by Crosland eight and a half years earlier when Jenkins had been appointed Chancellor.

Disillusioned by the British political scene, Jenkins resigned from the government and gave up his parliamentary seat at the end of 1976 to take up the post of President of the European Commission in Brussels. It happened that, during the first half of 1977, it was Britain's turn, in the form of Crosland as Foreign Secretary, to chair the EEC Council of Ministers. All looked to see how the two would get on. Their first European encounters, Jenkins wrote, were 'happily without friction'. But in February Crosland, a heavy drinker who suffered from high blood pressure (both conditions possibly exacerbated by his feud with Jenkins), suffered a fatal stroke, aged fifty-eight. This undoubtedly came to Jenkins, who claimed to have awoken from a dream about Crosland at the moment of the latter's death, as a traumatic shock: writing a eulogy for the *Observer* brought 'the intense closeness of our earlier relationship flooding back into my mind'. (Of course, no one but the two of them had known how close it had in fact been.) Some (including Jenkins himself) have speculated that, had they remained close rather than becoming rivals, they might have changed the Labour Party (and thus the course of British political history) in the 1970s – though it is hard to see how they could have sidelined Callaghan, a figure of immense cunning who had the credentials to unite all sections of the party.

The new Foreign Secretary, David Owen, was only thirty-eight. If not quite in the same league of brilliance, he was in many ways remarkably similar to Crosland – handsome and charismatic, combative and abrasive, and mentally 'quick on his feet'. As he had been an ardent 'Jenkinsite' since his election to parliament in 1966, he seemed (as Tony Blair would seem twenty years later) like Jenkins's political son. Just as Jenkins and Crosland had founded the Oxford University Social Democratic Club in 1940, so Jenkins and Owen (with Shirley Williams and William Rodgers) founded the Social Democratic Party (SDP) in 1981, hoping to 'break the mould of British politics'. But they soon fell out over who should be 'top dog'. After the disappointing SDP performance at the 1983 general election, Jenkins gave up its leadership to Owen, devoting his remaining years to writing elegant political biographies, enjoying the Chancellorship of Oxford University (to which he was elected in 1987), and, after Owen had declined to join the Liberal Democrats on their creation in 1988, performing an elder statesman role as that party's leader in the House of Lords.

One of the great reforms which took place under Jenkins's home secretaryship was the passing of the Sexual Offences Act of 1967 which implemented the Wolfenden recommendations on homosexuality. The government considered the measure far too controversial to be included in its official legislative programme – several of the cabinet, including its two leading members of working-class background, George Brown and James Callaghan, found it morally objectionable; Wilson feared it would 'cost Labour six million votes'; and even the libertarian Richard Crossman (who had frolicked with Auden at Oxford) feared it was 'twenty years ahead of public opinion'. There was no shortage of private members willing to sponsor a bill – the question was whether the government would allow sufficient time for it to go through. In the summer of 1965, a bill sponsored in the House of Lords by David 'Boofy' Gore, 8th Earl of Arran, and in the House of Commons by Leo Abse, Labour MP for Pontypool (the seat once held by Jenkins's father), failed through lack of time, though in its early stages it had garnered a majority in the Lords and only just fallen short of one in the Commons. Early in 1966, Humphry Berkeley, Conservative MP for Lancaster, proposed another bill, which this time won a clear majority in the Commons, but was lost when the general election (in which Berkeley lost his seat) was called in March. Jenkins, who had always proclaimed his support for Wolfenden, was now Home Secretary; and after Labour's landslide victory, he (in alliance with Crossman, now Leader of the House of Commons) persuaded cabinet colleagues that they could not indefinitely obstruct a measure that had already received a majority in both houses, and that they could now safely allow time for a bill without immediate fear of electoral consequences. 'I had to proceed by stratagem', wrote Jenkins in his memoirs; and although the government declared itself 'neutral' in the matter, he himself not only voted for the bill which was duly reintroduced by Arran and Abse but spoke in favour of it 'with all the authority I could command as Home Secretary'. He stayed up for the all-night sitting on 3–4 July 1967 at which the bill completed its stages, going on to an Independence Day celebration at the American Embassy.

All the politicians involved in promoting the bill represented themselves as heterosexuals pleading for tolerance towards an unfortunate minority which happened to possess a different nature; but in fact they all had personal experience of homosexuality. We have already noted the case of Bob Boothby, who had been largely responsible for initiating the Wolfenden inquiry, and who tirelessly supported the bill in the House of Lords. Both Berkeley and Abse have been described as 'heterosexual' in recent scholarly works; but the vain and mischievous Berkeley, a bachelor who lived with a housekeeper but spent much of his time abroad, was entirely homosexual, while the flamboyant Abse, married with two children, was actively bisexual (indeed, as a Freudian he believed that all men possess a homosexual streak). The eccentric Arran, also married with children, had been homosexual in his youth (as James Lees-Milne's diaries testify); he had also been close to his elder brother, briefly the 7th Earl, who had led a tortured homosexual life. And Jenkins himself could hardly forget the 'exceedingly close and intense friendship' he had once enjoyed with Crosland (who chose to absent himself throughout the long and tortuous passage of the bill).

# 15

# A STRAIGHT CHOICE

R obert ('Bob') Mellish (1913–98) was a typical traditionalist Labour MP of working-class background. He was
the son of a docker and himself started life as a docker
(though during the war he rose to be a major in the Royal
Engineers); from 1946 he represented the electors of
Bermondsey, who originally largely consisted of dockers and
their families, for thirty-six years. Having served as chairman
of the London Labour Party, and Minister of Works under
Harold Wilson, he was Labour's Chief Whip from 1969 to
1976, in which role he was known for his fierceness. A practising Catholic, he was married with five sons and regarded as
a devoted family man; like his friend George Brown (they had
both entered Labour politics via the Transport and General
Workers' Union) he had a reputation as a homophobe. With
the closure of the docks Bermondsey greatly changed in character, and by the late 1970s Mellish was having much trouble
from left-wingers in his constituency party. When the
Thatcher government offered him the post of vice-chairman
of the London Docklands Development Corporation, he

accepted and announced that he would not be contesting the seat in the next general election. He was appalled when the Bermondsey Labour Party selected Peter Tatchell, an Australian draft-dodger who had been a member of both the Trotskyite Militant Tendency and the Gay Liberation Front, to succeed him as candidate. Owing to his former membership of 'Militant' (which was incompatible with Labour membership) Tatchell had some trouble getting his candidature confirmed by party headquarters, and was indeed disparaged in the House of Commons by the party leader Michael Foot; but finally it was agreed to accept him as candidate. In disgust, Mellish resigned from the Labour Party, and soon afterwards also resigned his seat ahead of the general election, thus precipitating a by-election which took place on 24 February 1983.

Owing to the unusual circumstances which led to it, and the fact that it was seen as something of a test for the forthcoming general election (which took place the following June), the by-election aroused intense public interest. All three main parties were represented by unmarried men in their early thirties: Tatchell for Labour; the Welsh barrister Simon Hughes for the Liberals (who were then allied to, but had not yet amalgamated with, the Social Democrats); and Robert Hughes (no relation of Simon), a member of the Greater London Council, for the Conservatives. In addition, John O'Grady, a former leader of Southwark Borough Council, stood as the 'Real Bermondsey Labour' candidate with encouragement and support from Mellish. The campaign was marked by a torrent of homophobic abuse directed against Tatchell,* most of it coming from the O'Grady camp: O'Grady himself, often accompanied by Mellish, toured the constituency with a horse

---

* Tatchell agreed to a request from Labour HQ to remain silent about his sexuality during the campaign – but as he had never made any secret of it, this was a case of trying to lock the stable door after the horse had bolted.

and cart, singing a song which referred to Tatchell 'wearing his trousers back to front'. The Liberals joined in the baiting: their final campaign leaflet referred to 'a straight choice' between themselves and Labour. The result, unpredicted by the opinion polls, was a shock. Simon Hughes romped to victory with more than seventeen thousand votes, well over half the total cast. Tatchell came a pitiful second with fewer than eight thousand votes in what had been a safe Labour seat: even had he captured the two thousand or so votes cast for O'Grady, he would have come nowhere near winning. The Conservatives, traditional runners-up in the constituency, came fourth, narrowly retaining their deposit.

Following his humiliation, Tatchell abandoned mainstream party politics and became Britain's best-known gay rights militant. As a member of the 'OutRage' organisation, dedicated to 'outing' public figures who failed to support gay equality, he led disruptive protests at meetings of Anglican bishops, and wrote letters to various MPs implicitly threatening exposure, one of whom, the Ulster Unionist Sir James Kilfedder, promptly died of a heart attack. He also campaigned for a reduction in the age of consent to fourteen. He became a bogey-figure in the Conservative press – but they had to acknowledge his courage when, in Brussels in 2001, he attempted a citizen's arrest of the Zimbabwean President Robert Mugabe on account of the persecution of homosexuals in his country, getting beaten up in the process, and again in 2004 when he attacked Islam for its homophobia (which resulted in a temporary estrangement from his friend Ken Livingstone, then standing for re-election as Mayor of London).

Simon Hughes has remained MP for Bermondsey and its successor constituencies to this day, becoming a leading spokesman for the Liberals and their successor party (from 1988), the Liberal Democrats. In the leadership election which followed the resignation of Charles Kennedy in 2006 he stood as the candidate of the party's left wing. During the campaign another candidate, the party's home affairs spokesman Mark Oaten, a family man, stood down amid revelations in the *News of the World* that he had engaged in 'three-in-a-bed sessions' with rent boys. Hughes then denied in several interviews the longstanding rumours that he himself was gay, until the *Sun* announced that it possessed proof that he had used the gay telephone chatline Man Talk. He then admitted to being bisexual, explaining his earlier denials with the words: 'It's not just me. There are lots of people who have tried to keep their private lives private. I wasn't just doing it for me but for many others who are in the same boat.' He also apologised to Tatchell for the tactics used in his 1983 campaign, an apology which Tatchell graciously accepted, adding that he hoped Hughes would win his contest. Hughes came third in the leadership stakes, but in 2008 was elected President, and in 2010 Deputy Leader, of the Liberal Democrats, joining the coalition government in December 2013 as Minister of State at the Department of Justice.

Robert Hughes married in 1986 and served as Conservative MP for Harrow West from 1987 to 1997. In 1993 he was appointed a junior minister in the Major government, responsible for scientific and medical research, but resigned the post a year later after revelations in the *News of the World* that he had been having an affair with his (female) Commons secretary. He, it seems, had been the 'straight choice' at Bermondsey.

Bob Mellish was rewarded with a peerage for his work on the Docklands Development Corporation. He joined David Owen's Social Democrats, but attracted notice for blimpish remarks such as that he 'thanked God for the atom bomb'. Five years after his death, in a radio broadcast to mark the twentieth anniversary of the Bermondsey by-election, Tatchell claimed that

Mellish was in fact a 'secret bisexual', from whom Tatchell himself had received several unwelcome propositions. 'It's what we would now call sexual harassment. He was rather persistent ... I just gave him a polite firm "no". He actually said to me, "I wouldn't advise you to mention this to anyone, no one will believe you ..."'

# 16

# JEREMY AND NORMAN

Jeremy Thorpe (1929–2014), Liberal MP for North Devon from 1959 to 1979, and Norman St John-Stevas (1929–2012), Conservative MP for Chelmsford from 1964 to 1987, were among the most charismatic politicians of their generation, famed for their wit, flamboyance and dandified Edwardian dress. Despite their reputation as entertainers, both were extremely ambitious and indeed made outstanding careers. Thorpe served as leader of the Liberal Party from 1967 to 1976; Stevas (to give him the surname he was born with) became a leading member of the Thatcher administration on its formation in 1979. Both overreached themselves and experienced a dramatic fall from grace, slithering down the greasy pole they had struggled so long and hard to climb.

They had much else in common. Both (like others mentioned in these pages) were strongly influenced by formidable and ambitious mothers. Narcissism and fantasy loomed large in their personalities. Both began their political careers at university: at a time when those historic debating societies were still regarded as nurseries of the nation's rulers,

Thorpe served as a sparkling President of the Oxford Union while Stevas made an equally memorable impression as President of the Cambridge Union. (Stevas proceeded from Cambridge to Oxford and hoped to become President of the Oxford Union too, though he only succeeded in being elected to its secretaryship.) Both entered parliament via a career in the law. Their politics were similar, Thorpe being a conservative Liberal, Stevas a liberal Conservative (though in both cases their sense of compassion was overriden by a ruthless concern for their own self-advancement). Both became media pundits, whose views on the events of the day were listened to by millions on *Any Questions* and *The World at One*. Both were largely self-invented characters, who gave themselves the airs of superb aristocrats; and both were shameless snobs, who aspired to move in the grandest circles, and become trusted friends and advisers to royalty and heads of state.

There were also important differences. Stevas had a good academic mind, while Thorpe was a brilliant lightweight. Though both had expensive tastes, Stevas was born rich enough never to have to worry much about money, while Thorpe always struggled financially (and sometimes resorted to shady expedients to make ends meet). Stevas was a self-advertising Roman Catholic who gloried in the friendship of popes and his membership of various exclusive lay orders, whereas Thorpe's background was Protestant Irish, his grandfather having been a prominent evangelical Anglican cleric and denouncer of sin. And although both were homosexuals, they handled this aspect of their existence differently. Thorpe possessed an extreme risk-taking personality and was addicted to 'feasting with panthers'. He led an active queer sex life which, while secretive, was so louche and promiscuous that it always posed great risks to his career – and eventually destroyed it. He married twice, having a son by his first marriage, and represented himself to the world as a respectable family man. It might almost be said that he divided himself into two selves, each of which was hardly aware of what the other was up to. Stevas, who never married, and spent most of his life in a discreet relationship with one other man, was as cautious sexually as Thorpe was reckless, but as open about his proclivities as it was possible to be without compromising his career and getting into trouble.

Thorpe had two famous grandfathers (both of lower-middle-class origin), the said Archdeacon Thorpe and Sir John Norton-Griffiths, a flashy entrepreneur who became a Conservative MP and baronet, finally committing suicide when ruined after the Wall Street Crash. He never knew either of them, and the grandfather figure of his boyhood was Lloyd George, whose favourite daughter Megan had been a school-friend of his mother: the 'Welsh wizard', with his combination of political artfulness and sexual raffishness, became his role-model, and though Thorpe's own family background was staunchly Tory, from childhood his declared ambition was to become Britain's Liberal Prime Minister. His barrister father, a gentle, humorous (and probably sexually ambiguous) man from whom he inherited a talent for mimicry, died during the war, leaving the fifteen-year-old Jeremy under the influence of his mother, a strident, masculine, monocle-wearing woman. She taught him that he was the most important person in the world, that he could do no wrong, that he must succeed at all costs, and that almost anything was permissible if it helped him get on. Thorpe was not popular at Eton, where he was regarded as a show-off; but at Oxford his wit and showmanship won him general admiration, carrying him to the coveted Union presidency. After university, he earned his living as a barrister and broadcaster, but his sights were fixed on election to parliament as a Liberal – a considerable ambition at a time when the party held a mere handful of seats and was no longer regarded as a serious political force. He identified North Devon as a winnable seat where his colourful personality might prevail, and in 1959, after several years of vigorous campaigning, he captured it from the Conservatives, joining just five other Liberal MPs.

Thorpe demonstrated outstanding gifts as a campaigner, fund-raiser, parliamentary performer and constituency member, and soon became the best-known Liberal MP next to the leader Jo Grimond. When Grimond stood down in 1967, Thorpe, then thirty-seven, was the natural choice to succeed him. Though the darling of the party's rank-and-file, he was never much liked by most senior Liberals, who tended to find him devious, flashy, snobbish and superficial. On the other hand, he got on splendidly with the Labour Prime Minister Harold Wilson, who appreciated his wit and showed him much favour; and through his stylish media appearances he established himself as a popular and reassuring national figure. This paid dividends in February 1974 when Wilson's Conservative successor Ted Heath, facing a crisis caused by union militancy, called a snap election. In a series of masterly broadcasts Thorpe seduced many Tories away from their normal allegiance, causing the Liberals to win six million votes, almost one-fifth of the total and the greatest number in their history. Unfortunately, under the prevailing electoral system, this translated into barely one-fiftieth of the seats, fourteen in all. The election resulted in a hung parliament, and Heath approached Thorpe (whom he did not especially like, though they shared a passionate belief that Britain's future lay in 'Europe') with a view to forming a Conservative–Liberal coalition. Thorpe would have loved to accept, but was unable to secure a commitment from the Conservatives, upon which his colleagues insisted, to introduce proportional representation. Wilson returned to the premiership and was again most friendly to Thorpe, whom he sought to build up as a counterweight to the Conservatives.

In 1968, soon after becoming Liberal leader, Thorpe married Caroline Allpass, an attractive woman nine years younger than himself who had worked at Sotheby's. They had a son, Rupert; but there were rumours that the marriage was not as happy as it seemed, and in 1970 she died tragically in a car crash. In 1973 he made a second marriage to Marion, Countess of Harewood (*née* Stein), a handsome woman some years older than himself and a well-known personality in the music world, who had previously been married to the Queen's cousin George Lascelles, 7th Earl of Harewood. It would be unfair to say that he married purely for career reasons, for he enjoyed the company of women, and his wives rescued him from the emotional tyranny of his mother. But his nature was fundamentally homosexual; and from his early twenties he was addicted to the seduction of young men. (For him the preliminaries were as important as the somewhat perfunctory sexual act itself.) His known conquests included Devon farmers, journalists and policemen at the House of Commons, a cameraman filming his broadcasts, a footman at Buckingham Palace, a famous art expert and the heir to an Irish peerage. As Liberal leader he kept a friend in his entourage who discreetly procured male partners; but there were moments of madness when he cruised the streets and haunted gay clubs in search of 'trade'. Thorpe clearly enjoyed the dangers inherent in these encounters, and on the whole handled them with skill; but there were a number of close shaves, and one situation which ultimately defeated him. Norman Scott was a pretty stable lad of twenty when Thorpe met him in 1960. The following year they began an affair, during which Thorpe 'kept' Scott at a bedsit in the King's Road and spoilt him in various ways. Thorpe soon tired of Scott; but the latter, who suffered from a personality disorder, refused to be 'dropped' and proceeded to harass Thorpe for the next decade and a half, eventually going to live in his constituency with the object of spreading scandal about him. In 1976 Scott's 'story' became public. Thorpe defended himself vigorously, insisting that the relationship had been non-sexual, that Scott was just one of many unfortunates he had tried to help; but when, after several months, it became clear that his explanations had lacked frankness, he was forced to resign the party leadership.

Worse was to come. Sixteen months after the resignation it transpired that, while Thorpe was still Liberal leader, a 'hitman' had been hired to kill Scott, and had lured him to a lonely spot on Exmoor, but that the attempt had failed when the gun jammed. (He had already committed what some regarded as an even worse crime by shooting Scott's dog.) The press exposure of this sensational story began when the putative assassin, Andrew Newton, was released from prison after serving a sentence for 'being in possession of a firearm with intent to endanger life'. Subsequently it emerged that Newton had been hired by David Holmes, a bisexual crony of Thorpe who had been best man at his first wedding and was godfather to his son, and that the money used to pay Newton came out of funds innocently sent to Jeremy by a wealthy political donor he had recruited, Jack Hayward. As a result of the massive unfolding scandal, Thorpe lost his seat at the 1979 general election, and a few days later found himself on trial at the Old Bailey on charges of incitement and conspiracy to murder, together with Holmes and two other men who were peripherally involved in the affair. The case was circumstantially strong; but thanks to clever defence counsel, who succeeded in denigrating the characters of the main prosecution witnesses (Scott, Newton, and a raffish former Liberal MP named Peter Bessell who had for some years tried to 'manage' Scott on Thorpe's behalf), Thorpe (who wisely refused to go into the witness box) was acquitted, as were his co-defendants. But after the uncontested revelations about his sex life and the stratagems he had used to cover it up, and the exposure of his dubious financial dealings (he never produced any explanation of how the Hayward money had ended up with Holmes and Newton), he was discredited in the eyes of his party and the world. His efforts to resume his political career, or establish himself in another sphere, came to nothing, and in his early fifties he was diagnosed with Parkinson's disease. He did however show astonishing powers of resilience, and as the scandal receded into the distance he achieved a certain stature as a fascinating political survivor from another age.

Thorpe's fall from grace coincided with a rise in the fortunes of Stevas, who aspired to be the *éminence grise* of the new Conservative leader Margaret Thatcher. Stevas presented himself to the world as a quintessential Englishman, but there was nothing very English about his background. His father, whom he later described as an engineer, was a successful property developer and hotel owner of Greek nationality, who married an Irishwoman, Kitty O'Connor, employed in one of his hotels. (The 'St John' which Norman later tacked on to 'Stevas' was one of his mother's baptismal names.) After his parents' divorce he lived with his mother, who saw to it that he received a Catholic education: he briefly studied in Rome for the priesthood before concluding that the vocation was not for him. As a law student, he set out to win all the prizes: after getting a first-class degree at Cambridge, he went on to do a postgraduate degree at Oxford and a doctorate at Yale, picking up a host of prestigious awards along the way. He became a successful academic lawyer (who 'preached but never practised', as he wittily put it), teaching at Oxford and other universities on both sides of the Atlantic. His lasting achievements were to produce a report on the history of censorship in 1956, which influenced subsequent reform in that area of the law, and to edit the collected works of the great constitutional lawyer Walter Bagehot in fifteen impressive volumes published between the 1960s and the 1980s.

An active Conservative since his student days, Stevas was adopted in the early 1960s for the safe seat of Chelmsford in Essex (which twenty years earlier had been held by Jack Macnamara, the friend of Guy Burgess and Harold Nicolson). He enjoyed telling friends that he had gone to the selection meeting wearing what, by the standards of the day, was a distinctly 'pansy' outfit, including a brightly coloured shirt and tie, and shoes with tassels: he did not want the Chelmsford Tories later to feel they had been misled as to the sort of candidate they were selecting. A member of the selection committee afterwards remarked: 'They sent us three people to choose from, a woman, a drunk and a queer. Of course, we had to take the queer!' With his colourful personality and merry quips, he was popular with fellow MPs, though having been modest and deferential in youth he became increasingly haughty with the passing years. From 1972 to 1974 he served as a junior minister at the Department of Education, with responsibility for the arts, and seemed to make a great hit with his Secretary of State, Margaret Thatcher. When Thatcher became party leader in 1975, Stevas believed himself destined for great things. On becoming Prime Minister in 1979 she appointed him Leader of the House of Commons (in which role he created the modern system of select committees), allowing him to combine this with his old job of Arts Minister. He imagined that their relationship allowed him to take liberties with her. During one cabinet meeting he asked to leave early as he was going to a reception – when the Prime Minister pointed out that she had been invited to the same reception, he riposted that it took him longer to change. Behind her back, he called her 'Attila the Hen' and 'the Blessed Margaret', and made jokes at her expense. (When the prototype pound coin was shown to MPs, he caused hilarity by suggesting it should be called 'a maggie' as it was 'bold and brassy and thinks it's a sovereign'.) It came as a shock to him when, after twenty months in office, he was sacked in her first cabinet reshuffle in January 1981 – she had been irritated by his indiscretions and lukewarm support for her more strident policies, and did not see the need for a court jester.

However, being an accomplished networker, he managed to console himself with a variety of prestigious appointments, notably the chairmanship of the Royal Fine Arts Commission (1985–2000) and the mastership of Emmanuel College, Cambridge (1991–6), in both of which positions he operated in the most lavish and flamboyant style (becoming known at Emmanuel as 'Mein Camp'). On his retirement from the House of Commons in 1987 he was raised to the peerage as Baron St John of Fawsley (a title which caused some trouble at the College of Arms, as St John was not a surname borne by any of his forebears). He also revelled in his roles as a leading Catholic layman and friend of the royal family, frequently appearing on radio and television to comment on such matters as the divorce of Charles and Diana. (No one was ever sure to what extent he really possessed the confidence of royalty or acted as their unofficial spokesman: once, when accused of name-dropping, he admitted that 'the Queen said the same to me yesterday'.)

Lord St John claimed to be chaste and celibate, though for more than fifty years he lived in a discreet relationship with Adrian Stanford, a man six years younger than himself who had been one of his law students at Oxford in the late 1950s and later made a successful career in the city. (In 2009 they quietly entered into a civil partnership in order to spare the survivor death duties.) With his aesthetic preoccupations and outrageous mannerisms, he effectively advertised his tastes to the world, while being exceedingly cautious about indulging them (though the Liberal peer Lord Beaumont, who bought a house from him in Hampstead in the 1960s, found himself having to turn away a succession of 'gentleman callers' during the first months of his occupancy). Like Winston Churchill, he blossomed in the company of personable young men. At the Royal Fine Arts Commission, he engaged a succession of good-looking personal assistants; and at Emmanuel (where the somewhat puritanical governing body soon came to regret its choice) he showed unabashed favouritism to a coterie of handsome male undergraduates, whom he showered with invitations and allowed to bathe naked in the fellows' garden swimming pool.

Thorpe and Stevas were born in the same year and knew each other from 1950,* but (so far as one can tell) there was only one issue over which they joined forces. As young MPs in the 1960s, showing some courage, they campaigned together for the reform of the law relating to homosexuality, serving on the committee of the Homosexual Law Reform Society (founded in 1958 to press for the enactment of the Wolfenden recommendations), and lobbying the Labour Home Secretaries Soskice and Jenkins to facilitate the reforming legislation which was put forward by other parliamentarians and eventually

* They met at a boat race between representatives of the Oxford and Cambridge Unions in June that year, in which Stevas coxed the Cambridge Union boat and Thorpe, in one of his rare sporting moments, pulled an oar for the Oxford Union boat. The tone of the occasion can be judged from the fact that, halfway through the race, the two crews were met by a launch from which white-jacketed staff served them sherry: despite rowing with farcical incompetence, they nevertheless succeeded in their presumed joint aim of crossing the finishing line simultaneously. (David Walter, *The Oxford Union* [1984], p. 132.)

passed in 1967. That, however, seems to have been the limit of their collaboration, for they never much liked each other. Both at the Oxford Union and in the House of Commons, they were rivals in wit and showmanship; and perhaps they subconsciously recognised common qualities in one another which made them shudder. In their sex lives, Stevas was open but cautious, Thorpe secretive but reckless. Indeed, for all his posturing and malicious wit, there was an essential integrity about Stevas – whereas Thorpe lacked integrity, being one of those who, obliged by nature to be devious in one aspect of existence, become devious in most of the others.

# 17

# POLLY AND MANDY

Michael Denzil Xavier Portillo and Peter Benjamin Mandelson were perhaps the most intriguing (in the sense of mysterious and fascinating) politicians of the 1990s and early 2000s. They were both born in 1953, and had some surprising similarities in their backgrounds. Each was the last of a family of boys: Portillo was the youngest of five brothers, Mandelson the younger of two. Both had middle-class upbringings in suburban London, Portillo in Stanmore, Mandelson in Hampstead Garden Suburb. However, their parentage was somewhat unconventional. On their paternal side, both descended from colourful foreign refugees: Portillo's father, Luis Gabriel Portillo, was a Spanish professor and political radical, a friend of Lorca, who fled into exile in England after the Spanish Civil War; Mandelson's father, George 'Tony' Mandelson, advertising manager of the *Jewish Chronicle*, whose own father came from New South Wales, claimed descent from Russian-Polish Jews who had sought sanctuary in the British Empire when on the run from the Tsarist authorities owing to their revolutionary activities. Although they were both thought to resemble their fathers, they were closer to their mothers, strong-willed, defiant women who had risked estrangement from their families by marrying men of whom their parents disapproved: Cora Portillo (*née* Blyth) was the daughter of a wealthy Scottish linen manufacturer and art collector, and had met her husband (whose left-wing views she shared) while working for the relief of Spanish refugees; Mary Mandelson was the only child of the Labour statesman Herbert Morrison,\* and had married aged nineteen (somewhat disastrously – Mandelson was her second husband) largely in order to escape from a father and a family home she regarded as oppressive. Portillo said that he was 'certainly fifty per cent my mother's son' and had inherited 'a lot of her characteristics ... tenacity, endurance and grit'; Mandelson wrote in his memoirs that he 'doted' on his mother, whom he called 'the Duchess' as she seemed the incarnation of regality, and that her death in 2006 was 'the hardest blow' he suffered during his four years as a European Commissioner in Brussels.

They both attended excellent local grammar schools, where they were high academic achievers and demonstrated an early ability to make friends and influence people. Both became school prefects. Portillo was popularly known as 'Polly' (a variant of 'Jolly', which had been the nickname of his elder brother Jolyon); Mandelson (like his father) was 'Mandy' to his friends. They were both keen on amateur theatricals: Portillo appeared in school Shakespeare productions alongside the future Labour MP Diane Abbott (who would later be his regular fellow panellist on BBC's political discussion programme *This Week*); Mandelson played the eponymous role in the local

---

\* Herbert Stanley Morrison (1888–1965): Minister of Transport, 1929–31; Leader, London County Council, 1934–40; Home Secretary, 1940–5; Deputy Prime Minister, 1945–51; Foreign Secretary, 1951; life peer, 1959. The son of a policeman, and a vociferous homophobe.

amateur dramatic society's production of Rattigan's *The Winslow Boy*. Their schooldays coincided with the premiership of Harold Wilson (a friend of the Mandelsons who had been their neighbour in Hampstead Garden Suburb), and in keeping with their family backgrounds they both showed an early interest in left-wing politics. Portillo canvassed for the local Labour candidate at general elections, and protested against the Vietnam War; Mandelson resigned as a prefect to lead a revolt against the hierarchical school system, supported the local campaign to turn his grammar school 'comprehensive', and joined the Young Socialists and (briefly) the Young Communists. Both developed into striking-looking young men: Portillo was handsome in a sensual, Latin way; Mandelson was tall, with an impish expression.

They progressed to Oxbridge – Portillo to read History at Peterhouse, Cambridge, Mandelson to read PPE at St Catherine's College, Oxford. Here their paths diverged, for Mandelson, unlike Portillo, became engrossed in student politics: he was active in the University Labour Club and other left-wing societies, became chairman of his college JCR (the student representative body), and established a useful friendship with the Master of St Catherine's, the left-leaning historian Sir Alan Bullock. (His political activism was encouraged by his father, a strong Labour supporter; his mother hated politics, and although Peter was proud of the achievements of his grandfather Herbert Morrison, who died when he was eleven, they had rarely met owing to the family estrangement.) Meanwhile, at Cambridge, Portillo played no part in student politics, devoting himself to his academic work, the flamboyant social life of his college (which as the oldest Cambridge college has always regarded itself as being somewhat apart from the rest of the university), and the activities of the University Amateur Dramatic Club (ADC), of which he became treasurer. He was, however, strongly influenced by his principal academic mentor, the right-wing Peterhouse don Maurice Cowling, who converted him to the Conservative cause; he was also fascinated by Margaret Thatcher, elected as Conservative leader in 1975. Hence, on leaving their respective universities (Portillo with a first-class degree, Mandelson with an upper second), Portillo, recommended by Cowling, went to work for the Conservative Research Department (CRD), while Mandelson, recommended by Bullock, got a job with the TUC.

Matthew Parris, a colleague of Portillo at the CRD, later remembered him as 'an ambitious young man with a streak of ruthlessness, friendly up to a point but unreachable beyond it, possessed of an air of mystery which he did nothing to dispel, and scarily self-contained ... He was strikingly attractive, cool and bright. He had a sort of presence about him.' He also had a hint of vanity and narcissism: in an office where most were rather scruffy, he was always beautifully dressed; he was especially proud of his thick dark hair, and was often espied checking that it was perfectly in place. Portillo's main research brief was in the sphere of energy policy, the rock on which the previous Conservative government had foundered in 1974 amid the chaos of the miners' strike. By the time of the 1979 election he was regarded as a rising star, and secured the coveted job of briefing Thatcher before her campaign speeches, an experience which confirmed his already intense admiration for her. After Thatcher won the election, Portillo became special adviser to the Energy Secretary, David Howell. In 1981 he briefly left politics to spend a couple of years working in the oil industry and in television. (Mandelson also turned to TV around this time: soon after Portillo was appointed a researcher on Channel 4's *The Week in Politics*, Mandelson became a producer on LWT's *Weekend World*.) Returning to the fold, Portillo became a speechwriter to the party chairman Cecil Parkinson, and contested a marginal seat in Birmingham at the 1983 general election. He failed in that contest, but the following year was comfortably returned at a by-election in the apparently safe Tory seat of Enfield Southgate after its MP had been murdered by the IRA in the Brighton bombing. He placed himself firmly on the Thatcherite right, stood out among the young hopefuls owing to his striking personality, and was soon appointed an assistant whip. After the 1987 election he distinguished himself in two tricky junior ministerial posts, at the Departments of Social Security and Transport. Early in 1990, in one of her last reshuffles, Thatcher appointed him Minister of Local Government at the Department of the Environment, responsible for implementing the unpopular Community Charge. When Thatcher fell from power at the end of the year (Portillo was one of a band of loyalists who urged her not to resign but to fight on to retain the leadership), John Major kept him in the Local Government post, where he now had the task of dismantling the Community Charge, which he accomplished with his usual efficiency.

Portillo could claim some of the credit for the surprising Conservative victory at the 1992 general election: he had been in charge of the campaign in the London area, where the party did much better than expected. Although not much in sympathy with Major, he could no longer be left out of the cabinet, in which he served during the years 1992–5 in two thankless posts – as Chief Secretary to the Treasury when the government was having to slash expenditure, and as Employment Secretary when unemployment remained high. He was now the standard-bearer of Thatcherism. (At his fortieth birthday party in 1993, Thatcher declared: 'We brought you up; we expect great things of you; you will not disappoint us.') He presented an image which was glamorous, with a touch of Byronic charisma,* and robust, with a touch of Wagnerian melodrama. (He was indeed an ardent Wagnerian, like that other 'messianic' figure of the right, Enoch Powell.) When, in June 1995, Major, in an attempt to silence his eurosceptic critics, resigned as party leader and offered himself for re-election, Portillo seemed about to enter the fray, setting up a campaign headquarters and installing telephone lines. However, once his fellow right-winger John Redwood, the Welsh Secretary, had challenged Major, he decided not to join the contest. (He would certainly have stood, with Michael Heseltine as his probable main rival, had it gone to a second round – which it nearly did, Major having privately resolved to withdraw in the event of getting just four votes fewer than he in fact received.) Duly re-elected, Major rewarded Portillo for his hesitant loyalty with the post of Defence Secretary. At the party conference that October Portillo made a stirring speech, referring to Britain's glorious imperial and martial past and ending by citing the SAS motto 'Who Dares Wins': this was rapturously received by the party faithful, but went down less well with the public and press. (The speech was said to have been inspired by David Hart, an eccentric tycoon considered by some to exercise a Rasputin-like influence over Portillo.) As the Conservative government headed for almost certain defeat at the 1997 general election, Portillo could look forward to being front-runner in the further leadership contest which was likely to follow the disaster. However, in the most sensational news of the night, he lost his Enfield Southgate seat, his majority of more than fifteen thousand being translated into

---

* Some believed that Alan B'stard, the handsome, self-seeking, right-wing MP in the satirical TV series *The New Statesman* (1987–94), was vaguely based on Portillo. Bizarrely, one of the scriptwriters, Laurence Marks, though a Labour supporter, was a friend and constituent of Portillo, who offered some advice to the series on the workings of Westminster.

a Labour one of almost fifteen hundred on a swing of 17.4 per cent: the jubilation which greeted this result seemed to indicate that his 'gung-ho' image had been widely disliked. Retiring (temporarily, as it turned out) from the political field, Portillo accepted a job with the oil company which had employed him in the early 1980s, and embarked on his career as a presenter of television documentaries.

Like Portillo, Mandelson was intensely ambitious and self-controlled; but he had a more varied career as he climbed to the upper reaches of his party, and as Labour was out of power for almost two decades, he waited longer to taste the sweets of office. He only lasted eighteen months at the TUC, where his dour bosses were irritated by his attempts to seek the limelight – first by going to see the Prime Minister Jim Callaghan to present a report on youth unemployment, then by accepting the chairmanship of the British Youth Council and leading its delegation to the World Youth Festival in Havana (where he succeeded in having some Marxist rhetoric removed from its final communiqué). He then served for a term on the notoriously 'hard-left' Lambeth Borough Council, which enabled him to observe his main political enemies at close quarters. At the same time he worked for the Parliamentary Labour Party, helping to draft its transport policy review and gaining some useful allies, including the fiery left-wing MP John Prescott. From 1982 to 1985 he worked as a television producer for *Weekend World*, making more valuable contacts and honing his presentational skills. In 1985, largely owing to the recommendation of Prescott (who would rue the day), he was appointed Head of Communications of the Labour Party. Mandelson realised that Labour needed to present itself as a modern party committed to fairness and equality, while playing down its traditional union links and interventionist policies which had become unpopular with the electorate; he showed skill in putting out publicity which stressed the former while minimising the latter. He focused attention on the efforts of the leader Neil Kinnock to stand up to the unions, and introduced such presentational touches as the replacement of the red flag as the party's symbol with a red rose. He also identified two talented and attractive young MPs of centrist views, Gordon Brown and Tony Blair, as ideal purveyors of Labour's message, and contrived where possible to have them present the party's case on television, to the annoyance of more senior figures. Mandelson's rebranding exercise led to a significant upswing in Labour's fortunes, though they lost the 1987 election, and he gained a reputation (which he seems to have relished) as a devious manipulator, despised by many in his own party as 'the Prince of Darkness'. He was relieved of his job in 1990, soon after securing the Labour candidature in the safe seat of Hartlepool. He drew ever closer to Brown and Blair, advising them on how to promote themselves; after Labour had lost the 1992 election, the new leader John Smith found no place for Mandelson, but appointed his protégés Shadow Chancellor and Shadow Home Secretary. When Smith suddenly died in 1994, it was Mandelson who engineered the succession of Blair (whom he worshipped rather as Portillo had worshipped Thatcher), persuading the press to hail Blair as the best man to lead the party, and a reluctant Brown to stand aside in Blair's favour. During the next three years, still mostly operating behind the scenes, he was largely responsible for masterminding 'New Labour' (in effect a brilliant public relations concept which combined the attractions of Thatcherism with the compassionate elements of socialism) and piloting it towards its resounding victory at the general election of May 1997.

Having been swept to power, Blair owed a great debt to Mandelson, but he did not at first appoint him to the cabinet, wishing to continue to use him as a fixer and propagandist who could reconcile the factions within the government and ensure they all 'sang from the same hymn sheet'. He was given the innocuous title of 'Minister without Portfolio in the Cabinet Office', which concealed the fact that he wielded immense power, entitled to know everything that was going on in government and give whatever advice he wanted to ministers (which they ignored at their peril), without having to account to parliament for his actions. (It was a role of which Lord Esher would have been proud: like Esher, Mandelson also enjoyed the friendship and confidence of royalty, who frequently sought his advice.) Mandelson was deputy premier in all but name, which earned him the enmity of his former ally John Prescott, who (to appease the traditionalist left) had been given the actual title of Deputy Prime Minister. Blair had declared that the New Labour project would only be complete 'when the Labour Party learns to love Peter Mandelson'; but his Svengali remained far from popular among the party at large, as demonstrated when he stood for a vacant place on the party executive in September 1997 and was convincingly defeated by the radical left-winger Ken Livingstone. During fifteen months in his shadowy post Mandelson nevertheless performed valuable services for the government, minimising the effect of a series of scandals. It might have been better for him had he continued in the same role throughout Blair's first term, for the two cabinet positions he subsequently held – as Secretary of State for Trade and Industry (July–December 1998) and Northern Ireland (October 1999–January 2001) – both ended ignominiously after a short tenure. In each case Mandelson was brought down thanks to a weakness for hobnobbing with rich men. (He once declared that 'we [New Labour] are intensely relaxed about people getting filthy rich so long as they pay their taxes'.) His first resignation was prompted by the disclosure that he had accepted a six-figure loan from a colleague, the Paymaster-General Geoffrey Robinson MP, whose business activities his department was investigating, to help finance the purchase of a house in Notting Hill, and had failed to declare this either in the Register of Members' Interests or to the building society from which he had obtained a mortgage. His second resignation (which may be accounted a tragedy, as Mandelson's conspiratorial gifts ideally fitted him to resolve the problems of Northern Ireland) arose from the revelation that he had used his influence to expedite the passport application of the Indian businessman Srichand Hinduja, who had been a financial supporter of one of Mandelson's pet projects, the Millennium Dome. Mandelson might have survived both episodes (a parliamentary inquiry into the Hinduja affair later absolved him of improper conduct) but for the widespread hostility to him within party ranks. That was the end of his ministerial career under Blair, though the premier continued to rely on his advice, and in 2004 secured his appointment as European Commissioner for Trade, in which role he again caused controversy owing to his closeness to various tycoons. (Mandelson was a lifelong euro-enthusiast, one area of policy in which he took the opposite view to Portillo, who notwithstanding his continental associations – he frequently visited Spain and spoke the language fluently – consistently opposed both 'closer European union' and the single currency.)

Both Portillo and Mandelson made political comebacks. To a fanfare of publicity, Portillo re-entered parliament at the Kensington and Chelsea by-election of November 1999, and was soon afterwards appointed Shadow Chancellor by William Hague. However, during his two and a half years' absence he had become a very different political being: chastened by defeat, he had experienced a damascene conversion and was now a 'compassionate Conservative' who believed in 'diversity' and 'inclusiveness'. He proved ineffective at his shadow brief, as he found it hard to disagree with the policies of his opposite number, Gordon Brown. Although he remained loyal to Hague, tensions between them soon arose as Hague pursued a populist right-wing agenda; and some of Portillo's staff and supporters, eager for their hero to succeed to the leadership, worked to undermine Hague. After the Conservatives had suffered another disaster at the 2001 general election, and Hague resigned, Portillo stood in the contest for the new leader, the third time this prize had seemed within his grasp. His ardent admirers both inside and outside parliament believed that only he had the brains and charisma to unite the party and lead it to victory; but no one quite knew what he now stood for – certainly he could no longer claim to be the heir to Thatcher, who effectively disowned him. In the first-round ballot of Conservative MPs, he led the field; but in the second round, closely fought between Kenneth Clarke, Iain Duncan Smith and himself, he came third by just one vote, and was eliminated. (Had he got into the final round, which was now decided by the party membership in the country, he would almost certainly have won.) He retired from the House of Commons at the 2005 election, and left the Conservative Party. Mandelson had left the House a year earlier to take up his post in Brussels; but in 2008, when the Labour government wobbled as it faced the credit crunch with empty coffers, Gordon Brown, to the amazement of the public and press, invited him to rejoin the cabinet as Business Secretary, with a peerage. When the new Baron Mandelson faced the Labour Party Conference that October he was greeted with rapturous acclaim as a brilliant fixer who might save them from calamity. Indeed, during his twenty months in office he exhibited outstanding skills as a political manager and publicist, and was regarded by some as 'the real Prime Minister', especially after he had quelled a cabinet revolt against Brown in the summer of 2009 and been rewarded with an extraordinary array of new titles – First Secretary of State, Lord President of the Council, Minister for Outer Space . . . It is a tribute to his talents that Labour managed to avoid wipe-out at the general election of 2010 – his advice to Brown, against the latter's instincts, to appear in a series of televised 'leaders' debates' helped keep up the Liberal Democrat vote and deny the Conservatives a majority. But Brown, who had perhaps not forgotten how Mandelson had scotched his hopes of becoming leader in 1994, thwarted his ambition to go on to become European Commissioner for Foreign Affairs, the post going to another Labour peer, Baroness Ashton.

Both Portillo and Mandelson were attractive to women, and were certainly no misogynists. As a teenager in Stanmore, Portillo befriended Carolyn Eadie; their paths diverged when they went to university (Carolyn went to Oxford), but they kept in touch over the next ten years (during which Portillo was rumoured to have affairs with at least two other women), and in 1982, as he was about to seek adoption as a Conservative parliamentary candidate, he married her. Carolyn was now a successful 'head-hunter', and did not allow her role as the wife of a politician to interfere with her career – which was convenient for the household, as her earnings were far in excess of her husband's ministerial salary. Based on affection and shared interests, the marriage proved an endur-ing partnership. They had no children, possibly owing to Carolyn suffering an episode of breast cancer; their friends included two of Portillo's ministerial colleagues who were also childlessly married, Peter Lilley and Neil Hamilton, and the three couples often went on holiday together. Mandelson for his part got on particularly well with female colleagues and shared a flat with one of them – Kinnock's press secretary Julie Hall – in the early 1990s.

However, although they were both intensely protective of their private lives, it was common knowledge in the political and social circles in which they moved that Portillo, though enjoying relationships with women, had homosexual interests, while Mandelson was frankly gay. Portillo was attached during his twenties to three institutions in which homosexuality flourished – Peterhouse, the Cambridge University Amateur Dramatic Club (known as the 'AC/DC'), and the Conservative Research Department – and he did not hold himself entirely aloof from the opportunities offered, as Carolyn when she married him appears to have been fully aware. Mandelson had two long-term relationships – with Peter Ashby, a fellow researcher at the TUC, from the late 1970s to the late 1980s, and with Reinaldo Avila da Silva, a Brazilian some years younger than himself, from the mid-1990s: from time to time these attachments were the subject of prurient features in the tabloids, but as Mandelson always refused to rise to the bait or comment in any way, the effect of such exposure was limited.* Within the space of a year in the late 1990s, however, both their homosexual lives were sensationally brought to the attention of a wide public. In August 1998, Mandelson was inadvertently 'outed' by the journalist and ex-MP Matthew Parris in a

---

* Particularly distressing for Mandelson (as he writes in his memoirs) was an article which appeared in the *News of the World* just before the 1987 election, under the headline 'Kinnock's No.1 Man in Gay Sensation', revealing that Mandelson's lover Ashby had, during their relationship, had a brief affair with a woman resulting in a male child, then aged three, whom both Ashby and Mandelson were helping the mother to bring up. 'I have never cloaked [my private life] in secrecy: I simply regarded my life outside politics as having no relevance to my public role ... [T]he *News of the World*'s prurience ... made me more determined than ever not to make concessions to those who are interested in the relevancies of the bedroom over the Cabinet Room.' (*The Third Man*, pp. 101–2.) The boy, Joe Carbery, later became an adviser to David Miliband as Foreign Secretary.

discussion about gay politicians on BBC's *Newsnight*, occasioned by the Ron Davies affair (described in the Epilogue): it is an indication of the fear Mandelson inspired among editors that the huge press coverage which this incident provoked concentrated more on Parris's perfidy in 'outing' the minister than on Mandelson's homosexuality itself. And in the summer of 1999, Portillo, then about to seek adoption at Kensington and Chelsea, admitted in an interview with *The Times* to having had 'some homosexual experiences as a young person'. A businessman named Nigel de Villiers Hart then claimed in the *Mail on Sunday* that he had had an intermittent affair with Portillo lasting eight years, starting in Cambridge where they had overlapped as undergraduates and ending shortly before Portillo married Carolyn.* These revelations did not affect Portillo's successful bid for 'K. & C.', and indeed seem to have enhanced his standing with the public; but it is clear that concern among parliamentary colleagues about possible further embarrassing disclosures played a crucial role in Portillo's narrow failure to win the Conservative leadership two years later (as his rival Ken Clarke, for whom several MPs expected to back Portillo finally voted, later confirmed).

Although Portillo and Mandelson served together in the parliament of 1992–7, they were too busy with their respective roles in government and opposition to have much personal contact. But in 1998 Portillo interviewed Mandelson for a

---

* Hart, the son of a Tory squire in the West Country, was two years older than Portillo. After Portillo's marriage Hart continued to be friendly with both Portillos, going to live with them for six months in 1983 after suffering a business disaster. As a gay activist and sometime officer of the Campaign for Homosexual Equality, he was annoyed when Portillo voted in 1994 against the equalisation of the age of consent; but until Portillo himself revealed something of his gay past five years later, it never occurred to Hart to speak of their affair. However, after Portillo's 'confession' Hart found himself harassed by journalists who had been tipped off about the relationship, and decided to tell his story. He was suffering from AIDS at the time and died soon afterwards.

political television documentary, and they got on well, subsequently exchanging social invitations; and after Portillo's re-election to parliament the following year, Mandelson made a favourable reference in public to Portillo's new-found tolerant brand of Conservatism. During the interview (which took place before Mandelson had been 'outed' by Parris, and Portillo had 'outed' himself), Portillo asked Mandelson why he had so many problems with his own image when he had been so good at improving Labour's. Mandelson replied: 'Many of the people who get on in politics are the people who never cause offence to anyone. At the first sign of controversy they run for cover ... They are the majority. The minority are the strong personalities ... who are risk-takers. You have paid the price for being a risk-taker, and so have I.'

# EPILOGUE

It took a long time for social attitudes to catch up with the reform of the law. Crossman was not wrong when he suggested that the enactment of the Wolfenden recommendations was 'twenty years ahead of public opinion'. In 1966 Humphry Berkeley, who had recently proposed his reform bill, was defeated in the general election on a swing greater than the national average against his party, an indication (if one were needed) that the subject was a vote-loser. After the 1967 Act, further reform was slow in coming. Homosexuality remained illegal in Scotland until 1981 and in Northern Ireland until 1982; the age of consent remained at twenty-one until 1994, more than a quarter of a century after the original legislation. Although various MPs of all parties (such as Sir Charles Irving, the genial hotel owner and Conservative MP for Cheltenham who chaired the House of Commons Catering Committee)* were widely known to be gay, only two, both from the Labour Party, had the temerity to 'come out' before the 1990s. In 1977 Maureen Colquhoun, the feisty, left-wing MP for Northampton North, announced that she was a

---

* The 'Refreshment Department' controlled by the Committee employed many gay youths, who were known to organise discreet 'private parties' for like-minded MPs – see Parris, *Chance Witness* (Penguin, 2013), p. 299.

lesbian. She was promptly deselected by her local party; and although she managed to have herself reinstated by appealing to Labour's National Executive Committee, she lost her seat at the 1979 election. And in 1984 Chris Smith, the recently elected MP for Islington and Finsbury, told a public meeting convened to discuss a gay rights issue that 'I'm gay, and so are about a hundred other members of the House of Commons, but they won't tell you openly'. This was certainly brave: Smith had won his seat by just a few hundred votes; and only the previous year (as described in Chapter 15), Peter Tatchell, a sometime member of the Gay Liberation Front, had managed to lose the apparently rock-solid Labour seat of Bermondsey on a huge swing at a by-election.

In 1979, Margaret Thatcher became Prime Minister. Despite her Methodist upbringing and strait-laced image, she was quite broad-minded when it came to questions of personal morality, taking the view that it did not matter what people did provided they did not harm others or 'frighten the horses in the streets'. She was one of the few Conservative MPs who consistently supported Wolfenden in parliamentary votes. Moreover, she seems to have had a certain affinity with gay men: with her strident, maternal personality, she was looked up to by many of them as an 'icon'; and, consciously or unconsciously, she chose quite a number of them to serve her, including her first and last parliamentary private secretaries, Fergus Montgomery and Peter Morrison. When Matthew Parris, who had worked for her before her premiership and then become an MP, told her in 1986 that he was quitting politics, and added what she surely knew, that he was gay, she put her hand on his wrist and said sympathetically, 'That must have been very difficult for you to say'. Warned that the prospective chairman of the Association of Conservative Clubs was rumoured to be gay, she merely remarked: 'Oh really? How interesting. There are so many on our side.' On coming to power, she appointed the flamboyant Norman St John-Stevas to be one of her leading ministers.

However, in 1981 she sacked Stevas from her cabinet, largely owing to his unrestrained love of gossip; and during the 1980s public opinion in general and the Conservatives in particular became notably less tolerant of homosexuality, for three reasons. First, there was a general feeling that the 'permissiveness' of the 1960s and 70s had gone too far and that, while there was no going back, a halt should be called to social liberalisation. Secondly, from 1983 onwards the spread of AIDS inspired a widespread fear of homosexuals, believed to be the main carriers of the then usually fatal condition. It even claimed a member of the government – Nicholas Eden, 2nd Earl of Avon, the unmarried son of the former premier Anthony Eden, who at the time of his death in 1985, aged fifty-four, was a junior minister at the Department of the Environment. Thirdly, some left-wing Labour councils sponsored militant gay groups and published literature offering advice to schoolchildren on how to 'cruise' and adopt other aspects of a gay lifestyle, incidents which, though fairly isolated, were gleefully seized upon by the press. These factors resulted in growing public disquiet on the subject of homosexuality, leading the government to table what became Section 28 of the Local Government Act of 1988, which provided that a local authority 'shall not intentionally promote homosexuality or publish material with the intention of promoting homosexuality'. In practical terms, this measure was little more than advisory: it created no criminal offence, and during the fifteen years that it was in force there was only one occasion when a local authority was (unsuccessfully) taken to court for allegedly infringing its provisions. Nevertheless, many gay men and women regarded it as an insult that their inclinations should be stigmatised in this way; as Parris writes, 'there was something profoundly offensive about ... a law which singled out, from the infinite range of inappropriate causes a local authority might try to promote, one group in society, and prohibited teachers in state schools from talking positively about this group'.

In this atmosphere, almost all gay MPs in the 1980s remained closeted in the sense of not publicly admitting to their homosexuality, even if they were fairly well known to be gay, and actively supported gay rights. Chris Smith was the only real exception. One must however mention another parliamentarian who, while denying his homosexuality in public, nevertheless managed to pursue a colourful lifestyle which he took few pains to conceal. This was Allan Roberts, the thirty-five-year-old social worker who was elected Labour MP for Bootle in 1979. In 1981, the *News of the World* revealed that he had attended a party in a Berlin nightclub organised by the Motorcycle Leather Club, at which he had donned a dog collar and been whipped by a man in SS uniform before a crowd of delighted enthusiasts: he had subsequently required medical treatment for his wounds at a Berlin hospital, where he failed to pay the bill (which was altruistically settled on his behalf by his fellow MP Charles Irving, who also happened to be visiting the city). *Private Eye* reported that Roberts had once addressed Manchester City Council without employing his usual arm-waving technique, keeping his right hand in his pocket; when a supporter later approached him to shake it, a set of handcuffs was found to be dangling from the wrist. Despite such stories (on which he always refused to comment), Roberts, a robust, gregarious personality, retained the support of his local party and won huge majorities at the two subsequent general elections. In 1984 he successfully sued for libel over a report that Manchester City Police was investigating his sex life; he used his winnings to buy a pub, where he hosted parties which featured much sexual frolicking, heavy drinking and smoking of marijuana. He was promoted by his party to be a shadow spokesman on the environment, but died in 1990, aged forty-six, of causes which are unclear. At his memorial service on Merseyside no mention was made of his sexuality.

During the 1980s, two Conservative MPs ran into trouble because of homosexual accusations. Keith Hampson, the married, forty-year-old PPS to the Defence Secretary Michael Heseltine, was charged in 1984 with indecent assault after allegedly stroking the thigh of a 'pretty policeman' at an all-male strip club in Soho. He opted for a jury trial at which he pleaded not guilty, insisting that he had entered the establishment by mistake (though the owner testified that it was not the first time he had been seen there). The jury failed to reach a verdict, and Hampson was discharged; though he had been obliged to resign as Heseltine's aide, and received no further office, he remained MP for Leeds North-West until defeated there in 1997. Harvey Proctor, the forty-year-old, right-wing, bachelor MP for Billericay, was in 1986 the subject of allegations in the *People* newspaper (against which he had brought a successful libel action some years earlier) that he engaged in spanking sessions with underage rent boys: he had been tape-recorded during one of these with a youth of eighteen, who had assured Proctor (as the recording revealed) that he was in fact twenty-one. Proctor received strong support from his constituency party, but he continued to be hounded by both the press and the police, finally standing down from his seat before the 1987 election after he had pleaded guilty to a charge of indecent behaviour with a minor and been fined £1450.

During the 1990s, the pendulum swung back in favour of toleration: the annual *British Social Attitudes* survey suggested that, in 1983, 50 per cent of the public disapproved of homosexuality, the figure rising to 64 per cent in 1987 and returning to 50 per cent in 1993, declining steadily thereafter. John Major, who succeeded Thatcher as Prime Minister in 1990, was enthusiastically heterosexual but relaxed about homosexuality (coming as he did from a family involved in music hall and the circus), and sympathetic to the cause of gay equality. This cause was taken up by the Conservative MP and former health minister (and, as it subsequently emerged, former lover of Major) Edwina Currie, who in February 1994 tabled an amendment to the Criminal Justice Bill then going through parliament, proposing a reduction in the age of consent for homosexuals from twenty-one to sixteen, the same as that for heterosexuals. This was narrowly defeated in the House of Commons by 307 votes to 280; but a subsequent amendment providing for a reduction to eighteen was overwhelmingly carried by 427 votes to 162.

However, if the 1990s were a more comfortable decade for gay men generally, they presented a new terror for gay MPs – that of being 'outed' by the press, which was emboldened by two factors. One was the activities of the militant organisation OutRage, which sent letters (copied to the press) to allegedly gay MPs who had failed to support the vote on equality, urging them to declare their sexual nature; one of these, the Ulster Unionist Sir James Kilfedder, died of a heart attack on the day that the *Belfast Telegraph* revealed him to be one of the recipients.* The other was the slogan 'Back to Basics', adopted by the Conservatives at their annual conference in October 1993; this was merely intended as an appeal to greater civic-mindedness, but the Murdoch newspapers, now hostile to the unpopular Major government, chose to interpret it as launching a morality

---

* A decade later the same newspaper published an article by the Belfast-born journalist Leo McKinstry (the biographer of Lord Rosebery and doubter of his homosexuality) describing how, as a boy, he had rejected 'anguished attempts at intimacy' from the MP.

crusade, giving them a pretext to 'expose hypocrisy' by unmasking the wayward morals of Tory MPs. A witch-hunt followed, alleging sexual impropriety against a series of otherwise blameless parliamentarians. In May 1994, Michael Brown, MP for Brigg and Scunthorpe, was forced to resign as a government whip after the *News of the World* published photographs of him holidaying in the Caribbean with his twenty-year-old boyfriend. (Though the vote changing the age of consent had taken place, the change was not due to take legal effect for some months.) Soon afterwards he joined Chris Smith in publicly admitting his homosexuality. The same year David Ashby, the conscientious MP for Leicestershire North-West, was alleged by the *Sunday Times* to have 'left his wife because of friendship with another man'; he sued the newspaper for libel, breaking down in the witness box and losing the case, which left him financially ruined. Subsequently he became a supporter of gay rights, and was deselected by his local party. In 1995, the handsome Richard Spring, MP for Bury St Edmunds, was revealed by the *News of the World* to have engaged in a 'three-in-a-bed sex session' with a man and a woman he had met at a dinner party (to whom he had allegedly confided that he fancied both the Prime Minister's wife, Norma Major, and the Employment Secretary, Michael Portillo). As all those involved were unmarried (Spring was recently divorced from a wife by whom he had two children), freely consenting and 'of age' it is hard to see that this was anyone else's business; but it led to Spring's immediate resignation as PPS to the Northern Ireland Secretary, Sir Patrick Mayhew (though Spring remained an MP until 2010, when he was raised to the peerage as Baron Risby). Early in 1997 the *News of the World* struck again, alleging that Jerry Hayes, the charismatic MP for Harlow, married with two children, had had an affair with his eighteen-year-old male researcher six years earlier, when the age of consent was still twenty-one; Hayes insisted that the relationship had been platonic, and was supported by his family and local party, but lost his seat at the general election a few months later. On the eve of the election, the *News of the World* also revealed that Sir Michael Hirst, chairman of the Scottish Conservatives and a former MP and minister, married with two children, had a gay past: this led to his withdrawal as candidate for the supposedly safe seat of Glasgow Eastwood (and may have contributed to the total wipeout of the Scottish Tories at the polls).

1997 saw the great electoral victory of New Labour, which promised a new era of 'diversity' and 'inclusiveness' after what it represented as two decades of Conservative reaction and 'sleaze'. Labour candidates who triumphed in former Tory strongholds included two openly gay men, Stephen Twigg in Enfield Southgate (where he unseated Michael Portillo) and Ben Bradshaw in Exeter (where he won a large majority in the face of a homophobic Conservative campaign). Chris Smith became Culture Secretary and the first openly gay cabinet minister, his male partner being included in invitations to such official occasions as Buckingham Palace garden parties. The government's main strategist, Peter Mandelson, was generally known to be gay, a fact which became public after being mentioned by Matthew Parris on *Newsnight*. (The fascinating thing about Mandelson is that, although he came to office at a time when he could have been open about his sexuality, he continued to exhibit traits which had been typical of closet queens of the past such as Loulou Harcourt and Jeremy Thorpe – a flair for manipulation and intrigue; an addiction to risk; a streak of ruthlessness deriving from consciousness of his own vulnerability.) Great strides were made in reforming the law. The ban on homosexuals in the armed forces and the diplomatic service was lifted; the age of consent was reduced to sixteen in 2000; Section 28 was (after some obstruction by the House of Lords) repealed in 2003; civil partnerships were introduced, giving gay couples the same legal privileges as married couples, in 2004; and a series of measures enacted between 2003 and 2010 made it illegal to discriminate against people, or 'incite hatred' against them, on the grounds of their sexual orientation.

However, although the Blair government marked a new liberated era for homosexuals, it also witnessed one of the most bizarre gay scandals of the twentieth century, and the only one to result in the resignation of a cabinet minister. Ron Davies, born in 1946, Labour MP for Caerphilly from 1983, twice married with a daughter, was a robust male who 'appeared to typify the macho culture of the valleys'. He was a champion of Welsh devolution, and on being appointed Secretary of State for Wales in 1997 he lost no time in putting Labour's devolutionary plans into effect, presiding over a referendum which narrowly produced a 'yes' vote and steering through parliament the legislation creating a Welsh assembly and government. In September 1998 he defeated his rival Rhodri Morgan to become Labour's prospective candidate for the post of First Secretary for Wales when it came into being the following May. But Davies was destined never to hold that office. On 27 October 1998 he caused both amazement and puzzlement by announcing his resignation from the government on account of 'a moment of madness' on Clapham Common the previous night, which had led to his being robbed at knifepoint and relieved of his wallet, phone, car and Commons pass. The facts of the episode have never become entirely clear, but it would seem that Davies, having just returned from a stressful visit to his Welsh constituency, had visited a well-known London 'cruising spot', falling into the company of men who not only robbed him but attempted to blackmail him. In his resignation statement to the

House, Davies denied that he was gay, but added that 'we are all different, the product of our genes and experiences', and that the incident had indirectly resulted from the fact that as a child he had been bullied by his father; he subsequently admitted to being bisexual, and to receiving treatment for a personality disorder which impelled him to 'seek out risky situations'. Davies gave up his Westminster seat at the 2001 election. In 1999 he had been elected to the new Welsh Assembly over which he had once hoped to preside, but was obliged to stand down four years later after revelations in the *Sun* that he regularly visited another well-known cruising spot near a motorway lay-by: when confronted with the evidence, he claimed that he had been 'watching badgers'. He was divorced by his wife (eventually marrying for a third time), and resigned from the Labour Party (eventually joining Plaid Cymru).*

Meanwhile, following their 1997 defeat, the Conservatives had elected as their leader Davies's immediate predecessor as Welsh Secretary, William Hague. Hague was a thirty-six-year-old bachelor, and there were rumours (the truth of which he always denied) that he was gay, which subsided when, in December 1997, he married Ffion Jenkins, one of his former civil servants at the Welsh Office. They resurfaced years later, in August 2010, when a photograph was published of Hague, now Foreign Secretary, with Christopher Myers, a young friend he had appointed his special adviser at the Foreign Office: it emerged that they had shared a hotel bedroom during the recent general election campaign. Press speculation on the matter died down after Hague and his wife had issued a statement declaring that

---

* Another gay member of the Labour government in 1997 was the Chief Whip, Nick Brown. He was a close ally of Gordon Brown, and it is said that there were attempts to embarrass him on account of his sexuality as part of the 'dirty tricks' of the Blair–Brown feud. At all events, soon after being appointed Agriculture Secretary in 1998, Brown decided to come clean about his homosexuality, telling an audience of farmers: 'It's a lovely day, the sun is out – and so am I.'

theirs was a loving marriage, and that their desire to have children had been thwarted by her suffering a series of miscarriages. Hague's right-hand man during his leadership, said to be a close friend, was Alan Duncan, the personable MP for Rutland (and like Hague a former President of the Oxford Union), who in 2002 (after Hague had been succeeded as Conservative leader by Iain Duncan Smith) became the first Conservative frontbencher to declare his homosexuality.*

After his election as party leader in 2005, David Cameron was keen to show that the Conservatives now embraced sexual diversity and supported gay equality. He appointed Alan Duncan to the shadow cabinet, and issued a public apology for Section 28. Despite strong disapproval from the Conservative 'grass roots', the Conservative–Liberal Democrat coalition which came to power in 2010 legislated for 'same-sex marriage', which reached the statute book in 2014. Yet within eighteen months of the coalition taking office, two cabinet ministers had resigned for reasons not unassociated with the subjects discussed in this book. In May 2010 David Laws, the Liberal Democrat MP for Yeovil, gave up the post of Chief Secretary to the Treasury to which he had been appointed less than a month earlier when the *Daily Telegraph* revealed that he had claimed parliamentary expenses for London accommodation which in fact belonged to his 'long-term partner and secret lover', a situation disallowed by the expenses rules. A striking aspect of the affair was that, even among Laws's party colleagues, few had been aware of his sexuality: he explained that he had wished to keep it private out of respect for the feelings of his mother. And in October 2011 Dr Liam Fox, a former chairman of the Conservative Party, resigned as Secretary of State for Defence as

---

* Hague also made a reputation as an author and, like Lord Rosebery, published a biography of that great unmarried statesman, Pitt the Younger.

a result of his close (albeit non-sexual) relationship with Adam Werritty, a man seventeen years his junior who had been befriended by Fox while a university student, and who had subsequently lived in his flat and worked as his parliamentary researcher. Although Fox had married in 2005 (Werritty acting as best man and accompanying the couple on their honeymoon), the two men remained almost inseparable, and it was the startling revelation that Werritty, who possessed no official standing or security clearance, had been in constant attendance on Fox at the Defence Ministry, as well as accompanying him on most of his official trips and being present at many of his confidential meetings with foreign dignitaries, that obliged Fox to relinquish office.

While the campaign for gay equality had now triumphed beyond the dreams of its founders (indeed, some felt that the law, by making it difficult to utter any criticism of homosexuality and homosexuals, had compromised the right to free expression), a new form of intolerance had arisen, directed towards anyone deemed to have made 'inappropriate' sexual advances of whatever nature. As a result, some found themselves in trouble because of conduct which, a few years earlier, might have been regarded as merely indiscreet. One such was the Welsh Conservative Nigel Evans, MP for Ribble Valley from 1992 and a sometime Shadow Secretary of State for Wales, elected Deputy Speaker of the House of Commons in 2010. At the end of that year he confessed to being gay, saying that he was 'fed up with living his life as a lie' (he had been one of the 'closeted' MPs targeted by OutRage in 1994 for having failed to support the vote to equalise the age of consent). However, the strains of clandestine sexuality had induced in him a tendency to make playful passes at young men while under the influence of alcohol; and in 2013 a complaint arising from such behaviour led to his arrest on charges of rape and

sexual assault, and his resignation from the deputy speakership – though at his trial the following year he was acquitted on
all counts after most of the witnesses produced by the prosecution made it clear that, while rejecting his advances, they did
not consider themselves to have been 'assaulted'.

So the age of the political closet queen is not quite dead. In
a sense it will continue so long as there are politicians who
have homosexual feelings and enjoy homosexual experiences
while also wishing to lead a traditional family life with a wife
and children (a description which may be said to fit at least
one former cabinet minister sitting in the House of Commons
at the time of writing). Few would advocate a return to the old
days; but the need to keep one's sexuality secret tended to
foster qualities which may be missed in future.

# NOTES

## CHAPTER 1

27. McKinstry examines the evidence: Leo McKinstry, *Rosebery: Statesman in Turmoil* (John Murray, 2005), chapter 12

27. 'from my knowledge of what some of them may contain': Harcourt's diary for 8 March 1894, quoted in McKinstry, p. 304

29. 'I cannot forget 1895': quoted in Rosebery's *DNB* entry by John Davis

34. Esher quotations from Maurice V. Brett (ed.), *Journals and Letters of Reginald, Viscount Esher*, Vols 1 & 2 (I. Nicholson & Watson, 1934)

36. 'Elliot and I lay together': quoted in James Lees-Milne, *The Enigmatic Edwardian: The Life of Reginald, 2nd Viscount Esher* (Sidgwick & Jackson, 1986), p. 50

37-8. he could not recollect when he had not cared passionately for a male friend: Lees-Milne, p. 76

38. Teddie Seymour: Lees-Milne, pp. 87–91, 93–4, 103; *Journals and Letters*, Vol. I, p. 189

41. 'Priscilla': Lees-Milne, p. 158

43. 'the petted associate of half the public men of the time': A. G. Gardiner, *The Life of Sir William Harcourt* (Constable, 1923), Vol. I, p. 242

46. 'caught misbehaving': quoted in McKinstry, p. 276 & n.

47. Harcourt's 'harpie' tendencies, and interest in Esher's children: Lees-Milne, pp. 112, 119, 138, 337–8

47. Harcourt and Kühlmann: contemporary rumours of a homosexual element in their friendship reported to author by Professor Michael Dockrill of King's College, London

48. 'Harcourt said, "Come nearer, child."': Edward James, *Swans Reflecting Elephants* (Weidenfeld, 1982), pp. 26–7

48. Harcourt inquest: *The Times*, 1 March 1922

48. 'London is convulsed by the sordid tragedy': quoted in Lees-Milne, p. 337

49. Esher's daughters' feelings towards Harcourt: Philip Eade, *Sylvia, Queen of the Headhunters* (Weidenfeld, 2007), pp. 29–30

53. 'It sounds a very curious sort of illness': quoted in Jane Mulvagh, *Madresfield: One Family, One House, One Thousand Years* (Doubleday, 2008), p. 386

54. 'They say – what say they?': *ibid.*, p. 381

54. Jowitt and Lady Aberconway surprised: Christabel Aberconway, *A Wiser Woman?* (Hutchinson, 1966)

54. 'Ld Beauchamp in the act with a boy': A. O. Bell and A. McNeillie (ed.), *The Diary of Virginia Woolf*, Vol. 5 (Hogarth Press, 1984), p. 211

55–6. Beauchamp warned not to bring lover to Canberra: Harold Nicolson MS Diaries (Balliol College, Oxford), 15 January 1937

59–60. Lord Beauchamp and Madresfield models for Lord Marchmain and Brideshead: see Paula Byrne, *Mad World: Evelyn Waugh and the Secrets of Brideshead* (Harper, 2009)

## CHAPTER 2

62. Montagu marriage unconsummated: Naomi B. Levine, *Politics, Religion and Love: The Story of H. H. Asquith, Venetia Stanley and Edwin Montagu* (New York UP, 1991), p. 387

64. 'I (unlike many) never found him physically repulsive': Polly Keynes and Richard Keynes (eds), *Lydia and Maynard: Letters between Lydia Lopokova and John Maynard Keynes* (Deutsch, 1989), p. 256

64. 'To know him was to delight in him': Winston S. Churchill, *The World Crisis: 1911–1914* (Thornton Butterworth, 1923), p. 233

64. Montagu's love for 'Bron': Montagu to Lady Desborough, 17 April 1917, Hampshire Record Office, DERV C1882/1 (brought to author's attention by Richard Davenport-Hines)

65. 'I never knew a male person who was more addicted to gossip': John Maynard Keynes, *Complete Works*, Vol. X, p. 42

66. Asquith bombards Venetia with love letters: Michael and Eleanor Brock (ed.), *H. H. Asquith: Letters to Venetia Stanley* (OUP, 1982)

67. Edwin 'a closet homosexual': Bobbie Neate, *Conspiracy of Secrets* (John Blake, 2012), chapter 16

67–8. 'a marriage of convenience': John Joliffe (ed.), *Raymond Asquith: Life and Letters* (Collins, 1980), p. 202

68. paternity of Venetia's daughter: Levine, pp. 670 ff.

## CHAPTER 3

73–4. Kipling thinks Balfour's sexuality suspect: see Piers Brendon, *Eminent Edwardians* (Secker, 1979), p. 80

74. Balfour's love for May Lyttelton unconvincing: R. J. Q. Adams, *Balfour: The Last Grandee* (Murray 2007), pp. 27–33

75. Balfour's sado-masochistic relationship with Lady Elcho: *ibid.*, pp. 46–8

75–6. 'a kind of exhilaration at the catastrophe': quoted in David Gilmour, *Curzon: Imperial Statesman* (John Murray, 1994), p. 352

77. 'Tell Arthur I love him': Adams, pp. 201–2

77. suggestion that Wyndham died in male brothel made by Simon Blow (Wyndham's great-great-nephew) in *Spectator*, 18 January 2014

77. 'the beauty of a statue and the tenderness of a woman': Curzon's appreciation of Wyndham in *The Times*, 10 June 1913

77. 'he pirouettes like a dancing-master': quoted in Wyndham's *DNB* entry by Alvin Jackson

78. 'a hermaphrodite': A. J. P. Taylor, *Beaverbrook* (Hamish Hamilton, 1972), p. 154

78–9. Bruce affair: Randolph S. Churchill, *Winston S. Churchill*, Vol. I (Heinemann, 1966), pp. 248–51

80. 'incapable of love': *ibid.*, p. 425

81. 'his wife could never be more to him': Mark Pottle (ed.), *Lantern Slides: The Diaries and Letters of Violet Bonham Carter, 1904–14* (Weidenfeld & Nicolson, 1996), p. 162

82. 'a well-run household': Sir John Colville, *The Churchillians* (Weidenfeld, 1981), p. 122

82. Marsh a foot-fetishist: see James Lees-Milne, *A Mingled Measure* (Murray, 1994), p. 59

83. 'Few people have been as lucky as me': Churchill to Marsh, 20 August 1908 in Randolph S. Churchill, *Winston S. Churchill*, Vol. II, Companion Part 2 (Heinemann, 1969), p. 836

83. 'Ruth to Winston's Naomi': Sir Edward Marsh, *A Number of People* (Heinemann, 1939), p. 171

83. 'joyous, fearless, versatile': *The Times*, 26 April 1915

84. Surviving early correspondence between Churchill and Sinclair in Ian Hunter (ed.), *Winston and Archie* (Politico, 2005)

84. 'the head-boy's fag': Max Hastings, *Finest Years: Churchill as Warlord* (HarperPress, 2009), chapter 1

86–7. 'No doubt Churchill's spontaneous offer … why Winston liked him': Andrew Boyle, *Poor Dear Brendan: The Quest for Brendan Bracken* (Hutchinson, 1974), p. 102

89. housekeeper's diary reveals homosexual goings-on: *ibid.*, pp. 344–5

89–90. Garrett Moore believed Bracken in love with him: information from his son, 12th Earl of Drogheda

89. Lindemann's sexuality: Adrian Fort, *Prof: The Life of Frederick Lindemann* (Cape, 2003), p. 163

91. Churchill and Guy Burgess: see Tom Driberg, *Guy Burgess: A Portrait with Background* (Weidenfeld, 1956), pp. 43–8

92. Churchill and Heath: Philip Ziegler, *Edward Heath* (HarperCollins, 2010), pp. 84–5

94. 'I once went to bed … very musical': related by James Lees-Milne to the author, 1979 (it is unclear whether Lees-Milne – who frequently met

Maugham as a fellow resident of the French Riviera in the 1950s – heard
this directly from him or from another source)

## CHAPTER 4

95. 'love between men': Jan Morris, *Farewell the Trumpets: An Imperial Retreat* (Faber & Faber, 1978), chapter 1

99. Curzon's platonic friendships: Kenneth Rose, *Superior Person: A Portrait of Lord Curzon and his Circle in Late Victorian England* (Weidenfeld, 1969)

99. 'fine, stalwart, bronzed figures': quoted in David Gilmour, *Curzon: Imperial Statesman*, p. 37

100–1. Curzon's campaign against homosexuality among native Princes: Gilmour, pp. 190, 239; Kenneth Ballhatchet, *Race, Sex and Class under the Raj* (Weidenfeld, 1980), pp. 119–21; Richard Davenport-Hines, *Sex, Death and Punishment* (Collins, 1990), pp. 113–4

105. Kitchener 'worshipped General Gordon ...': Ronald Hyam, *Empire and Sexuality* (Manchester UP, 1990), pp. 38–9

106. what Diana Cooper told Wilson: A. N. Wilson, *The Victorians* (Hutchinson, 2002), p. 598

109. 'circumstantial evidence': Hyam, p. 39

113. 'having been brought up in a religion': unpublished memoir of Miss O'Sullivan quoted in Lothian's *DNB* entry by Alex May

114. love for Pepys Cockerell 'the deepest possible': quoted in John Charmley, *Lord Lloyd and the Decline of the British Empire* (Weidenfeld, 1987), p. 40

## CHAPTER 5

122. 'big and gauche': James Lees-Milne, *Caves of Ice: Diaries, 1946–7* (Chatto, 1983), entry for 15 September 1946

122. 'it would probably be more appropriate': J. A. Cross, *Sir Samuel Hoare: A Political Biography* (Cape, 1977), p. 10

123. Hoare 'persuaded Wolfenden of the importance of the work': Patrick Higgins, *Heterosexual Dictatorship* (Fourth Estate, 1996), p. 7

124. 'dark face, heavily lidded eyes': Peter Stansky, *Sassoon: The World of Philip and Sibyl* (Yale UP, 2003), pp. 23–4

126. Sassoon-Esher correspondence: James Lees-Milne, *The Enigmatic Edwardian*, pp. 280 ff

129. 'he brought to bear on the property of the public': Cecil Roth, *The Sassoon Dynasty* (R. Hale, 1941), p. 255

130. Channon described him as a Jew who hated Jews: Robert Rhodes James (ed.) *Chips: The Diaries of Sir Henry Channon* (Weidenfeld, 1967), entry for 3 June 1939

131. Malet called Sassoon 'Phil': Stansky, p. 113

131. 'whatever these confidences may have been': *ibid.*, p. 139

131–2. 'So you waited all the day': *ibid.*, pp. 81–2, 111–12

132. Sassoon implored Cartland to become his private secretary: Barbara Cartland, *Ronald Cartland* (Collins, 1942), p. 139
132. 'she has set me too dizzying a standard': Stansky, p. 68
133. 'removed from the ordinary passions': Nigel Nicolson (ed.), *Harold Nicolson: Diaries and Letters 1930–1939* (Collins, 1966), entry for 1 June 1931
133. 'I prefer to work under Sam Hoare': Stansky, p. 119
133. 'You know how happy I have been': *ibid.*, p. 124
134. 'There was no one in my lifetime like Philip Sassoon': *The Times*, 5 June 1939

## CHAPTER 6

136. fascinating autobiographies: Tom Driberg, *Ruling Passions* (Cape, 1977); Boothby [sic], *Recollections of a Rebel* (Hutchinson, 1978). There memoirs are complemented by biographies published a decade or so later – Francis Wheen, *Tom Driberg: His Life and Indiscretions* (Chatto, 1990); Robert Rhodes James, *Bob Boothby: A Portrait* (Hodder, 1991)
137. John Pearson on Boothby: *Notorious: How the Kray Twins made themselves Immortal* (Random House, 2010), chapter 11
137–8. Macmillan happy to nominate Boothby for peerage: National Archives, PREM 11/2455
139. 'I have known many homosexuals': Boothby, pp. 212–3
140. 'They disclosed that HN was homosexual': James Lees-Milne, *Through Wood and Dale: Diaries 1975–1978* (John Murray, 1998), entry for 10 July 1978
140–1. 'The frequent allegation that Boothby was homosexual': Rhodes James, pp. 40, 370–1
144. 'an expert at bribing policemen': Roy Jenkins, *A Life at the Centre* (Macmillan, 1991), p. 90
145–6. public records released in 1995: National Archives, PREM 11/4689
147. the Krays blackmail Boothby: Pearson, chapters 11–12
147–8. 'which he was wise to say': quoted in Wheen, p. 352

## CHAPTER 7

149. Lennox-Boyd's otherwise discreet biographer: Philip Murphy, *Alan Lennox-Boyd: A Life* (Taurus, 1999)
150. 'the person I have loved most': Rhodes James (ed.), *Chips: The Diaries of Sir Henry Channon*, entry for 18 December 1934
151. Channon's 'adored' Princess Paul of Greece: *ibid.*, 10 August 1936
153. Butler writes in his memoirs: R. A. Butler, *The Art of the Possible* (Hamish Hamilton 1983), p. 76
154. 'an act of pure, disinterested, sisterly friendship': Driberg, *Ruling Passions*, p.187
154. a guardsman expired of a heart attack: Bryan Connon, *Somerset Maugham and the Maugham Dynasty* (Sinclair Stevenson, 1979), p. 196

156. she was happy to have a homosexual husband: information from Lady Selina Hastings
156. the union involved role-reversal: information from Piers Brendon
157–8. Lennox-Boyd's sons surprised to learn of his homosexuality: information from Sir Mark Lennox-Boyd
158. Quotations from Lees-Milne: Michael Bloch (ed.), *James Lees-Milne, Diaries* (3 vols, John Murray, 2006–8), entries for 5 April 1948, 10 April 1948, 20 April 1948, 20 January 1949, 20 March 1983, 28 July 1983
158–9. Lennox-Boyd accepted advice to travel with wife rather than Beattie: Murphy, pp. 81–2

## CHAPTER 8

162. a selection of his journals ... published in three volumes: Nigel Nicolson (ed.), *Harold Nicolson: Diaries and Letters* (Collins, 1966–8)
164. 'a quick visit to a picture gallery between trains': Nigel Nicolson, *Portrait of a Marriage* (Weidenfeld & Nicolson, 1973), p. 141
165. Nicolson enjoyed discussing Byron's homosexuality: see James Lees-Milne's diary for 17 February 1942
165. the 'compromising' letter discovered in John Murray archives: Fiona McCarthy, *Byron: Life and Legend* (Murray, 2002), pp. 565–8
165. Nicolson's homosexual love letters curious to read: see Michael Bloch, *James Lees-Milne: The Life* (Murray, 2009), pp. 61–2
165. Macmillan apparently unaware of Nicolson's homosexuality: see Lees-Milne's diary for 22 February 1978
166. the Wellesley marriage: see Lady Jane Wellesley, *Wellington: A Journey Through My Family* (Orion, 2008)
166–7. the Lees-Milne marriage: see Bloch, *James Lees-Milne: The Life*
168. friendship between Nicolson and 'Hinch' in wartime House of Commons: see Nicolson's published diary for 28 June 1944
168. 'like a very jolly able-bodied seaman': James Lees-Milne, *Caves of Ice: Diaries 1946–1947* (Chatto, 1983), p. 13
168. Robert's searing memoir: Robert Montagu, *A Humour of Love* (Quartet, 2014)

## CHAPTER 9

169. Nicolson in tears: published diaries, 8 May 1945
171. 'The reason Victor never married': Thelma Cazalet-Keir, *From the Wings* (Bodley Head, 1967), p. 29
172. 'Victor's mania for knowing important people': Nicolson MS Diaries (Balliol College, Oxford), 7 April 1937
172. biography of Cazalet: Robert Rhodes James, *Victor Cazalet: A Portrait* (Hamish Hamilton, 1976)
173. Bernays and Beauchamp: Nicolson MS Diaries, 15 January 1937; Nick

Smart (ed.), *The Diaries of Robert Bernays, 1932–1939: An Insider's Account of the House of Commons* (Edward Mellen, 1996), pp. 257, 319

173. 'he is as fond of me as I am of him': Bernays Diaries, p.292

174. 'of course it was not a "grand passion"': quoted in Bernays Diaries, pp. 114–5

175. 'out to destroy' him: Nicolson MS Diaries, 28 May 1940

175–6. Macnamara adopted at Chelmsford thanks to Howard-Bury: Sir William Teeling, *Corridors of Frustration* (Johnson, 1970), pp. 114–15

176. Macnamara and Guy Burgess: Goronwy Rees, *A Chapter of Accidents* (Chatto & Windus, 1972), pp. 122–4; Miranda Carter, *Anthony Blunt: His Secret Lives* (Macmillan, 2001), p. 162

176. Macnamara requiring 'much experience of public affairs and public behaviour': Nicolson MS Diaries, 28 May 1936

177. wartime meetings of Nicolson and Macnamara: *ibid.*, 26 November 1939, 12 February 1940, 10 April 1940, 19 January 1941

177. Macnamara entertained by Churchill: Nicolson published Diaries, 14 October 1942

179. Cartland and Ruth Leonard: Barbara Cartland, *Ronald Cartland*, pp. 154–5

179. 'a particular friend': Peter Coats, *Of Kings and Cabbages* (Weidenfeld & Nicolson, 1984), p. 7

180. Latham entertains fellow gay MPs: *ibid.*, pp. 5–7

180. Latham and Eddy Sackville-West: Michael De-la-Noy, *Eddy: The Life of Edward Sackville-West* (Bodley Head, 1988), pp. 164–7

181. 'Poor Paul, he has not had a happy life': Nicolson MS Diaries, 31 July 1941

181–2. Lees-Milne Diaries, entries for 29 May 1943 and 28–9 April 1946

## CHAPTER 10

185. 'the young widow and her infant son': R. J. Minney, *The Private Papers of Hore-Belisha* (Collins, 1960), p. 22

185. 'In his rooms he had an abundance of purple cushions': *ibid.*, p. 26

186–7. H.-B. and Channon: *Chips: The Diaries of Sir Henry Channon*, entries for 27 January 1935, 31 January 1935, 22 November 1936, 6 December 1936, 27 April 1937, 12 May 1938, 14 December 1938

187. 'a bronze bambino in a niche': Minney, pp. 80–82; H. B. Liddell Hart, *Memoirs*, Vol. II (Cassell, 1965), pp. 75–6

187. 'snug and luxurious ... a sort of *chapelle ardente* to his mother's memory': *Chips*, entries for 12 May 1938 and 14 December 1938

188. 'my new S. of S. is doing what I put him there for': quoted in Iain Macleod, *Neville Chamberlain* (F. Muller, 1961), p. 284

190. 'My mind was centered on the War Office': Minney, p. 270

190. 'A fine day's work for the Army': Brian Bond (ed.), *Chief of Staff: The Diaries of Lieutenant-General Sir Henry Pownall*, Vol. I (Leo Cooper, 1972), p. 203

191–2. H.-B.'s visits to Ireland in search of Bracken's origins: Boyle, *Poor Dear Brendan*, pp. 17–18; information from the late Florence O'Donaghue

193. Haydon cigarette case episode: Minney, pp. 108, 114
193. 'a confirmed bachelor because of his undimmed devotion to his mother':
Minney, p. 296
193. H.-B. and Bruce-Lockhart: Kenneth Young (ed.), *The Diaries of Sir Robert Bruce-Lockhart*, Vol.2 (Macmillan, 1980), entry for 19 February 1957
195. 'She had a proper admiration for her son's abilities': Anne Gold (ed.),
*Edward Boyle: His Life by his Friends* (Macmillan, 1991), p. 114
196. Churchill and Boyle: *ibid.*, p. 68
198. Boyle and d'Aranyi: *ibid.*, p. 50
198. Chataway unaware of homosexual interest: *ibid.*, p. 105
198. 'he fell impatiently silent': Sir Michael Howard to the author, 20 September 2014
199. 'His rotund shape and bubbling good nature': Gold, pp. 60, 105
199. H.-B. and Rees-Mogg: William Rees-Mogg, *Memoirs* (2011)

## CHAPTER 11

201–2. Desmond Kilvington: see Simon Ball, *The Guardsmen* (HarperCollins, 2010), also Crookshank's *DNB* entry by same author
203. 'Jezebel': see D. R. Thorpe, *Selwyn Lloyd* (Cape, 1989), p. 17
203–4. Booth's encounter with Lloyd: Tony Booth, *Stroll On: An Autobiography* (Sidgwick & Jackson, 1989), p. 71
204–6. Ian Harvey, *To Fall Like Lucifer* (Sidgwick & Jackson, 1971)
206. wedding cake made of cardboard: information from Lady Selina Hastings
208. 'parties with teddy boys at Margate': Bob Edwards to the author, August 1994
209. 'I broke the law with my eyes open all my life': quoted in Matthew Parris and Kevin Maguine, *Great Parliamentary Scandals* (Robson, 2004), p. 146
210. Powell's confession revealed by Eric James (after Powell's death) in a letter to *The Times*, 10 February 1998, p. 19
210–11. Powell's letters to his parents from Australia of 22 May and 16 June 1938 in Churchill College Archives, POLL 1/1/1 (I am grateful to Peter Brooke for drawing my attention to this material)
213. 'vain and foolish' Eden 'managed' by his wife: Richard Davenport-Hines (ed.), *Letters from Oxford: Hugh Trevor-Roper to Bernard Berenson* (Weidenfeld & Nicolson, 2006), p. 211

## CHAPTER 12

217. 'He had learned from his mother': Philip Ziegler, *Edward Heath* (HarperCollins, 2010), chapter 12
219. 'When I look at him and he looks at me': *ibid.*, chapter 24
219. letter from 'Freddy' to 'Teddie': *ibid.*, chapter 2
219. Heath's 'disturbing experience': Andrew Roth, *Heath and the Heathmen* (Routledge, 1972), p. 11

221. Czech *agent provocateur* the subject of a documentary on BBC Radio 4, *The Heath Caper*, broadcast on 25 June 2012

222–3. Jeremy Norman, 'Sir Edward Heath' in *No Make-Up: Straight Tales from a Queer Life* (Elliott & Thompson, revised edn 2011)

## CHAPTER 13

225. 'A look from thee': quoted in Tim d'Arch Smith, *Love in Earnest* (Routlege, 1970), p. 141

225–6. Margaret Cole on her husband in *The Life of G. D. H. Cole* (Macmillan, 1971), pp. 91–4

227. 'a strong homosexual strain is clear': Ben Pimlott, *Hugh Dalton* (Macmillan, 1985), p. 198

228. 'waving an immense steaming penis in his face': quoted in Paul Delaney, *The Neo-Pagans* (Macmillan, 1987), pp. 49–50

228. Dalton invited to discuss homosexuality with Hirschfeld: information from Richard Davenport-Hines

229–30. 'who kept me in a little whitewashed room for a fortnight': quoted in Anthony Howard, *Crossman: The Pursuit of Power* (Cape, 1990), p. 24

230. 'an exceedingly close and intense friendship': quoted in John Campbell, *Roy Jenkins: A Well-Rounded Life* (Jonathan Cape, 2014), p. 66

230. 'held hands and recited verse because … they had loved each other': quoted in Brian Brivati, *Hugh Gaitskell* (Richard Cohen, 1996), p. 14

230. 'there was a scintilla of platonic homosexuality': Woodrow Wyatt, *Confessions of an Optimist* (Collins, 1985), p. 179

230. 'Hugh Dalton was in love with Tony': *ibid.*, p. 225

230. 'Thinking of Tony … I weep': quoted in Susan Crosland, *Tony Crosland* (Cape, 1982), p. 54

230. Dalton's lovesickness for Crosland: Nicholas Davenport, *Memoirs of a City Radical* (Weidenfeld, 1974), p. 171

231. 'This is how Rome fell!': quoted in Peter Paterson, *Tired and Emotional: The Life of Lord George-Brown* (Chatto, 1993), p. 32

231. Crossman squirms with embarrassment: see Richard Crossman, *Backbench Diaries* (Hamish Hamilton, 1981), p. 991; Richard *Davenport-Hines, An English Affair: Sex Class and Power in the Age of Profumo* (Harper, 2013), chapter 8

233. 'the strange and unnatural happenings at Government House': Christopher J. Walker, *Oliver Baldwin: A Life of Dissent* (Arcadia 2003), chapter 15

235. 'Gavin, still very much the lord of the manor': quoted in D. J. Young, *Bright Young People* (Chatto, 2007), p. 234

235. 'a pansy pacifist of whose tendencies it might be slander to speak': Ben Pimlott (ed.), *The Second World War Diary of Hugh Dalton* (Cape 1986), p. 509

236. 'the bed-and-breakfast candidate': Brian Sewell, *Outsider II* (Quartet, 2012), pp. 184–5

238. Thomas would 'dangerously over-react and panic if there was the slightest sign of a crack in the thin ice': Leo Abse, *Blair: The Man who Lost his Smile* (Robson, 2003), pp. 55–7

240. two books about Victor Grayson: D. McCormick, *Murder by Perfection* (John Long, 1970); David Clark, *Victor Grayson: Labour's Lost Leader* (Quartet, 1985)

240. 'Lewis Harcourt took an overdose': Noel Annan, *Our Age: Portrait of a Generation* (Weidenfeld & Nicolson, 1990), p. 163

## CHAPTER 14

243. 'Thereafter we saw each other nearly every day': Roy Jenkins, *A Life at the Centre* (Macmillan 1991), p. 30

243. 'Roy was not by nature gay': Campbell, *Roy Jenkins*, p. 33

243. 'pansy Beau Geste': *ibid.*, p. 34

245. 'from being David and Jonathan': *ibid.*, p. 66

245. Crosland's repressed homosexuality in adult life: see Bryan Magee, 'Tony Crosland as I Knew Him' in *Political Quarterly*, Vol. 10, No. 2 (2010), pp. 182–3, and Woodrow Wyatt, *Confessions of an Optimist*, p. 179

246. Jenkins and Crosland act as ushers at Driberg wedding: Jenkins, pp. 90–1

246. 'Hugh loved his looks and eternal undergraduate youthfulness': Wyatt, p. 225

250. Crosland's friends dismayed to observe him compromising principles: Magee, pp. 183–5

251. 'the intense closeness of our earlier relationship': Jenkins, p. 457

252. 'cost Labour six million votes': Crossman, *Backbench Diaries*, entry for 15 May 1961

252. 'twenty years ahead of public opinon': Richard Crossman, *Diaries of a Cabinet Minister*, Vol. 2 (Hamish Hamilton, 1976), entry for 3 July 1967

253. 'I had to proceed through stratagem': Jenkins, pp. 208–9

253–4. Abse and Berkeley described as 'heterosexual': Campbell (p. 297) refers to Abse's 'flamboyant (though heterosexual) showmanship'; Michael McManus, in chapter 5 of *Tory Pride and Prejudice* (Biteback, 2011), describes Berkeley as 'the heterosexual Conservative MP for Lancaster'

254. Arran's youthful homosexuality: see James Lees-Milne, *Holy Dread: Diaries, 1982–1984* (Murray, 2001), entry for 20 March 1983

## CHAPTER 15

258–9. Tatchell claims Mellish 'a secret bisexual': *They Fought and Lost*, BBC Radio 4, February 2003

## CHAPTER 16

268–9. Stevas and Stanford enter into civil partnership: *Daily Mail*, 19 March 2013.

# CHAPTER 17

272. 'certainly fifty per cent my mother's son': quoted in obituary of Cora in the *Herald*, 19 April 2014

272. 'the hardest blow': Peter Mandelson, *The Third Man: Life at the Heart of New Labour* (Harper, 2010), pp. 45, 411–12

274. 'an ambitious young man with a streak of ruthlessness': Matthew Parris, *Chance Witness: An Outsider's Life in Politics* (Penguin, 2013), pp. 174, 181

280–1. Portillo and Hague: see Simon Walter, *Tory Wars* (Politico's, 2001)

284. 'some homosexual experiences as a young person': *The Times*, 9 September 1999

284. Nigel Hart story: *Mail on Sunday*, 12 September 1999; *Guardian*, 13 September 1999

284. Clarke confirms that Portillo supporters switched to him: *Daily Telegraph*, 7 January 2002

# EPILOGUE

287–8. 'Oh really? How interesting.': quoted in McManus, *Tory Pride and Prejudice*, chapter 6

289. there was something profoundly offensive': Parris, *Chance Witness*, p. 356

289–90. Allan Roberts: *ibid.*, chapter 12

290–1. *British Social Attitudes* survey quoted in McManus, chapter 10

290–3. political sex scandals of the 1980s and 90s described in entertaining detail in Matthew Parris and Kevin Maguire, *Great Parliamentary Scandals*

294. 'appeared to typify the macho culture of the valleys': *ibid.*, p. 385

295–6. suggestions concerning William Hague: see Rob Wilson, *The Eye of the Storm* (Biteback, 2014), pp. 282–5

# INDEX

# PICTURE CREDITS

Ronnie Cartland: private collection
Leslie Hore-Belisha: private collection
Sir Edward Boyle: private collection
Enoch Powell: © TopFoto.co.uk
Edward Heath: © National Portrait Gallery, London
G. D. H. Cole: © National Portrait Gallery, London
Tony Crosland: Rex/Associated Newspapers
Jeremy Thorpe: Duffy/Getty Images
Norman St John-Stevas: © AP/TopFoto
Michael Portillo: © 2004 Credit: TopFoto/UPP
Peter Mandelson: Rex/Herbie Knott